LOYALTY

LOYALTY

*An Essay on the
Morality of Relationships*

George P. Fletcher

OXFORD UNIVERSITY PRESS
New York   Oxford

Oxford University Press

Oxford   New York
Athens   Auckland   Bangkok   Bombay
Calcutta   Cape Town   Dar es Salaam   Delhi
Florence   Hong Kong   Istanbul   Karachi
Kuala Lumpur   Madras   Madrid   Melbourne
Mexico City   Nairobi   Paris   Singapore
Taipei   Tokyo   Toronto

and associated companies in
Berlin   Ibadan

Copyright © 1993 by George P. Fletcher

First published in 1993 by Oxford University Press, Inc.,
200 Madison Avenue, New York, New York 10016

First issued as an Oxford University Press paperback, 1995

Oxford is a registered trademark of Oxford University Press

Library of Congress Cataloging-in-Publication Data
Fletcher, George P.
Loyalty: an essay on the morality of relationships / George P. Fletcher
p. cm.   Includes index.
ISBN 0-19-507026-7
ISBN 0-19-509832-3 (pbk.)
1. Loyalty.
I. Title.   BJ1533.L8F54
1993   92-460

2 4 6 8 10 9 7 5 3 1
Printed in the United States of America

In memory of
Gerald Goldfarb
1940–1989
Loyalty's teacher

and for
Rachel Rose
1988–
Loyalty's gift

Contents

Preface

The central arguments in this book were a long time in coming. If I asked about the subject of loyalty some ten years ago, I undoubtedly would have reacted as many of my liberal friends react today. I would have identified patriotism with the breast-beating zealots who threatened my generation with those billboards: "America, Love It or Leave It." I would have thought, ten years ago, that schoolchildren's pledging allegiance to the flag was tantamount to their reciting prayers in public schools—a clear violation of the neutrality that provides the framework for American pluralism. At the very minimum, I would have taken an ethic of loyalty to smack of the rhetoric of anti-Communist fanaticism, McCarthyism, and all the excesses that defined the enemies of free thought as I was coming of age.

It is not clear to me whether I have had a change of heart or whether a decade of greed (as Barbara Ehrenreich has dubbed the 1980s) simply made me more conscious of the moral importance of commitments to those with whom I share a common fate. In retrospect, President John F. Kennedy's inaugural appeal in 1961—"Ask not what your country can do for you, but what you can do for your country"—rings clearly as an appeal to our national loyalty. It is an appeal to responsibility that resonates with my basic sentiments far more than the ethic of self-interest that dominates current obsessions with tax cuts as the way to solve our problems.

Whatever the deep roots of my sentiments, some experiences of the last few years helped to crystallize my thought around the theme of loyalty. The first was a conversation with David Hartman, a rabbi in Jerusalem, with whom I had the pleasure of studying in March and April 1987. I had explained to Rabbi Hartman that I had done most of my philosophical work on the Kantian theory of law and morality. Hartman turned to me, quizzically, and said, "Fletcher, don't you know that Kant's universalistic ethics cannot accommodate

special relationships. Hartman had in mind the covenantal relationship between God and the Jewish people, but the same objection
applies to all special relationships, as between friends, between
lovers, and among citizens in the same polity.

Several themes in this book derive, directly and indirectly, from
that conversation with David Hartman. First, I include in my analysis of loyalty the question of religious loyalty that would presumably
get lost in most secular philosophical studies. Further, as a consequence of that conversation about covenant, I began to rethink the
promise and power of Kantian morality and the Enlightenment
ethics of impartiality in general. This book would probably never
have taken shape unless I had grown skeptical of the entire tradition
of impartial ethics and had come to recognize that the normal commitments of our lives—expressed as "loyalties"—provide a sounder
basis for the moral life than an Enlightenment ideal that is, as I will
argue, incapable of realization.

This process of re-evaluating moral theory dovetailed with another
experience that led me to see the connections between national identity and the analysis of interpersonal loyalties. My interest in the
Pledge of Allegiance and the instilling of national identity in our
schoolchildren comes from an indelible experience I had a few years
ago as I was entering the United States from Canada. The background
to the border episode is an unusual feature of my family biography, of
which I happen to be proud. My father, born in Széchény, Hungary,
under the name Fleischer Miklos and reared as the privileged scion of
a wealthy landowner, entered the United States in the mid-1920s by
swimming across the Rio Grande. After having worked as an illegal
immigrant for at least ten years, he went to Canada then returned to
the United States, thereby establishing a legal date of entry and
enabling him to qualify for citizenship in 1941. The officials at the
casual Canadian border winked, no doubt, at the passing of my father
and countless other aliens who had no proof of American citizenship.

As I found myself in the Toronto airport, walking toward the
checkpoint they call the border, my father's first legal crossing came
back to me. I started thinking in the accents and rhythms that
marked his speech as Habsburgian. The guard asked a question routine for travelers without passports: Where were you born? I replied,
"Cheecahgo"—precisely as my father pronounced "Chicago," with
the flat "e" and broad "a" that only Hungarians can get right.

I was in trouble. My slip into a time warp, my affected accent, as well as my 1930s long German overcoat and Left Bank beret, all marked me as a suspicious foreigner. With a passport in my hand, I could have entered without much discussion, but I chose the luxury of going north and crossing back into the land of my birth without the usual papers. There would be no winking at this crossing. For the first time in my life, I encountered someone who seriously doubted whether I was an American, whether I belonged here. Bringing my speech back to normal Yankee did not help. Neither my New York driver's license nor my credit cards impressed the man guarding the gate. Perhaps he could try to determine whether I was a spy by asking me esoteric questions about Americana, the way soldiers in World War II movies uncovered German spies with trick questions about baseball. Snobbish antifan that I am, I doubt if I could have named any second baseman in the majors.

As I was getting desperate, something remarkable happened. The immigration official asked me to recite the Pledge of Allegiance. Like Sarah asked to give birth, I laughed. I was too old, I had not uttered those lines in at least twenty-five years. Surprisingly, as I started, the secular American prayer to the flag came back to me. One word followed another until, with a sense of mastery, I came to Eisenhower's emendation "under God," and then I was home free. I was back in the seventh grade engaged in one of the rituals that made me into an American.

As I pondered this incident in the years following, I began to wonder whether without the Pledge and other patriotic rituals, we Americans of diverse origins would share a common emotional bond to a country that, intellectually, we are prepared both to criticize and defend. My pride in being an American certainly does not follow from recitations of the Pledge in school. My sense of privilege derives much more from growing up in a country that permitted me, the son of a *mojado,* to nourish an unlimited sense of possibility. Yet the making of Americans from immigrant children and the descendants of slaves is not an easy task. And today, with the growing sense of defensiveness and hostility expressed by many American ethnic groups, the casting of a common cultural loyalty is becoming ever more difficult. Patriotic rituals, I have come to believe, are necessary to nurture and maintain a common national identity and a sense of responsibility for the welfare of the nation as a whole.

Some of my arguments will strike my anticipated reader as provocative and even wrongheaded. Certainly my students thought so as I presented earlier drafts in seminars on jurisprudence at the Columbia Law School. They were always polite as they confronted my passions and forced me to rethink my positions. As a result of their skepticism, I rewrote the entire manuscript several times. I was enormously aided in the restructuring of the argument by the comments of Maurice F. Edelson. I am also indebted to Jack Kint, Micah Green, Jonnette Hamiton, Mark Lopeman, and my assistant Robert Jystad, all of whom offered detailed criticism as the manuscript evolved from draft to draft. Frank J. Dalton, Merav Datan, and Rebecca J. Fletcher kindly helped me to prepare the manuscript for publication. I am very grateful to Cynthia Read, my editor at Oxford, who believed in the project after seeing it in rather imperfect form and helped me to tighten the argument. Appreciatively acknowledged as well are the Rockefeller Foundation, which provided me with ideal conditions for writing at Villa Serbelloni in Bellagio, Italy; my colleagues at the Gruter Institute for Law and Behavioral Research, who encouraged my turning toward the human sentiments driving the law; and my deans at the Columbia Law School, Barbara Black and Lance Liebman, for their support and encouragement.

Several colleagues have given me invaluable guidance. John Kleinig generously shared with me the work that he has done on loyalty. Joseph Raz proved to be a remarkably perceptive critic, first in a long conversation on the steamy summer streets of London in July 1990 and then in the fall of 1991, when he came to Columbia and we taught a joint seminar on loyalty. Herbert Morris, Ruti Teitel, Anne-Marie Roviello, Meir Dan-Cohen, Sanford Levinson, and Kent Greenawalt offered me helpful comments. And Bruce Ackerman, as always, was there as a foil for argument and affirmation of the project's value. Portions of the manuscript were offered as papers and lectures in Toronto, Montreal, Frankfurt, and Brussels, and I appreciate the seriousness with which my arguments were received.

Now you must decide how important loyalty is to you.

New York   G.P.F.
July 1992

LOYALTY

CHAPTER 1

The Historical Self

We all live in networks of personal and economic relationships—of friends and acquaintances, of families and nations, of corporations, universities, and religious communities. The ties so nurtured range from the trivial to the sublime. At minimum, we buy from these groups or live with them and work with them. In some cases these encompassing ties generate the interactions that make our daily lives meaningful. From time to time, we object to the way other people in the group are acting. We do not like the way we are treated, the service or the product we receive, the political actions or moral positions taken by others in the "community." What do we do?

We have the choice either of leaving to search for other relationships or another community that more adequately fits our expectations or of staying and working to improve the environment that shapes our lives. Leaving has become the increasingly popular option. In the marketplace, where all that is at stake is the performance of the product or the quality of the service, the best thing to do is to leave—that is, to find the competitor who better supplies the needed good.

The exemplar of the marketplace has conquered neighboring arenas. Today we think about relatives, employers, religious groups, and nations the way we think about companies that supply us with other products and services. If we don't like what we are getting, we consider the competition. Conventional free market theory teaches that leaving is a virtue. The willingness to "switch rather than fight" engenders competition and forces inefficient producers to "shape up" or "ship out." The marketplace works to ensure that only the fit survive; and the condition for promoting the competent is the willingness of consumers to favor the better producer.

The values of the marketplace apply today not only in the choice of material products like toothpaste and automobiles but in our relationships with people. Most scholars and scientists have become consumers of university services, and when a competitor offers a higher salary, a better-equipped laboratory, or more interesting colleagues, there is no reason not to entertain the offer. Academic stars have become like baseball stars, willing to play for the highest bidder. There is no doubt that the free-floating academic class forces their producers—university administrations and the financial sources that back them up—to offer more to stay abreast of the competition.

The mentality of "trading up" can be made to apply to friendships, marriages, and other attachments. Shifting loyalties is an increasingly common way of coping with a weak friendship, a shaky marriage, a religious community that takes the wrong stand on an important issue, or a nation that has come into the hands of the wrong political party. The beauty of the marketplace mentality is that one can act solely on the basis of consumer preferences and by the force of one's decisions induce those harmed to work harder to maintain their share of the market. If academics flee low-paying English universities for the United States, the move might induce conservative governments to respond with better funding for higher education. If in 1970 a whole generation of young Americans had taken refuge from the draft in Canada, the White House would have had to choose between an unpopular war and maintaining a country to govern.

In an illuminating monograph,[1] Albert Hirschman challenges this way of thinking, even as applied to the core cases of choosing between products and job offers. *Exit*, or leaving, is contrasted with *voice*, the medium used by those who stay and fight. The starting point of the argument is that voice, defined as "any attempt to change . . . an objectionable state of affairs,"[2] is sometimes more effective than exit, even as a stimulus to better economic performance. The options of voice range from making a personal complaint, mobilizing the opinions of others, negotiating, reasoning with and forming alliances against management, and, not to be ignored,[3] using legal devices, such as stockholder remedies and conduct-changing tort claims. In exercising any of these options, the consumer takes on a greater personal burden than simply pulling out, shifting ties, and moving on. Voice in place of exit can help an endangered firm survive—by providing, first, necessary feedback on the breakdown in performance and, second, a cushion of time and support that will permit the firm to recover.

However useful voice may be, in organizational politics as well as the marketplace, exit is likely to prevail. This is particularly true in the American way of thinking, based as it is on the mentality of the frontier—on the solving of problems by pulling up roots and starting over. Voice requires creative thinking, patience, a willingness to gamble on an investment of time and energy. Those who exit cannot be faulted for assuming that newly planted roots will yield greener grass.

This is the point at which, in Hirschman's thinking, loyalty enters as a virtue both in the marketplace and in institutional life. Whether we are talking about shopping, investing, or staying with a group of people, loyalty tends to check our preference for exit over voice. The hallmark of loyal behavior is "the reluctance to exit in spite of disagreement with the organization of which one is a member."[4] Loyalty fulfills its function, Hirschman reasons, when the costs of exit are otherwise nil and there are close substitutes—that is, a comparable product to buy or a similar club, firm, university, or city to join. Within a few months of the Berlin Wall's crumbling in November 1989, a million East Germans, 6 percent of the population, left for the West. Not only was the Federal Republic's "product" similar in history and language to life in the East, but the costs of exit were minimal. Only loyalty to the socialist way of life could have saved the German Democratic Republic as a separate state, and it was clear from the outset that economic welfare was more important than the state's preservation.

Feelings of loyalty raise the cost of exit by exacting a psychological price. The price may be irrational, but it serves a rational purpose of ensuring, in Eric Erikson's *bon mot*, that people "actively stay put."[5] In a word, loyalty is the beginning of political life, a life in which interaction with others becomes the primary means of solving problems. Loyalty is the means by which politics triumphs over self-interested economic calculation. In personal relationships, loyalty expresses the relationship's assuming an external force, holding lovers or friends in a bond that transcends temporary disaffection.

Against the background of Hirschman's defense of loyalty, con-

sider a significant concession Alasdair MacIntyre makes in an otherwise sympathetic treatment of loyalty and patriotism: "Patriotism
turns out to be a permanent source of moral danger. And this claim,
I take it, cannot in fact be successfully rebutted."[6] Obviously, he has
in mind the slippery slope toward fascism, of blind, unthinking
adherence to "my country right or wrong."[7] Blind adherence to any
object of loyalty—whether friend, lover, or nation—converts loyalty
into idolatry. There is a moral danger in thinking that any concrete
person or entity could become the ultimate source of right and
wrong, but the moral danger is no greater in the case of patriotism
than it is in friendship, erotic or filial love, or political commitment.

To counteract this danger, exit remains a critical supplement to
the loyal voice. The commitment to voice could become a moral
trap unless there are limits beyond which exit becomes the sensible
turn. Further and more practically, the ever-present threat of exit
renders the loyal voice a more powerful medium for institutional
correction.

Friendship and Loyalty

In thinking about the nature of loyalty, we cross philosophically
untraveled territory. The prior treatments of the subject in the literature skip over foundational matters.[8] Yet one subject close to the
core of loyalty has received considerable attention since Aristotle.
Friendship, writes Aristotle in the *Nicomachean Ethics*, "is a virtue or
implies a virtue and is besides most necessary with a view to
living."[9] Reflecting on Aristotle's treatment of friendship, we begin
our investigation of the foundations of loyalty.

In Aristotle's system, character dispositions are called virtues if
they contribute to our *telos*, or end as human beings—an end that
today we call "human flourishing" or more commonly, the good life.
The precise connection between friendship and virtue remains vague,
however, for Aristotle appears to be ambivalent about whether friendship is but one of the virtues or whether it is the universal precondi-
tion for the good life.[10] The better reading, it seems, is that rooting
the personality in a nexus of relationships is the condition for the
evolution of personality toward *eudaemonia,* or happiness.

Aristotle concedes that friendship comes in lower and higher forms. The lower variety is based on pleasure, as is often the case in youthful comraderie,[11] or on utility, which is so often the case with networking in business and political life. The higher form of friendship, transcending both pleasure and utility, rests on each partner's reciprocally wishing each other well and conferring benefits on each other as an end in itself.[12] This higher form of friendship, we need to add to Aristotle's account, requires an implicit understanding of continuity and reciprocal reliance. A friend must be more than someone who transiently wishes another well.

Friendship rests on loyalty, but not in the same demanding way that exclusive relationships do. One can be friends with many, though not so large a number that one's attentions and caring become too diffuse to sustain friendship. As Aristotle says, "It would seem impossible to be a great friend to many people."[13]

Friendship and all forms of loyal bonding presuppose relationships rooted in shared histories. As Aristotle says, friends must have "eaten salt" together.[14] "One must . . . acquire some experience of the other person and become familiar with him, and that is very hard."[15] The best way for two people to become friends is to repair a car together. The point is almost too obvious: Loyalties crystallize in communal projects and shared life experiences.

Generalizing from friendship to all relationships of loyalty, we perceive the role of two terms that mark off these moral commitments from others: First, the question of loyalty does not arise in the abstract but only in the context of a particular *relationship*. Further, by definition, these ties generate *partialities* in loyalties, loves and hates, dispositions to trust and distrust. In the realm of loyalty, inequality reigns: Outsiders cannot claim equal treatment with those who are the objects of loyal attachment.

People bring their histories to their loyalties, which implies that the reasons for attachment to a friend, family, or country invariably transcend the particular characteristics of the object of loyalty. As John Ladd points out in his article on loyalty in the *Encyclopedia of Philosophy*: "More purely personal characteristics of [the object of loyalty], such as his kindness, courage, amiability, honesty, or spirituality cannot serve as the *grounds* for loyalty."[16] If the same personal characteristics are found in another person and if they were sufficient to ground loyalty, then, regardless of historical ties to the other person, one should be loyal to him or her as well. But we know that this is not the case. Our loyalties are relational and partial. The objective characteristics of the other may incline us in our sentiments, but only as these characteristics play against receptivities that are rooted in our personal biographies.

The same analysis of objective judgment applies in understanding loyalty to nations or countries. Many thoughtful civil libertarians claim that their loyalty to the United States is defined by their rational respect for the Constitution. But what if it could be shown to them that in many critical areas—for example, free speech or equality for women—the constitution of some other country, say Italy or Germany, is in fact superior? Would they then shift their loyalties to the objectively superior constitution? I think not. The personal, historical dimension of loyalty breeds a faith in the country and the Constitution that goes beyond the current rulings of the Supreme Court.

Betrayal

Loyalty, by definition, generates interest, partiality, an identification with the object of one's loyalty rather than with its competitors. Loyalty is expressed in relationships that generate these partialities. The minimal demand of loyalty is the maintenance of the relationship, which requires the rejection of alternatives that undermine the principal bond. A loyal lover is someone who will not be seduced by another. A loyal citizen is someone who will not go over to the enemy in a time of conflict. A loyal political adherent will not "sell out" to the opposition. Some of the strongest moral epithets in the English language are reserved for the weak who cannot meet the threshold of loyalty: They commit adultery, betrayal, treason.[17]

There are always three parties, A, B, and C, in a matrix of loyalty. A can be loyal to B only if there is a third party C (another lover, an enemy nation, a hostile company) who stands as a potential competitor to B, the object of loyalty. The competitor is always lurking in the wings, rejected for the time being, but always tempting, always seductive. The foundational element in loyalty is the fact not present—the counterfactual conditional statement that if the competitor appears and beckons, the loyal will refuse to follow.

In the way we draw the lines of our loyalties, we define ourselves as persons. We distinguish ourselves from others, who understandably might attach themselves to the competitor waiting in the wings. The objects of our loyalties play an active part in setting us apart and making us distinctive. If we express our loyalty to a country, to another person, or even to a company or a baseball team, these objects of our loyalties play a reciprocal part in defining who we are. The same is true of my principles. I am loyal to them, and they are also operative on me. They are *my* principles—not principles in the abstract—and therefore they contribute to the contours of my personality.

Loyalty comes with a built-in element of contingency. The person who reflects about his loyalties should realize that things might have been different. He might have been born in a different country or of a different religion; she might have married a different man or worked for a different company. This sense of contingency, the sense that one might succumb to the tempter in the shadows, should breed tolerance for the loyalties of others.

The prediction that the loyal will reject temptation provides the minimal condition for loyalty. The maximum condition is an element of devotion, an affirmative feeling toward the object of loyalty. In the context of citizenship, loyalty seems to be a minimalist condition.[18] It is a quiet, passive virtue. It requires that one not join the enemy, typically the military enemy. Patriotism, by contrast, is loyalty *plus* affection. The sentiment required for patriotism comes close to love in human relationships. Some patriots regret, in the disarming declaration of Nathan Hale, that they "have but one life to lose for [their] country."[19] As in loving, the good of their country becomes the patriots' own good.

We might be inclined to think that loyalty turns on an unrefined human attachment, a habit of running with a certain pack. We might be inclined to draw analogies between the herd instinct of animals and the human commitment to stand by friends, lovers, and family. Of course, in a trivial sense, dogs and horses can be devoted to their human masters, and many animals are monogamous and devoted to their offspring. But it would be a serious mistake to think that these biological patterns capture what we mean by loyalty.

The complexity of loyalty, I argue, is characteristically human. The way to see this is to think about disloyalty and betrayal. Betrayal is the stronger term, and it implies something more than an absence of loyalty or a shift in loyalties. Animals often change the objects of their attachment and devotion. Some animals will be attached to whomever feeds them last. So far as their attachments can be called loyalties, these ties of devotion shift with changing patterns of care. The loyalty of animals expresses attachment, but not the principled rejection of tempting alternatives.

Betrayal is characteristically human. There is nothing suspect about the *shifts* in loyalty that occur among animals as well as humans. Humans engage in such shifts when they divorce and remarry or emigrate and acquire the nationality of an adopted country. Betrayal, however, is one of the basic sins of our civilization.

Dante reserves a special place in hell for those who betray trust by committing fraud and embezzlement. The thief who pretends to be our friend not only deprives us of our goods but "snaps the ties of close regard."[20] In Blackstone's eyes, treason "[is] the highest civil crime which (considered as a member of the community) any man can possibly commit."[21]

The difference between a shift in loyalty and betrayal inheres in a simple fact. Betrayal occurs only when one breaches an obligation of loyalty. A shift in loyalty represents not a breach but the extinction of the duty toward one object and its revival toward someone else. How could animals be under duties of loyalty? Some more advanced mammals may behave loyally toward their human masters, but we would be hard pressed to attribute duties of loyalty to them. A junior monkey may engage in deception in order to copulate with a female under another's dominance, but it would be odd to think of either the deceiving male or the female as guilty of sexual betrayal.[22]

For the purposes of this argument, the line between humans and animals does not express a conceptual point. Young babies also shift their loyalties without incurring the label of betrayal, and the general thesis would hold even if it turned out that dolphins should be regarded as closer to humans than to other animals. Why do the characteristics of domesticated animals and babies prevent them from bearing duties of loyalty? Is it the lack of a sense of time? their lack of syntactical language? their incapacity to think abstractly or counterfactually, to understand that they ought to be doing something else? We need not isolate a single distinguishing characteristic to realize that animals and babies could not bear duties of loyalty. As a matter of social practice, we attribute obligations only to those beings that can understand that they are under an obligation. Our shared assumption is that animals lack this understanding.

The Loyal and the Liberal

The centrality of personal commitment and partiality in loyal relationships distinguishes loyalty from an entire body of moral theories that derive from eighteenth century moral philosophy. Grouped today under the vague term "liberalism," these moral theories have in common a set of views that center on the principles of "individualism," "impartiality," and "equality." Admittedly, the term "liberalism" means different things to different people. We cannot avoid its use entirely, but it seems clearer to focus on the label "impartial morality" to capture the set of views opposed to the demands of loyalty. More specifically, we shall consider the claims of impartial morality as they have crystallized in two prominent, conflicting ways of thinking, one rooted in English and the other in German moral thought. The progenitors of these theories are two eighteenth century philosophers, Jeremy Bentham and Immanuel Kant.

Bentham and Kant share a commitment to impartiality in moral judgment. Their underlying assumption is that we all exist as individuals prior to our attachments and that therefore we can act freely, unbound by pre-existing relationships. Whether our conduct is moral or not depends, for these two representatives of impartial morality, on different and indeed opposing considerations. The debate between these two schools, which continues today in the public sphere as well as in university forums, has shaped our conception of morality. When MacIntyre claims loyalty and patriotism represent a "permanent source of moral danger,"[23] and Paul Gomberg asserts, even more strongly, that "patriotism is like racism,"[24] they draw implicitly on the tradition of Benthamite and Kantian impartial morality as the benchmark of morality.

The mode of impartial moral thinking most familiar to Americans is Bentham's utilitarianism, which in various forms and modalities holds that the right moral decision is the one that has the most beneficial impact upon the welfare of all sentient beings who experience pleasure and pain. If, as Adam Smith argued, individuals seek to maximize their personal utility in the marketplace, then entire societies ought arguably to do the same. It follows that the right decision for any individual would be to do that which the society as a whole, if acting as a single individual, would choose in its long range self-interest. The key point is that according to utilitarianism, the right decision is the one that is the best for society as a whole.[25]

Some people argue that utilitarianism can accommodate loyal attachments as acts that serve the long-range interests of both those who are loyal and those who are the objects of loyalty. It is good, the argument goes, for each child to have some people devoted to his or her welfare. We all benefit from the possibility of concentrated care by our parents.

It is fairly easy to show, however, that utilitarianism cannot explain why in all cases we should be loyal to our children or family members rather to other people equally in need who would make more of a contribution to society. If I must choose between two drowning children—one my own rather slow-witted offspring and the other my neighbor's very gifted scion—there is no apparent reason why society is better off if I save my own.[26]

William Godwin argues that it would indeed be better to save the person who would make the greater social contribution. He reports coming upon a house on fire. He learns that his mother as well as Archbishop Fenelon are trapped inside. He has time to enter the house and rescue one person. He opts for the archbishop on the ground that the archbishop will contribute more to the general welfare of society. As he explains his decision: "What magic is in the pronoun 'my' that should justify us in overturning the decisions of impartial truth?"[27] The impartial truth is that not sentiment, not gratitude, not loyalty—only the welfare of society counts. The archbishop should be saved, because he more than Godwin's mother matters to the group as a whole.

The correct moral decision, according to Bentham and his followers, ignores the personal and relational dimension signaled by the pronoun "my." In making a moral decision, it should not matter whether it is the actor's mother or a stranger's mother who is in mortal danger. Ignoring personal attachments is necessary to achieve the ideal of moral impartiality. In the end all mothers are to be treated equally. Any distinction between persons—between a mother and an archbishop—depends on how valuable that person is to the society as a whole. Though Kant would reject classifying people on the basis of their utility to the group, he shares Bentham's and Godwin's commitment to the ideal of impersonal and impartial moral judgment.

As utility for all is Bentham's benchmark, Kant begins his moral thinking by reflecting on the impartial demands of human reason. Reason is the common denominator of all humanity, the divine spark that distinguishes us from animals. Reason as abstracted from sensual drives engenders unity in the species; the particularist drives of our sensual selves take us in our own directions, each person according to his or her own physical constitution.

The virtue of Kant's moral theory is that it provides a compelling foundation for the familiar postulate that "all men [and, obviously, women] are created equal." Bentham too treats all people, mothers and archbishops alike, as equally capable of being useful to others. But those who are not useful to others have no claim to being considered as the one who should be saved in an emergency. Kant's argument for human equality gets its grounding not in the impact that people have on each other, but on the universality of human reason. We share reason not only with other human beings but with divine beings, God and the angels, who have no corporeal existence. Because reason brings us into a mode of existence above the animals, who are driven solely by sensual impulse, reason confers a unique dignity on human beings. This dignity is beyond all price, all trade-offs; it is of absolute value. The assertion of absolute value in each human being, in turn, provides the foundation for treating all human beings as intrinsically equal.

What this equality requires in practice has generated philosophical cacophony in contemporary debates among philosophers who think of themselves as liberals. Need everyone receive an equal share of the pie, as Ackerman assumes?[28] Or is it sufficient that the government treat its citizens with equal concern and respect, as Dworkin claims?[29] Or perhaps, as in Rawls's theory, equality in social and economic interests is merely the starting point from which all deviations must be justified.[30] In one version or another, however, liberal theory endorses some version of impartial morality.

In some stylized arenas, such as athletic competitions or law courts, we are undoubtedly required to treat everyone as equal. Philosophers like William Godwin would extend the principle of impartial justice to all social and personal relations. It is wrong, allegedly, to consider the loyalties entailed by the pronoun "my." The ideal mode of behavior would be to treat the children of others exactly as one treats one's own children, the mothers of others as one treats one's own mother. This would be the utopia of impartial, egalitarian morality, a world in which the emotions of attachment never interefere with the virtue of evenhanded treatment.[31]

Whatever may be the case among private individuals, committed liberals maintain, governments are bound to treat everyone equally, to accord them equal concern and respect. But who counts in the calculation of "everyone?" To whom does one owe a duty of justice? all five billion people on the planet? "Obviously not," would be the expected reply. Yet the foundations for this reply are not so obvious. Some class of persons—citizens, residents, or some similar group— is entitled to equal protection of the laws in their government's actions. There is ongoing controversy about who constitutes this class, whether, say, undocumented aliens in the United States are inside or outside the protected sphere. Perhaps the duties of protection and impartial justice run only to those people who, in turn, are loyal to the government. The principle of equal treatment may have its roots in a bond of feudal reciprocity: The government serves and cares for those who may be expected to care for and serve the government.[32]

The basic difference between the moral teachings of impartial morality and of loyalty are easily seen if we engage in the thought experiment of Robinson Crusoe on a desert island. Bentham and Kant have much to teach the solitary individual, living in isolation from others. Bentham would teach him to use his time and resources wisely, in order to maximize his overall happiness and pleasure in life. Kant would insist that he respect the demands of reason and universal humanity. The categorical imperative would require him not to deceive himself, to develop his talents (by studying philosophy, no doubt), and he would be enjoined not to commit suicide. The critical point, for these two leading liberal thinkers, is that respecting the distinguishing feature of one's own existence—be it the capacity for pleasure or the accessibility of reason—is no less important than respecting these qualities in others. Robinson Crusoe poses no problem for the liberal, impartial moral thinker.

But for the solitary individual, without bonds to others, the notion of loyalty is irrelevant. Loyalty gets its grip in relationships with others. It is a mistake to reduce the notion to vacuity by speaking of "loyalty to oneself." The most that this phrase could mean is that loyalties to others should not inhibit one's actions.

If loyalty is expressed in relationships and only in relationships, then we should work toward a clearer understanding of what this critical term means. At minimum, a relationship requires two interacting beings. In Martin Buber's idiom, there must be an "I" and a "Thou."[33] To enter into a Buberian relationship, I must suspend my temptation to master the other as object of my power and cease to see the other solely as a source of sensual gratification. For Buber, relationships (*Beziehungen*) inhabit a realm beyond the senses. Their existence testifies to a world of unity beyond the physical realities that separate us. This metaphysical point, with its Kantian overtones of a world beyond the senses, reminds us that relationships are not matters of consumption. They cannot be reduced to the economic model of inputs that satisfy our preferences. They must meet Aristotle's conditions for the higher forms of friendship.

The focal point of loyalty is a relationship-based entity that transcends the individuals who constitute it. Families, tribes, and nations live on, so long as some members survive, and the biographies of individuals in whom the group is inscribed become in turn part of the ongoing and living history of these collectives. Admittedly, it is more difficult to make this claim for one-to-one relationships. Marriage (or other deep loves) do not, in any operative sense, survive the death of one of the partners. Yet I have encountered many survivors who think of the relationship as staying with them, integrated into the background of their lives.

For our purposes, the aspect of relationships that matter is that they enter into the individual's sense of identity. In oversimplified terms, the ethic of loyalty takes relationships as logically prior to the individual, while liberal morality thinks of the individual, existing wholly formed, choosing to enter into relationships. For the former, the family and the nation define the individual; for the latter, the individual chooses to contribute to the identity of the family and the nation. Carol Gilligan has called this distinction to our attention in developing her argument about differences between the way young boys and young girls think about moral issues.[34] In her scheme, abstract liberal universalism appeals to the male side of our personalities; the contextualized emphasis on relationships appeals to our female side. That the ethic of loyalty is so late in emerging from the shadows of philosophical thinking may reflect the preference of a male-dominated tradition for abstract and universal modes of moral thinking. The theory of loyalty brings a needed reorientation of moral inquiry.

Obligations of the Historical Self

Our identity bears upon our obligations. At stake in the debate between impartial morality and the ethic of loyalty is whether our histories matter in determining what we ought to do. Need we act loyally toward the groups and individuals that have entered into our sense of who we are? If we do act loyally, do we do so as a matter of inclination or habit or by virtue of a well grounded duty of loyalty? This, in one fashion or another, is the question that dominates this book. It recurs in thinking about why animals cannot, conceptually, betray their masters, in analyzing treason as a crime, pondering adultery as a sin, and explaining idolatry as a theological vice.

To get a grip on the question whether our personal histories entail duties of loyalty, we should think first about the way in which liberal theory generates obligations. The moral philosophies of Bentham and Kant, as presented above, root their theories of obligations in the common traits shared by all humans. Bentham claims that our common denominator is our capacity for pleasure and pain, and infers that everyone has an obligation to act in a way that takes account of the pleasures and pains of everyone else. The Kantian claim that every human is rational and therefore bears a common humanity generates an inference to respect that humanity as an end in itself.

As the universal self so described entails obligations, the historical self generates duties of loyalty toward the families, groups, and nations that enter into our self-definition. These duties may be understood as an expression of self-esteem and self-acceptance. To love myself, I must respect and cherish those aspects of myself that are bound up with others. Thus by the mere fact of my biography I incur obligations toward others, which I group under the general heading of loyalty.

We do not choose our historical selves in any direct and immediate sense. We are born into a particular culture, acquire a mother tongue, receive exposure to certain political and religious ideas, learn a national history—all without significant choices on our part. The responsibility for our initial sense of historical self is left to our parents, those who run our schools, the media, and the religious leaders who have an impact on us. Of course, some choice is left to us as adults to leave our native cultures and attempt to assimilate as immigrants or converts in a new world. Whether the assimilation succeeds depends, in large part, on the will and talents of the individual and the receptivity of the receiving culture. It is obviously easier to assimilate as an immigrant to the United States than to most other national cultures. The possibility of engaging in this structural change, engendering a whole new set of loyalties, represents the limited control that we have over our historical selves.

In some areas, of course, we reach our critical decisions as adults, and we can alter our commitments to friends, marital partners, religions, and professions in midlife. The range of our freedom in making these structural changes depends, as well, on the receptivity of the culture in which we seek to act. As compared with Western countries, it is not easy to restructure one's religious commitments in Iran or one's professional loyalties in Japan.

The logical relationship between the historical self and loyalty runs both ways. As the historical self inculcates a sense of loyalty, loyalties, especially to nations, derive exclusively from the historical self. I cannot decide from one day to the next to be loyal to someone with whom I have no history. Fond as I am of French culture and cuisine, I cannot decide tomorrow that I shall be loyal to François Mitterrand and the French nation. My connection to the French remains that of a fond observer. I may continue to appreciate French culture as an outsider, but on the fringes of the culture, looking in, I am not in a position to be either loyal or disloyal to the French people.

However much Alexis de Tocqueville admired America, he could not suddenly declare his loyalty to us. Six thousand French regulars fought under General Rochambeau in the American Revolution, but this was not an act of loyalty to the emergent American republic. A Virginia farmer can put aside his plow and take up arms as an act of loyalty, but a Parisian who comes to fight in the same cause does not make the same statement about where he stands. Even if he believes firmly in his heart that the Americans should win (and not as does his government, that for political reasons the English should lose), he fights as an outsider. The soundness of his cause influences how hard he fights, but his fighting neither expresses nor confirms his historical self.

Fighting in foreign wars can sometimes be an act of loyalty. The Americans who went to Spain in the mid-1930s to fight in the Abraham Lincoln brigade made a statement about who they were and about the internationalist ideas that defined their lives. American Jews who went to fight in the 1948 Israeli War of Independence also gave testimony to their Jewish and Zionist consciousness.[35]

The scant literature on loyalty underestimates the centrality of the historical self in affirmations of loyalty. In a major work on the subject, Josiah Royce defines a loyalty as "the willing and thoroughgoing devotion of a person to a cause."[36] The stress on willing devotion suggests that anyone can commit himself or herself to any cause, Americans to the French or the French to Americans. But this, as I have argued, gives insufficient weight to the historical self as limitation on the range of our loyal commitments.

The duties of the historical self provide us with the best account of why we must share our wealth with the poor. If alleviating the suffering of the poor is not simply a matter of charity but of recognizing that as human beings they have some claim against our assets, we have to ground the obligation somewhere. The place to begin is with the recognition of a common humanity, but then the question is whether that common humanity is best perceived as an expression of our historical selves or of a universal self. My claim is that the historical self gives us the most plausible account of why we should treat others as our brothers sharing a common fate and fortune.

The most significant effort in recent years to develop a theory of common ownership is John Rawls's theory of justice, which defends the principle that all members of a given society are entitled to a minimal share of social and economic goods.[37] The problem, as Rawls puts it, is not how the poor should justify their claim to a share of the economic pie but rather how the rich can justify their keeping the share that comes to them in the form of wages and return on capital. The rich may justifiably retain their incremental wealth, Rawls teaches, only if departures from equal distribution benefit all segments of society, including representatives of the class least well off. The rich deserve their disproportionate wealth only if paying them more is necessary to secure their energies and talents for the sake of the entire society.

Rawls comes to this remarkable result only because he assumes, in the Kantian tradition, that principles of justice must meet the expectations that people would have if, as abstract disembodied beings, they did not know whether they would turn out, in the real world, to be rich or poor, strong or weak, quick or dull. The expectations behind this "veil of ignorance" express the judgments of a universal self, a rational self attributed to all human beings. The rational universal self would insist that all wealth and opportunity be distributed equally unless a disproportionate award to some would, in the end, benefit all. Thus a theory of justice rooted in our common humanity supports an obligation to help the homeless and unemployed; they may insist that disparities in wealth benefit them as well.

The unanswered question is, Who are the people who, behind the veil of ignorance, are entitled to demand a fair share of the world's resources? Do future generations count? Do fetuses have a full vote? If the parties affected by justice are limited to the living, does the relevant pool encompass the whole world? Does Rawls seriously maintain that the rich in the Netherlands cannot justify their wealth unless it also directly benefits the poor in Sri Lanka?[38]

It seems that Rawls simply assumes that national borders are "given" at the outset of the discussion. He seems to be concerned about justice within particular societies, but this is obviously an arbitrary limitation on the analysis. If there is a duty to care for the destitute at home, there must also be some obligation—though perhaps a less demanding one—to help the suffering abroad. Recent events have demonstrated some extraordinary acts of international caring. The unification of Germany on October 3, 1990 and the commitment of more than a trillion dollars to the economic development of the East would not have occurred if conventional boundaries had been determinative. Israel's lightning airlift of 15,000 Ethiopians in May 1991 expressed a capacity to reach out dramatically to people of a different color who speak a different language.

Yet there is something significant about these examples that does not fit readily into Rawls's theory or into any theory based on the universal self. The commitment that Germans feel toward their "*Brüder*" in the former GDR (however much grouching there may be in the aftermath of unification) does not extend to other peoples. The Israeli airlift was directed to fellow Jews in danger. These rescue operations reflect a sense of duty; the source of commitment lies in a shared sense of history and oppression.

We pay too little attention to the conditions necessary to form a community of reciprocally caring people, committed to counting each other as equal in their common project. Michael Walzer recognizes the centrality of the problem of membership in working out a theory of distributive justice, but allows his justification of nation states to rest on the intuition that "most people" prefer distinctive cultures and that therefore they must form states and regulate entry into their extended families.[39]

The theory of loyalty can help us understand the proper structure of communities within which one expects reciprocal caring and benevolence. Loyalties circumscribe communitarian circles, all the members of which take others within the circle to be the objects of their concern.[40] The circle might not be larger than a family, but it can well extend to a tribe, to ethnic groups, to neighborhoods, and to nations. Loyalty to the group and its purposes provides the basis, then, for counting some people in and others out, for believing that insiders count for more and outsiders for less. Rawls's theory makes sense within a circle of reciprocal loyalty and caring, but can hardly support a theory of justice for the planet as a whole (not to mention the problem of future generations). It might be an ideal to extend our loyalty to everyone on the planet, but nourishing utopian visions about faraway places sometimes makes people indifferent to the real suffering next door.

Immanuel Kant, whose theory of the rational universal self supports Rawls's argument, was in fact sensitive to the natural limitations on human sentiment. Kant's views on law and politics differ markedly from his vision of a universal humanity underlying our moral ideals. When it comes to actual decisions in the real world, Kant displayed a commonsense pragmatism wanting in much contemporary moral philosophy. Laws must address people as they really are, not as we wish them to be in a moral utopia. This understanding of the human condition led him to endorse the values of loyalty and patriotism. He writes, "The only conceivable government for men who are capable of possessing rights . . . . is a *patriotic* government."[41] This striking appeal for patriotism from a leading liberal philosopher should make us sit up and take notice. "A *patriotic* attitude," he explains, is one where everyone in the state, not excepting its head, regards the commonwealth as a maternal womb, or the land of the paternal ground from which he himself sprung and which he must leave to his descendants as a treasured pledge.[42]

In a patriotic society, where all individuals share a common past and purpose, each can identify with the others and find in them an equal partner in a common cause. The rooting of the self in a culture of loyalty enables individuals to grasp the humanity of their fellow citizens and to treat them as bearers of equal rights. The private self-seeking that dominates our consumer society gives way to a shared sense that no one can be free and secure in one's rights unless all are. "Each regards himself as authorized to protect the rights of the commonwealth . . . ., but not to submit [the common property of all] to his personal use at his own absolute pleasure."[43] When we take people as they are, we are led to understand and to appreciate the critical role of loyalty in buttressing theories of social justice.

Loyalty is a critical element in a theory of justice; for we invariably need some basis for group cohesion, for caring about others, for seeing them not as strangers who threaten our security but as partners in a common venture. There is no easy response to the idealist who insists that all five billion people constitute one community, with one cause. The answer must begin with an understanding of how we as human beings are constituted and what our natural limits of sympathy may be.

Divergent Senses of Loyalty

My project in this chapter has been to give an account of the core sense of loyalty as an obligation implied in every person's sense of being historically rooted in a set of defining familial, institutional, and national relationships. For most purposes, this analysis of loyalty holds true. But two tangents off this core meaning require special elaboration.

One is the suspect sense of loyalty that troubled us so deeply during the McCarthy anti-Communist scare of the 1950s. It is captured in the ongoing use of the term "loyalty oath" to refer to a declaration that one will uphold the Constitution of the United States.[44] Someone who had been a member or supporter of the Communist Party was presumptively disloyal. There was no suggestion that this "disloyalty" was tantamount to treason or a betrayal of the United States. Rather, the thought seems to have been that present and past Party members, or those who refused to take an oath to support the Constitution, were likely to commit espionage or otherwise betray their country. With regard to those black-listed in Hollywood, the fear was that filmmakers would use their talents to undermine the attachment and devotion of Americans to their country.

When in 1954 the physicist J. Robert Oppenheimer was denied a security clearance on grounds of loyalty, no one suggested that he had already breached his duty of loyalty to the country. The only serious evidence against him was that he had assisted a friend in covering up a questionable political past. Yet the fear was that Oppenheimer was "soft" on issues of national security. He was regarded as sufficiently unreliable to justify fear of security-endangering behavior in the future. This tangential sense of loyalty underscores the degree to which the suspect is identified with the national cause.

In questions of loyalty and fidelity to the national cause, questions are often raised about people who stand slightly outside the mainstream, those to whom the insiders can attribute dual loyalties. Jews, Catholics, and other "marginal" citizens have often been put in this position. Homosexuals are often suspected of having greater loyalties to their friends than to their patria. The most dramatic example of loyalty-inspired bigotry is the framing of Alfred Dreyfus, a career Army officer, for treason against France in 1894. The minimal evidence mustered against Dreyfus, namely, an incriminating letter that he allegedly signed, found an audience among those inclined to suspect an Alsatian Jew of espionage. The way in which the passions of insiders encourage suspicions of dual loyalty and of the untrustworthiness of outsiders properly makes us dubious about loyalty as a virtue. Though persistently troublesome, this sense of loyalty—meaning political reliability—is best understood as a deviation from the central ethic of loyalty.

A second tangential sense of loyalty swings in a different arc. We speak often of the professional loyalty owed by lawyers to their clients, physicians to their patients, and corporate managers to their firms. These professional loyalties derive solely from contract, from voluntary commitments, not from an historical self.

Professional loyalty is expressed in the intensity of care and attention to the client or patient. As Charles Fried argued in a controversial article of the 1970s, a good lawyer "will lavish energy and resources on his existing client, even if it can be shown that others could derive greater benefit from them."[45] Their commitment should be to the client or patient before them, not to those waiting in the halls and not to the society as a whole. A third party could tempt the lawyer away from his commitment to his clients. The competitor might be an opponent in a lawsuit, or, metaphorically, the society as a whole, whose interests would be realized, for example, by convicting a criminal defendant as charged. Loyalty to the client means that the lawyer will not favor these competitive interests at the client's expense.[46]

In a more recent discussion of loyalty, Fried turns to his own role as Solicitor General under President Ronald Reagan.[47] He discusses his own sense of commitment in executing the programs of the President and the Attorney General. His loyalty to the administration was "enjoined by law and a proper conception of the President's establishment."[48] The President is entitled to loyalty, for he chooses whom to appoint to serve him. This sense of loyalty dovetails well with professional loyalty, with the duty of the lawyer to realize the objectives of his or her client. Yet it has nothing to do with friendship, with the historical self, with bonds that run deeper than contract.

Both of these divergent senses of loyalty—loyalty as political reliability and professional loyalty—deepen our grasp of the core cases of loyalty to friends, lovers, family, community, and nation. The basis of loyalty, as I have argued, is the historical self. In neither of these divergent cases does the individual's historical self prove pivotal. Suspicion of outsiders and marginal citizens in national security cases derives not from the historical sensibility of the suspect but rather from the fears of the dominant group. That Oppenheimer and Dreyfus are suspected of disloyalty tells us little about them, more about their accusers. Similarly, in cases of contract-based professional loyalty, the historical self of the lawyer or physician is irrelevant. All that matters are the conventions of her profession and her commitment to the client or patient.

The result of our initial inquiry, then, is to establish the centrality of the historical self in understanding loyalty. History breeds relationships, and these bonds, like friendship, generate a system of ethics different from the universal imperatives of liberal morality. In discussing loyalty we are in the realm of the affective and partial. The basic idea is that the argument begins with our historical roots. We can understand the individual only by locating him or her in a matrix of relationships and crystallized commitments.

Yet all this leaves many questions unanswered. Not all relationships are the same. There must be important differences between loyalty in one-to-one relationships of love and loyalty in political organizations. If it is plausible to talk about loyalty to God, there must be differences between loyalty that is unreciprocated and loyalty that is exchanged, like feudal fealty, for protection. And there are important differences in the degrees of loyalty exacted in particular relationships. Sometimes the minimum commitment of nonbetrayal sustains the relationship; sometimes affirmative duties of devotion are demanded. To probe these complexities, we turn to some case studies. We could find these cases in real life, but in fact the recurrent theme of loyalty in biblical and dramatic literature provides a rich and more accessible repository of our culture's perception of loyalty and its importance to us.

CHAPTER 2

Three Dimensions of Loyalty

In acting loyally, the self acts in harmony with its personal history. One recognizes who one is. Actions of standing by one's friends, family, nation, or people reveal that identity. The self sees in its action precisely what history requires it to do.

A moment of authentic reconciliation with one's past can come upon one suddenly, as when Moses realizes that he is a Jew and binds himself to the fate of his people:

> He went out unto his brethren, and looked on their burdens. And he spied an Egyptian smiting a Hebrew, one of his brethren. And he looked this way and that way, and when he saw that there was no man, he slew the Egyptian, and hid him in the sand.[1]

The biblical account is unclear about how Moses, who had grown up in the house of Pharaoh, developed what we would call a Jewish consciousness. But he sensed his kinship with an oppressed people and came to their aid. His act expresses the demands of an inner tie to his own people. An Egyptian might have done the same thing, perhaps out of a sense of universal brotherhood. For an Egyptian, however, the intervention would have been an act of justice, not of loyalty and self-realization. The difference is important.

Moses' act of loyalty toward a single oppressed "Hebrew, one of his brethren" changes the course of his life. As he flees to the desert to escape arrest, the follower of the biblical narrative knows that this is a man who is capable of leading his people. Dramatic acts of loyalty—as well as of betrayal—enable us to recognize depths of character in the unfolding tale. In the legends of ancient cultures as well as on the modern Western stage, the theme of loyalty focuses a magnifying glass on heroes and villains.

The Loyalty of Love

Loyalty is better suited for the theater than for subtle and intricate psychological novels. It lends itself to a medium in which the storyteller seeks to cast the image of a character in a few bold strokes. On the stage and in legends told by the campfire, tales of personal and familial loyalty abound. Lear's descent into madness is embedded in a frame of undisputed betrayal by Goneril and Regan and the unflagging loyalty of Cordelia. Hamlet's unwavering attachment to his father's honor frames his prolonged reflections whether he should act or not act to right the wrong of family betrayal.

Even as sophisticated moderns accustomed to psychological complexity, we are disarmed by the simple expressions of loyalty that inform dramatic moments. Cordelia's simple response to Lear's final recognition of her honest devotion is memorable but hardly eloquent. "No cause, no cause," she responds to his confession that she had reason not to love him. Her loyalty is no discovery, either to her or the audience; it is the premise that enables us better to understand the complications of Lear's misplaced trust in Goneril and Regan.

Ibsen's picaresque character Peer Gynt romps across the world, forgetting that as a young man he betrothed and then abandoned the lovely Solveig. She waits patiently for him, though he, in turn, hardly makes an effort to bind himself to the mast to avoid the temptations of the sensual world. At the end of his journey, he comes upon her, still waiting for him in the cottage they briefly shared. Facing death, he asks her pathetically, "Where has Peer Gynt been? . . . Where I've been: Myself, entire, complete—Peer Gynt with God's stamp on my brow?" As we smile at the prodigal Peer's naiveté, Solveig's answer disarms: "In my faith. In my hope. In my love." The moment is as transparent as Cordelia's declaration of filial loyalty. One sees Cordelia and Solveig expressing a self that comes alive in their attachments.

The theater and the telling of heroic legends have much to teach us about the nature and structure of loyalty. Is there a difference between loyalty to one's people (Moses) and loyalty to a lover (Solveig)? Do these loyalties to people differ fundamentally from loyalties to a cause or to the ideas bounded up in religious piety? In an effort to chart these dimensions of loyalty, let us turn to a variety of dramatic examples, the most illuminating of which is Sophocles' *Antigone*, a crucible of loyalty and betrayal, religious devotion, and secular obligation.

The background of the play is the incestuous marriage between Oedipus and Iocasta: Antigone and her sister Ismene are the sole surviving offspring; their two brothers, Etiocles and Polyneices, have slain each other in the battle for Thebes, the former fighting for the homeland and the latter joining forces with the invading army of Argos. Iocasta's brother Creon succeeds to the throne of Thebes. In an apparent effort to consolidate his power, he decrees that the loyal Etiocles shall receive an honorable burial but that Polyneices, who "came to burn [the gods'] pillared shrines and sacred treasures," should receive no burial at all. In his view, Polyneices was guilty of treason, and traitors deserve no better. The penalty for disobeying Creon's decree is death by stoning.

From the outset, Antigone is resolved to disobey the decree and abide instead by her perception of the Greek god Hades' imperative to provide her brother with a proper burial. As the action is reported to us, she twice slips past the guards overseeing the body, performs the required rites, and sprinkles dirt on Polyneices' corpse. Yet there is no dramatic conflict in these acts. They are the premise for the dialogues that constitute the action on stage.

Antigone is enmeshed in relationships that could claim her loyalties. Creon is her uncle. She is engaged to Creon's son Haemon. Yet neither these attachments nor the opposition of her confidante Ismene overcomes the imperative to stand by her fallen brother. When Antigone proposes that they disobey the decree, Ismene responds, "What can your meaning be?" Ismene's only thought is that the burial is "forbidden in Thebes." But for Antigone the opposing imperative is clear: "I will do my part . . . to a brother. False to him I will never be found." Ismene rejects what her sister terms a sharing in "the toil and the deed."

After the deed, Ismene seeks to reclaim her relationship to her sister. In front of Creon she declares herself willing to share the guilt and suffer the same fate as her sister. But Antigone rejects the offer:

"A friend in words is not the friend that I love." It is too late for Ismene to be loyal. Complicity in the deed would have been a way to side with Antigone as well as Polyneices. But once the moment has passed, Ismene's desire for self-destruction cannot recoup the opportunity for shared assertion.

Creon too is caught in a potential conflict between his role as ruler of the city and his familial tie to the fallen Polyneices. His conflict is resolved by suppressing his familial relationship; the fate of his nephew means nothing in comparison to his commitment to rewarding civic virtue and punishing traitors against Thebes. That the two protagonists resolve their conflict in arguably oversimplified, opposing directions creates the frame for the play's dramatic conflict.

As critics have debated the play throughout the centuries, their question has always been, Who was right? Moderns tend to read the play as a vindication of Antigone's loyalty to her brother and her willingness to defy a secular order for the sake of a higher duty. Yet there is also a case to be made on behalf of Creon's championing loyalty to the city over loyalty to family. Behind this dispute lies a more basic question whether there is a right answer to the conflict. Perhaps there is no clear resolution of the conflict, no way to determine whether Antigone's understanding of Hades' command should have prevailed over Creon's earthbound concentration on civic loyalty.

Those who read the play as a moral conflict tend to think that there must be one right answer, for it is in the nature of morality, as understood in the Kantian tradition, that moral action is necessitated by a single prevailing duty. Recently Martha Nussbaum has argued that the play expresses the tragedy of irreconcilable conflict.[2] There is no clearly correct choice, she argues, between Antigone's contradictory duties to Hades and to Creon. The tragedy consists in the necessity of a choice, and the recognition that however Antigone chooses, she will be sacrificing a significant value. Understanding the play as a conflict of loyalties supports Nussbaum's reading; the competing demands of loyalty both have a claim on the self. Antigone is citizen of Thebes as well as sister to Polyneices. Her identity as citizen entails a duty of loyalty to the city as well as to her family. Yet there is no reason to suppose a single loyalty—like a single moral duty—will dominate and eliminate the conflict. The most one can expect, as the play teaches us, is that one duty may have an edge, though the conflicting duty remains morally compelling.

The dramatic intensity of *Antigone* unfolds not in the deed but in the arguments offered by Creon (and sometimes the chorus) to defend his decree and the efforts by everyone else (Antigone, Ismene, Haemon, the chorus, and later the oracle Teiresias) to convince Creon that his decree was wrong. Creon defends himself not only by attacking Polyneices' loyalty but by claiming absolute authority as ruler. The chorus applauds him when he says that "disobedience is the worst of evils," and then he seemingly defends the inevitability of the decree: "An offense against power cannot be brooked by him who has power in his keeping." Whether this particular decree was necessary to maintain his authority, Creon insists that stable government requires submission to the state's decrees: "Whomsoever this city may appoint, that man must be obeyed, in little things and great, in just things and unjust." Yet Creon also has a moral argument on his side—a point to which I will turn presently.

Significantly, Creon is the only character who refers to the decree as law. Antigone reserves the term "law" for the commandments "the gods have established in honor." The other principals in the debate treat the decree simply as an act of Creon's will, bearing no resemblance to the inevitability of nature's laws. Though Creon stands relatively alone in the exchanges, he can play the familiar card of stable government and the consequent duty of all to submit to the law as decreed by established secular authority.

Ismene, Antigone, and Haemon take up distinct positions in their efforts to convince Creon that he has erred. Ismene appeals to Creon's personal interest in the welfare of his house: "But will you slay the betrothed of your own son?" The king responds crudely, "There are other fields for him to plough." Once again Ismene has missed the meaning of loyal attachments. She fails to act when loyalty requires it, and she mistakenly thinks that a man obsessed by his power and statecraft would bend for the sake of his son.

Antigone never mentions Haemon and indeed never invokes any argument other than the supremacy of Hades' law and her "longer allegiance to the dead than to the living" for, as she says, with attention to their fate, "in that world [of Hades, she] shall abide forever." The same line of thought takes on a different hue, however, in the final colloquy between Creon and Antigone. He makes a supreme moral defense of the decree by insisting that it would be unjust to honor the disloyal brother with the same burial accorded the loyal

Etiocles. "But the good does not desire a like portion with the evil." Antigone sidesteps the argument of justice: "'Tis not my nature to join in hating, but in loving." If she cherished the life of Polyneices as much as that of Etiocles, she must recoil at distinguishing between them in death.

In response to Antigone's resting her case on the imperatives of love, Creon begins a series of seemingly misogynistic remarks about the evils of deferring to women. "If you must needs love, love them," he responds to Antigone, "While I live no woman shall rule me." The way to read these and other similarly distempered remarks about women, I suggest, is to see in them a rejection of Antigone's ethic of love and fraternal loyalty. These are values that mean little to the ruler of Thebes, as his remarks to Ismene already revealed. His value of civil loyalty transcends the flesh and blood attachments that move Antigone to commit her deed. As Nussbaum argues, the only relevant family for Creon is the population of Thebes, the only relevant loyalty, loyalty to the city.[3] Antigone, as woman, as sister, represents an alternative system of values, a challenge to the supremacy of civic loyalty.

Creon charges Antigone with deviating from the opinion—or at least the behavior—of the mass of Thebans. Significantly, he takes this to be a cause for shame: She should be embarrassed to find herself alone and isolated in her supposed deference to a higher authority. But Antigone has already made it clear that she feels no shame. She volunteers that the burial rites were carried out in public. "There is nothing shameful," she insists, "in piety to a brother."

In his challenge to Creon, Haemon turns this theme on its head and charges that it is indeed his father who stands alone. In response to the claim that Antigone is "tainted with the malady" of "show[ing] respect for evildoers," Haemon responds, "Our Theban folk with one voice denies it." Despite the force of this and other arrows aimed at his father, Haemon's challenge remains a model of filial loyalty. He repeatedly reassures his father that it is he for whom Haemon truly cares. He never mentions his love for Antigone, insisting always it is for Creon, "and for [himself] and for the gods below" that he pleads. His appeal embodies the notion of loyal opposition. His loyalty runs not to the external figure of an authoritarian king, but to his essentially wise father. In the end, he makes little progress in moving Creon from his resolve to execute the decree. His exit, with the threat "not shall you ever set eyes upon my face," carries foreboding of the impending denouement of the conflict.

In fact, as Haemon despairs and disaster is about to befall Creon's house, the ruler begins to show traces of regret. He modifies Antigone's punishment to give her a chance of survival. Instead of stoning, he decrees that she should be put in a cave with a supply of food and water, to test whether by "praying to Hades, the only god whom she worships, . . . she will obtain release from death." Creon is in the throes of recognizing his error. He creates this ambivalent punishment so "that the city may avoid a public stain." There would, of course, be no stain if the punishment were in harmony with the laws of this world and the next. But his willingness to change comes too late. The world comes askew; blood and doom seize the ruling house of Thebes. Creon leaves the stage bemoaning "the crushing fate" that has "leapt upon [his] head."

This play provides a remarkable grid for understanding the complexities of loyal relationships. Loyalties to kin and lovers interweave with the demand of attachment to the people of Thebes and the gods Zeus and Hades. The question remains whether in the end the motivating force for Antigone's decision was a personal loyalty to the gods or a moral conviction, inspired by her religious belief, that it was simply not "right" to allow him to lie there "unwept, unsepulchered, a welcome object for the birds . . . to feast on him at will." In the play itself, there is little evidence that Antigone gets Hades' command right. No other character confirms her reading of Hades' will.[4] Creon never rejects the conventional pantheon enthroning Zeus and Hades. Yet what Creon hears as a command to reward the loyal and punish the disloyal, Antigone hears in the idiom of family attachments.

There seems to be not only a transparent command of the gods that drives Antigone, but her judgment that the command, as she understands it, is morally right. Yet many loyal actions seem to be motivated solely by an emotional, almost instinctive attachment, untempered by moral reflection about the right thing to do. This deep personal loyalty is expressed not only by Solveig's waiting for Peer but by Cordelia's adhering to her father despite his fuming and irrational rejection. The personal attachment, the nonrational embracing of the other as part of oneself, dominates all other explanations of these devoted women. It is indeed a role that, beginning with Queen Penelope in the *Odyssey*, seems often to be attributed to female heroes.

An unmatched example of this selfless devotion to others is found in the legends of the Jews (the *Midrash*), one in particular that improvises on the biblical tale of Jacob, Rachel, and Leah.[5] Jacob works seven years to win the hand of his beloved Rachel. Laban, his employer, feels compelled to find a mate first for his older, less attractive daughter Leah ("of weak eyes") and therefore sends her veiled to Jacob's tent on the wedding night. Laban's deception (like Rivka's earlier deception of Isaac favoring Jacob over Esau) was arguably an act of loyalty. The rabbis improvised a tale of loyalty that goes far beyond the biblical story. According to the *Midrash*, Jacob suspects that Laban might cheat him and therefore he teaches Rachel special signs that she should use in bed, under the wedding veil, to indicate that it is really she with whom he is consummating the marriage. But Rachel cannot bear to see her sister humiliated, and so (with less than full loyalty to the poor Jacob) she shares the secret signs with her sister. Not only that, as she confesses to God, but:

> Moreover, I hid under the bed where he was lying with my sister, and he would speak to her and she would be silent, and I would answer everything he said so that he would not recognize my sister's voice, and thus I did this kindness for her. I was not jealous of her and I did not permit her to be humiliated.[6,7]

The self-sacrifice in Solveig's and Cordelia's loyalty does not leave them selfless or indeed, in any sense, less well off. They are not like Cyrano, who resigns himself to losing Roxanne and therefore savors his art as poet as he suffers unrequited love. They are not like Sydney Carton in *A Tale of Two Cities*, whose love for Lucie Manette moves him to accept the guillotine so that she and Charles Darney may escape from France and live. Those who express their loyalty in patiently waiting exult in the significance their own lives acquire. As Solveig views her relationship to Peer, he comes alive in their embracing love. Rachel's loyalty to her sister is also life affirming, for she then challenges God to be more patient with his wayward people.[8]

In the loyalty expressed by Solveig, Cordelia, and Rachel, ideology and rectitude are absent. There is no claim of truth or divine command that, as in Antigone's case, justifies the action. There is no point to the loyalty except the loving attachment to the other. It cements the relationship of two people or perhaps an entire family, but it remains contained within them. Nothing more is at stake than the welfare of those bound together.

Group Loyalty

A distinct form of loyalty, notable in political and corporate life, adds a factor of ideological commitment to the emotion of attachment. Effective mass action, in groups ranging from labor unions to fighting armies, depends ultimately on the subservience of foot soldiers to their leadership. This subservience is likely to remain firm if it not only feeds on fear but is nourished by reciprocal loyalties within the group, and by hierarchial loyalty to the leadership. Creon correctly thanks the citizens of Thebes for being loyal to him after the death of Oedipus, thus assuring continuity and stability in government. If the first is the loyalty of love, then this is the loyalty of group action.

While the loyalty of love typically runs in one direction (Peer and Lear need not do anything in particular for Solveig and Cordelia), political loyalties display intricate reciprocity. The leadership can act in reliance on their followers, and the followers acquire a sense of themselves as serving a goal larger than a single life. If they do not stand in a personal relationship with the group's leadership, they are tied to the group by a shared understanding that they are members of the union or party, or citizens of the nation. The cause, the idea, as well as the personal object of their loyalty, brings meaning to their lives. In the grip of a cause, one lives not for consumption and pleasure but for the victory of the crusade, the company, the union, the party, or the nation.

Though the cause must prevail, enormous personal gratifications accrue to those who are part of the struggle. When it is all for one and one for all, a larger life pulsates in every individual. A million people taking to the streets in Leipzig to protest the condition of their lives brings like-minded souls into a harmony of purpose. Whatever the outcome of their shared mission, the politically bonded ground their lives in a sense of higher purpose.

The bedrock idea in group loyalty is not *relationship* but *membership* in a group competing with other groups. Membership makes one an insider; it confers identity within a matrix of relationships both to other members and to the leadership of the organization. Membership crystallizes in two stages: entry and identification. One may join a political party or a labor movement, and one is born into a family, a tribe, or a nation. Whether entry is voluntary or involuntary, it has an objectified form, an institutional shell. Lists are kept, passports issued, heads counted. Without doing more, one remains a member of the group that treats one as a member.

Beyond entry, a second stage is required for membership to enter into one's sense of identity. In the course of time, one thinks of oneself as Democrat or Republican, liberal or conservative, left or right. These labels become so much a part of personal identity that those who are accustomed to them insist on using them even after they have lost their traditional meaning. No one knows exactly what it means to be a leftist or liberal today, but there are many who never give up (or never accept) the label. The same process of identification occurs in corporate and university life, most remarkably in Japanese culture, where it may be easier to change wives than to change corporate homes. These group identities bear a strong resemblance to the sense of self that develops in a family or nation. It is a commonplace of these corporate bodies to invoke the images of family and community—sometimes in excess of the actual bonds—in order to cultivate this sense of identity.

Loyalties arise, I argue, not just from the fact of entry but from the crystallization of the self in the second stage of membership. The genesis of these group loyalties parallels the deepening of attachments in personal relationships. Yet there is one important difference. Where entry has a formal quality, where membership is marked by being inscribed or born into the group, betrayal does not dissolve the bond between the member and the group to which he owes loyalty. In the case of friendship and love, betrayal undermines the relationship. Being a lover or a friend is, as it were, contingent on ongoing loyalty. Yet membership in a group is defined by the formal conditions of entry, not by acts of loyalty. Polyneices remains the nephew of Creon, even though he fights against Thebes. Citizens who betray their countries remain citizens, and they are punished as citizens, as insiders.

These group loyalties, nourished by an evolving sense of self, bring with them the "permanent moral danger" that MacIntyre fears.[9] The greatest abuses of individual rights have occurred in the name of someone's church, party, or nation. For all those who marched with Martin Luther King, Jr., there were millions more seduced by the *Führer*. For every prophet there are countless mountebanks, and in every loyal follower may lurk the mindless zealot yearning to be a slave. For all the virtues of loyalty to community and nation, the countervailing vices of xenophobia and racism put us on guard.

The moral challenge for every devotee of a cause is to find the proper balance of loyalty and independent moral judgment. In *Antigone*, Ismene emerges as the exemplar of the nonthinking loyalist. She is not enthusiastic about Creon's decree, but she lacks the distance and the courage even to think about whether it warrants resistance. The model of loyal resistance is Haemon's deferential but persistent and increasingly bold attack on his father. If the play were rewritten to conform to the conditions of the Third Reich, we would find Antigone being executed early, apprehended in an effort to harbor her Communist brother. Ismene would engage in what the Germans call *innere Emigration*, a spiritual emigration compatible with outward deference to arbitrary laws. Most significantly, Haemon would stand with Colonel Claus von Stauffenberg as a German patriot, executed for an attempt to assassinate Hitler in July 1944. His loyalty to his nation would be expressed in an attack from within the house of power.

The disconcerting fact is, however, that Haemon commits suicide rather than patricide. At the moment that he could have turned against his father, he thrusts himself upon his sword. Perhaps this is but a dramatic moment auguring the violent doom that will descend upon the house of Creon. Yet to turn against his father, Haemon would have had to express a deeper loyalty to Thebes as his fatherland, and this impersonal commitment to the state behind its king seems wanting in the political motivations of those struggling against Creon.

Haemon's suicide bears resemblance to an incident recently disclosed in Nikita Khrushchev's taped memoirs.[10] After the ruling clique in the Kremlin decided to invade Hungary in October 1956, Anastas Mikoyan, who had been in Budapest when the decision was taken, was so disturbed that he threatened to commit suicide. According to Khrushchev, Mikoyan was convinced that "armed intervention was not right and that it would undermine the reputation of our government and party."[11] Arguing fervently with Khrushchev was an act of loyalty to him and to the party.[12] Suicide would have been nothing but an act of despair.

Loyalties generally lead people to suspend judgment about right and wrong. In a loving relationship or in the loyalty of group action, the loyal person defers to the judgment of the other, the person or group with whom one is bound in a relationship of loyalty. The recurrent problem is working out the limits of this deference. Some abstract sense of right and wrong, a "shock to the conscience," can set the point beyond which one will not go. For our immediate purposes, however, the intriguing question is whether conflicting loyalties can by themselves circumscribe limits to the willingness to suspend judgment about right and wrong. Specifically, can one interpret Antigone's willingness to disobey Creon's decree as a matter of loyalty to Zeus and Hades? As she tells us, it is critical that Hades "desires these rites." Does it follow that her disobedience of the civil order was an expression of a higher loyalty?

Loyalty to gods and God

In general, it makes good sense to think of one's relationship with God as a commitment of loyalty. The faith of the believer is constantly subject to temptation by a false power who seeks to seduce the believer into idolatry or counterfeit forms of worship. In this sense, the devil is a competitor to the God of Israel. At the outset of the book of Job, the devil wagers with God that Job will not remain loyal. In the critical moment of his suffering, Job's wife urges him to turn his back on God ("Curse God and die"), but Job remains steadfast in his faith. The devil tempts Jesus in the desert with a show of supernatural powers, but Jesus remains loyal.

The original sin in the Garden of Eden lends itself to interpretation either as a sin of disobedience or of disloyalty. The problem with the former is that it is not clear why Adam and Eve must obey God's word, particularly to the point of abstaining from acquiring knowledge of good and evil. Nor is it clear why God should be angry about his creatures' transgressing an apparently arbitrary order. The story makes more sense if one thinks of it as a tale of betrayal rather than disobedience. God expects his created beings to remain solely in relationship with him, closing themselves off from independent sources of knowledge. God appears here not as a law-giver, not as king, but as father, as the natural object of human affection and loyalty. Adam and Eve are put to a test of their loyalty, and they fail. The serpent offers Eve a broader horizon, and she accepts, then inducing Adam to follow the path of independence.

Then God reenters the garden. As God searches for Adam, one expects an affirmation that Adam remains steadfast in his relationship with his parent-creator. One searches the text in vain for the response *Hineni*—"I am here"—with which Abraham responds to God when his loyalty is tested at Mt. Moriah.[13] God tests Abraham with the command to sacrifice Isaac, his sole hope for the future. The command runs contrary to natural morality as well as God's own earlier pronouncement that Abraham's seed will prosper. Yet Abraham confirms that he is still in a relationship with God: *Hineni*—"I am here.". But upon eating of the fruit and discovering their nakedness, Adam and Eve are no longer there for God. "And they heard the voice of the Lord God walking in the garden . . . : and the man and his wife hid themselves from the presence of the Lord God amongst the trees of the garden."[14]

Banishment from the garden now becomes inevitable. The original relationship is breached and recast forever. God can no longer be simply parent to his created beings. They enter into a world of dominance, scarcity, competition. Adam rules over his wife; "by the sweat of his brow" he must earn his bread; their children will become locked in homicidal conflict. The ongoing questions of justice infuse all human actions, and the role of God expands gradually from father to self-binding authority over nature[15] to "Judge of all the Universe."[16]

Although the themes of law and justice eventually become dominant in God's relationship to human beings, the role of loyalty remains critical in understanding the religious life, particularly of Jews. In its biblical foundations, God is king, father, and protector of his people, who in turn owe him a duty of loyalty. This duty is breached initially in Eden, and then repeatedly when the Jews turn to other gods, worshiping the golden calf, Baal, or Peor. They go whoring after foreign gods, as the prophets unceasingly remind us. Idolatry stands in relation to God as adultery to one's lover and treason to one's country. But what, we may ask, is the basis for this duty of Jews to worship the god of Exodus, a god who only hints at his true name ("I am what I am"), over all other gods?

The covenant (a seemingly voluntary contract) at Sinai is central to the Jewish conception of their duty to be loyal and to worship the God who appeared to them. Christians borrowed this basic idea in an effort to cast their new relationship forged at Calvary in language already familiar to them from the legends of the Jews. The covenant signals entry into relationship with God. It also presupposes membership of the Jews in the community that covenants with God. The covenant is a mode of entry, yet the Jews' duty of loyalty to God is hardly based on voluntary contract. The Jewish self-understanding of the biblical story reveals that the Jews had no choice in the matter. According to the legends of the rabbis, as God offers the Jews the covenant at Sinai, he holds the mountain over their heads; if they refuse he will destroy them.[17] Entry into the covenant was an offer the Jews "could not refuse." The Jews are "chosen" in the sense that they do not choose themselves.

The better explanation of the Jewish duty to worship the God who reveals himself at Sinai lies in the historical genesis of the Jewish people. When God presents himself in the Bible, he identifies himself historically: "I am the God of they father, the God of Abraham, the God of Isaac, and the God of Jacob."[18] At the outset of the Ten Commandments, God recites his unique intervention in political history: "I am the Lord thy God, which have brought thee out of the land of Egypt, out of the house of bondage."[19] The emphasis on saving the Jews from their enemies and taskmasters reminds one of a feudal lord's claim to fealty. Protection lies at the root of the feudal relationship. God heard the cry of the Jewish people and came to their aid. As Jews conceive of their history, that is the event that brought them into being. When the covenant with its detailed laws of behavior was offered at Sinai, there was no plausible choice but to accept.[20]

The historical self finds expression in all three dimensions of loyalty. In personal and family relationships, the child acquires a sense of personality incorporating others as intimate faces in his or her biography. In the genesis of group loyalties, parallel changes occur in the adult sense of self. Membership in a company or a political party, citizenship in a nation or a community, enter into the foundations of personality. In the relationship between God and man, God's historical link to the Jews becomes the means by which God identifies himself. As remembering Sinai is an indispensable part of a Jew's sense of self, meditating on the historical moment at Calvary is part of what it means to be Christian. Loyalty sometimes takes the face of fidelity to friends, sometimes of fealty to nation, sometimes of faith in God. In all three dimensions of loyalty, the historical self generates a duty to stand by those who have become a critical part of one's biography.

These three dimensions of loyalty are distinguished in part by the directions and planes of attachment. In the personal loyalties of friendship and love, the lines of obligations bind individuals in an intimate relationship. In cases of group loyalty, the members of the group are horizontally loyal to each other and, in addition, vertically loyal to their leader. In the case of loyalty to God, the commitment is unidirectional. God reciprocates, in the Judeo-Christian tradition, partly as father, partly as feudal lord and leader, who responds to loyalty primarily as protector and lawgiver.

These planes of loyalty are distinguished by the role of rectitude in maintaining loyalty. In loving relationships, the sense that one is doing the right thing plays a minimal role in the nurturing the bond. In political action, the loyalty of participants to each other reinforces a sense of righteousness in holding firm to the cause. Religious loyalties vacillate between an uncritical submission to God's word and a critical sense that only that which is right should be treated as God's command.

That there are three dimensions contributes to maintaining the proper balance among them. The tension between loyalty to an individual and loyalty to the nation minimizes the "permanent moral danger" of each. Sartre did say that if he had to choose between his mother and the French Resistance, he would choose his mother.[21] But there may be many cases in which loyalty to the national cause requires one to leave one's family and take up arms. Religious loyalties can trump the claims of nation, as witnessed by Antigone's choice,[22] and legends abound in which a divine command displaces loyalty to children, as evidenced by Agamemnon's sacrificing Iphegenia[23] and Abraham's willingness to carry through God's command to sacrifice Isaac. Abject submission to God's word is so troubling precisely because it seems that personal loyalties should enter into the way we perceive and interpret the divine command. Abraham should have loved his son enough to have heard God with a clarity more consistent with our sense of right and wrong.

The interplay of these three dimensions of loyalty implies that in making difficult life choices we typically act counter to some loyalties in order to further others. If Antigone must choose between the demands of the civic loyalty and the perceived word of the god Hades, she cannot but make the choice with a sense of regret. If Sartre turns his back on the nation for the sake of his mother, he cannot but carry with him a sense that he should have done more for France. In the realm of conflicting loyalties, there are no clear choices. There is only the ongoing process of self-definition expressed in siding with one of the conflicting demands. The inevitable betrayal of some for the sake of others captures Nussbaum's thesis of moral tragedy as produced by irreconcilable claims.[24] The tragedy is better understood when the dimensions of loyalty come into proper focus.

When a duty of loyalty arises, it is not clear precisely what the duty demands, when our conduct is sufficient to be loyal. In all three dimensions, the duty of loyalty vacillates between minimal and maximal demands. Minimal loyalties consist in not betraying the object of one's loyalty, not committing adultery, not fighting for the enemy, not worshiping foreign gods. The demands of loyalty sometimes expand to exact more than the negative act of nonbetrayal to include affirmative attention and devotion to spouse, nation, and a jealous God. To get a grip on this concept that oscillates between a passive minimum and a fervent maximum, we should think first about the clearest cases of minimal loyalty.

CHAPTER 3

Minimal Loyalty: "Thou Shalt Not Betray Me"

The worst epithets are reserved for the sin of betrayal. Worse than murder, worse than incest, betrayal of country invites universal scorn. Betrayal of a lover is regarded by many as an irremediable breach. For the religious, betrayal of God is the supreme vice. The specific forms of betrayal—adultery, treason, and idolatry—all reek with evil.

All of these forms of betrayal have become commonplace in modern life. Adultery is routine. Idolatry is no longer thought to be a vice. And espionage, though still punished and punished severely, has become a crime of conscience. As an expression of political conviction, a generation of intellectuals, led by Anthony Blunt, shared secrets with the Kremlin. In some quarters it has become chic to downplay the loyalties traditionally inherent in citizenship. When Jonathan Pollard delivers classified information to Israel, many Americans find it hard to see evil in the deed of selling secrets to a political ally. Mordechai Vanunu, an Israeli, delivers secrets about his country's nuclear capacity to a British newspaper and the act appears to many to be a breakthrough for world peace.

Precisely because national betrayal is no longer clearly perceived, the courts and other officials overcompensate for public doubts with apparently excessive punishment. In 1951, Judge Irving Kaufman sentenced Julius and Ethel Rosenberg to death, even though their guilt seems not to have been proven at trial.[1] His justification of the death penalty by recalling the extent of American suffering in Korea remains a model of irrational thinking about sentencing. In 1987 another federal judge condemned Jonathan Pollard to life imprisonment, even though the tangible harm to the United States is still subject to debate.

Betrayal and treachery may harm the traitor himself by depriving him of the people who share his culture and history. Yet these acts do not entail victims the way other crimes do. Murder, theft, rape, arson, robbery, and the other hard-core felonies leave damage in their wake. The decedent is killed; the property taken; the body violated. Crime consists in an attack against a tangible human interest. The crime succeeds when the goods of life, limb, property, and freedom fall hostage to the aggressor's intentions.

Treason is different. It lies not in the concrete realm of causing harm but in the ethereal realm of breaching a relationship of required loyalty. The breach consists, in the language of the U.S. Constitution, in "adhering to the enemy, giving them aid and comfort." Adhering implies emotional identification. According to the Constitution, the United States may exact emotional attachment. The nation, through its government, may insist on minimal loyalty: If the nation has enemies, no citizen may identify with them and give them sustenance.[2]

The term "enemy" has come to receive a narrow reading. For the time being, at least, it is interpreted to cover only enemies in declared wars. Saddam Hussein's Iraq was the enemy in the Gulf War, but neither Vietnam nor North Korea was an official enemy in the wars fought on their territories. There are at least two reasons, then, why Pollard could not have been guilty of treason in selling secrets to Israel. First, Israel was an ally, and second, even if Israel had not been an ally, there was no Congressional declaration that put it off limits. It was highly questionable, then, at the time of sentencing Pollard, for Secretary of Defense Casper Weinberger to submit a memorandum to Judge Robinson that labeled Pollard a traitor.[3]

The language of treason and treachery incites passions. It is hard, in principle, to know how to punish treason. Is it a crime worse than homicide, worse than rape? If the death penalty is unconstitutional as applied in rape cases, does it follow that it should be equally suspect in cases of treason? There is no law on this question, for we lack an appropriate methodology for thinking about the gravity of treason.

Just punishment requires a sense of proportion, which in turn requires sensitivity to the injury inflicted. In the metaphoric formula of Exodus: "Thou shalt give life for life, eye for eye, tooth for tooth."[4] The more the victim suffers, the more pain should be inflicted on the criminal. In the context of betrayal, the gears of this basic principle of justice, the *lex talionis*, fail to engage the problem. The theory of punishment does not mesh with the crime when there is no tangible harm, no friction against the physical welfare of the victim. Traitors betray, but their breach of faith is complete without anyone suffering actual harm. Their disloyalty disturbs us, but not because of traces left by their treachery in the physical world.

There is every likelihood that Weinberger's branding Pollard a traitor contributed to Judge Robinson's decision to impose a life sentence. The harm represented by sharing secrets with an ally in the Middle East could hardly justify a severe penalty under the *lex talionis*. Only by assimilating Pollard's crime of espionage to the grave sin of treason could one think that life imprisonment was a fitting response.

Adultery has the same structure as treason. The breach of the relationship occurs when one partner emotionally identifies with another man or woman. As Jesus teaches in Matthew 5:28: He who "looketh on a woman to lust after her hath committed adultery with her already in his heart." Lusting after another man or woman is a mode of adhering—not necessarily to an enemy but to a person off limits. Though Jimmy Carter's confession that he had lusted after other women met with polite derision, he was drawing on common assumptions about loyalty in marriage.

Though still nominally criminal in some states, adultery is almost never prosecuted. The tendency today is to think that betrayal in marriage should fall outside the scope of the criminal law. Adultery is not quite a "victimless offense," as are many other forms of alleged sexual misconduct, such as homosexual sodomy and incest between nonprocreating adults. Yet the potential harm is not regarded as a matter of public concern.

The potential harm of treason does, of course, concern governments that wield the power of criminal prosecution and punishment. Yet we have no guidelines for knowing how to punish the spiritual event of adhering to the enemy. Without a theory to guide us, we are likely to fall prey to emotional attacks on the disloyal. Breaching the bonds of loyalty takes on the quality of an absolute wrong, and no punishment seems excessive to counteract this fissure in the ties that bind us together.

The analogue in the 1950s to Weinberger's attack on Pollard was Judge Irving Kaufman's rationale for sentencing Julius and Ethel Rosenberg to the electric chair, again for the espionage of sharing military secrets with a former ally. Kaufman held the Rosenbergs accountable for Stalin's acquiring the atom bomb, and as an alleged consequence, entering the war in Korea against the United States. He described their crime as "treason" and as a "betrayal resulting in more than 50,000 casualties."[5] Looking back on the execution of the Rosenbergs, one can only wonder about the way in which the anti-Communist fervor sweeping the country fell on Jewish outsiders, subject to the ever-ready accusation of dual loyalty and weak national devotion. The passion of punishing an absolute wrong claims its victims.

The History of Treason

The law's treating treason as an absolute wrong dates back to the first significant criminal statute enacted in English history, passed by Parliament under Edward III in 1351. The archaic language of this statute bequeathed the terminology of treason to the entire English-speaking world. The crime is defined to include not only adhering to the enemy but "compassing the death of the King" or other members of the royal household.[6]

Compassing the death of the king is a matter of intention. The intention to kill the crown breaches the duty of fealty required under the feudal system. The king undertakes to protect his subjects, and in return they must be faithful and loyal, in mind as well as deed. Compassing is more than merely desiring the death of the king, but it appears to be less than actually "acting out" the intention to kill the king. Thomas Hobbes described the crime of compassing as one that "lyeth hidden in the breast of him that is accused."[7]

As a practical matter, the state could not prosecute for treason without some act evidencing the treasonable act of compassing. The same statute that punishes "compassing" demands that betrayal in the heart must be "provably attainted by open deed." There must be some act in the open, an act witnessed by others, that establishes the inner breach in either compassing the death of the king or adhering to the enemy. This came to be known as the requirement of an overt act. A good example is the prosecution in 1634 of Crohagan, an Irish priest, who reportedly said in Portugal, "I will kill the King [of England] if I come upon him."[8] When he came to England two years later, he was arrested and convicted of treason on the basis of what he had said in Portugal. His words provided sufficient evidence of compassing the death of the king. The required overt act appears to be his speaking the words that evidenced his intention.

The question whether words alone could constitute sufficient evidence of treason became a central focus of seventeenth- and eighteenth-century debates about the nature of treason. The leading commentator of the early seventeenth century, Sir Edward Coke, had observed just before Crohagan's case: "And it is commonly said, that bare words may make a Heretic, but not a Traitor, without an overt act."[9] This scholarly opinion appears to be a preliminary, though partial, victory for free speech; it implies that no one could be convicted of treason just for uttering hostile thoughts toward the king.[10] According to this view, the required overt act would have to consist in steps taken toward carrying out the hostile intention.

A subsequent commentator, William Hale, agreed with Coke. But if Coke is right about free speech, what does one make of Crohagan's conviction? Was it to be accepted as a sound precedent interpreting the statute of 1351? Hale accepted the conviction and reasoned that Crohagan had committed an overt act different from uttering his threatening words against the king. His coming to England supposedly in furtherance of his plan constituted the "open deed" by which his intentions were "provably attainted."

Others disagreed with Coke's libertarian view on the relationship of spoken words to treason. A leading royalist commentator of the early eighteenth century had concluded: "Words are the natural way for a man whereby to express the imagination of the heart."[11] Though these sentiments restricting freedom of speech are historically suspect,[12] several American colonies enacted treason statutes that linked "adhering to the enemy" with expressions of support for King George III. New York made it a felony "to attempt to persuade any inhabitant to renounce allegiance to the State or acknowledge allegiance to the King."[13] Virginia made it a crime, punishable by five years' imprisonment, "to maintain and defend the authority . . . . of the King or Parliament of Great Britain."[14] Acts of speech are recurrently invoked as the best evidence of "what lyeth hidden in the breast" of the suspect: "What other proof can there be had of it than words Spoken or Written," wrote Hobbes.[15]

It is not so clear, however, exactly what thoughts must be attributed to the heart of the traitor. The disloyal yearnings of would-be adulterers typically run toward the same sexual goal, but disloyalty to country comes in a variety of degrees and forms. There was no doubt that Iva Toguri, known as Tokyo Rose, adhered to the enemy as she made radio broadcasts for the Japanese during World War II.[16] But did Jane Fonda "adhere to the enemy" in Vietnam when she broadcast from Hanoi and attempted to persuade American flyers to desist from their bombing missions? It is one thing to commit oneself to the Japanese war effort with a view to defeating the United States. It is quite another to take measures to induce the United States' withdrawal from a foreign military adventure. Jane Fonda could believe (as I am sure she did) that she was acting in the long range interests of the country to which she owed allegiance and to which she remained loyal.[17] Tokyo Rose could not make the same claim.

Crimes of the Heart

The required link between the outward act and the inner intention has become a philosophical puzzle at the core of Western reflections not only about law but about morality and sin. Think about the Tenth Commandment: "Thou shalt not covet thy neighbor's wife."[18] When does the act of coveting occur? Is it simply a matter of desiring in the heart? Or, by analogy to the statute on treason, need the coveting be "provably attainted by open deed?" Theologians and ethical teachers have taken a variety of positions, but I am inclined to favor the teaching of Maimonides that there is no violation of the commandment without the manifestation of coveting in an act designed to satisfy the desire.[19]

Maimonides' interpretation of the Tenth Commandment reflects a legal orientation to the moral sin of coveting. It stresses the external side of action rather than the internal side of feeling and intending. The same emphasis on external acts characterizes Maimonides' analysis of idolatry.[20] Though the disloyalty to God is committed in the heart, Rambam would treat the crime as punishable only if manifested in acts of "weird worship."

The relationship between the internal and external aspect of criminality received its clarification first in the work of Immanuel Kant and, in this century, in the writings of Gustav Radbruch. In both law and morals, Radbruch reasoned, we need to consider acts as well as intentions and inner sentiments. Characteristically, the difference is that the law requires some external event and relies on intention and internal sentiments as a guide to understanding the meaning of the external event. Accident and arson differ not in whether the house burns but in the aims of the smoker who drops a cigarette. The difference between being kicked and being tripped—a distinction that, as Oliver Wendell Holmes, Jr., commented, even a dog senses[21]—lies in the attitude of the actor. The physical impact may be the same, but the quality of the act turns on the animus of the person kicking or tripping.

In the world of morality, by contrast, the relationship between internal and external is transposed. What counts, morally, is whether the bond of love, friendship, or trust is breached or maintained. External events are not important in themselves. They have moral significance only so far as they provide evidence to confirm or disconfirm the inner sentiment. Forgetting an anniversary is significant only so far as it says something about the strength of the marriage.

Crimes of betrayal blur this sharp demarcation between the law as external and morality as internal. As clothed in the crimes of treason and adultery, the figure of disloyalty enters where morality generally fears to tread. It passes as an external crime, but its essence is in the spirit. Fidelity of the heart, steadfastness of mind, constancy of character—these are the marks of loyalty to nation and to lover. Yet in a practical world, the inner side of morality gives way to the external exigencies of proof and the need to convict the guilty even as we secure the rights of the innocent.

As the law of treason has come down to us from the fourteenth century, the tension between the internal and the external remains unresolved. The constitutional definition of treason eliminates the crime of "compassing the death" of the king or any other head of state; these crimes have been reclassified as sedition, internal subversion—now concentrated on the aggressive act of attempting to overthrow the government. What remains in the Constitution from the original statute on treason is "waging war" against the country and "adhering to the enemy, giving them aid and comfort."[22]

In keeping with the original demand that the treason be "provably attainted by open deed," the Constitution requires either that the defendant confess in open court or that two witnesses testify to the "overt act" constituting the treason. When charged with espionage for passing secrets to the Soviet Union, the Rosenbergs tried to take advantage of this constitutional rule by arguing that the charge against them was, in essence, treason and therefore they could not be convicted unless there were two witnesses to some overt act of disloyalty;[23] they lost the argument and were executed on the basis of Greenglass' testimony alone, demonstrating the value to the government of prosecuting for espionage rather than treason. The "two witness" requirement, which carries forward the biblical conception of legally defined modes of proof, is usually taken as a sign that the framers were bent on avoiding the misuse of treason prosecutions against political dissenters.

Thus the Constitution bequeaths to us a mélange of internal sentiments ("adhering") and external events ("giving aid and comfort" and "overt act"). The "giving [of] aid and comfort" could be seen not only as an external act but as a tangible harm inflicted on the United States, a harm comparable to the damaging impact demanded in the traditional crimes of homicide, theft, and arson. Working out the proper relationship among these criteria of treason has plagued the jurisprudence of the Supreme Court.

In the first major case on treason to reach the Justices in Washington, a German immigrant, Anthony Cramer, faced charges of adhering, during World War II, to the Third Reich, giving the enemy "aid and comfort."[24] This case as well as the parallel prosecution of another immigrant, Hans Haupt, was the fallout of an effort by German agents to carry out acts of sabotage in the United States. Eight saboteurs had penetrated U.S. waters in a submarine in the summer of 1942. Their purpose, apparently, was to destroy the American aluminum industry. After landing by rubber boat near Jacksonville, Florida, part of the group fanned out, making contact with sympathetic German immigrants in New York and Chicago.

The FBI followed two of them to New York City where they met several times with Cramer, first at Grand Central Station, then for over two hours at the Twin Oaks Inn. Cramer was a good friend of one of the saboteurs named Thiel and of Thiel's fiancée Norma Kopp, who still lived in New York. Cramer left the restaurant with Thiel's money belt packing $3,600 of the Third Reich's money. Though they could not hear the conversation inside, the FBI agents arrested Thiel and the other German outside the Twin Oaks Inn. They were handed over to a military tribunal, which tried them and prosecuted them as enemy aliens.[25] Cramer was arrested a few days later, and because he was a naturalized U.S. citizen, he was held to answer on charges of treason.

There was no serious doubt about whether Cramer "adhered to the German enemy" or, in the words of Justice William O. Douglas, whether he had treasonous or traitorous intent.[26] He had made several incriminating statements to Norma Kopp, which she was required to disclose at trial. Thus the jury learned that Cramer knew how the saboteurs reached U.S. soil and that they had a mission hostile to U.S. interests. In his own statements to the FBI, Cramer claimed that, so far as he knew, the purpose of the mission was solely to undermine American morale.

The problem in Cramer's trial was not the state of his heart but the impact of his actions. Did he do enough to render aid and comfort to the enemy? Perhaps his taking Thiel's money belt and holding it in safekeeping might have been enough to secure his conviction.[27] But the Constitution requires two witnesses to the overt act of treason, and apparently the government did not have two witnesses to Cramer's handling the money belt, for they dropped this charge at the trial. The focus of the government's case was the seemingly innocuous act of meeting and conversing with the foreign agents in a cafeteria and thereby giving them the "psychological comfort" of "mingling normally with the citizens of a country with which they were at war."[28] The trial court was convinced that this was enough aid to be treasonous; Cramer was convicted and sentenced to 45 years in prison.

Cramer's appeal to the Supreme Court reads like a philosophical debate about the relevance of internal and external evidence on the issue of disloyalty.[29] The great liberals of the Court, Justices Hugo Black and Douglas, proved to be the most willing to take a moral approach (in Radbruch's sense) to the crime of treason. All that mattered, in their view, was that Cramer had a treasonable intent and took some act (the overt act required by the Constitution) that showed his intent had moved from fantasy to action. The essence of the crime was the attitude of disloyalty, and if the jury had concluded that Cramer was so motivated when he met his compatriots, the Supreme Court, they argued, should not upset the verdict of guilt.

Unfortunately, juries are easily swayed by circumstantial evidence of a disloyal heart. As one reviews the evidence used against Cramer, the feeling inevitably arises that a prosecution for treason can become a boundless probe into the private life of the suspect. Evidence was heard at the trial that Cramer once slammed the door in the face of a bond salesman raising money for the war effort; he was a member of an organization that later became the German-American Bund; he went to the 1936 Olympic games in Berlin and wrote letters home, in German, critical of the "American army as a world conqueror."[30] In a trial conducted in the xenophobic mood of a world war, this kind of evidence could readily convince a jury of decent Americans that Cramer was disloyal in his heart and that his meeting with German agents had a hostile purpose. Justices Douglas and Black voted to affirm the conviction.

Remarkably, a majority of the Court voted to reverse the conviction. Deaths on the battlefields of Europe did not sway their judgment. Justice Robert Jackson's opinion for the Court reflects the law's proper concern with the external side of treason. Whatever the state of Cramer's heart and mind, whether he was loyal or not, his acts did not amount to the minimal threshold of treasonable behavior. Though the jury found Cramer guilty, they did not have the final word on the law and the Constitution. There were external elements to crime that went beyond the treasonable intent of adhering to the enemy. There had to be an actual rendering of "aid and comfort" to the enemy. And acts of "social intercourse" and "mingling with the citizens"[31] of an enemy country, even citizens bent on a mission of sabotage, were simply not enough to constitute the rendering of actual aid and comfort. Something more was required. The exact quantum of required aid was left open, to be resolved another day.[32]

Jackson's and the majority's courageous reversal of a treason conviction in wartime drew heavily on the constitutional text as seen from the perspective of the traditional legal principle that crimes must occur in the external world. If the Constitution specified "aid and comfort" as a requirement that went beyond the state of the suspect's loyalty, then this requirement had to be taken seriously. And if crimes characteristically require either some act that is dangerous to others or some actual harm to others, then treason should also be interpreted narrowly to come as close as possible to the traditional notion of crime.

Significantly, as the war ended and another case arising from the same German sabotage mission finally found its way to the Supreme Court, the majority on the Court shifted. Admittedly, the facts in the *Haupt* case[33] were slightly different. The Haupt family had come to Chicago in 1923. Hans and Erna Haupt took American citizenship and swore allegiance to the country; their son Herbert acquired derivative citizenship and later elected to remain German.[34] When the war broke out in 1939, Herbert left the United States and by a circuitous route arrived in Germany where he was trained as a saboteur. After landing by dinghy on the Florida coast, he made his way back to his parents' home and they took him in. His father helped him to buy a car and, more incriminatingly, to return to his job at an optical company that made military instruments, including the Norden bombsight.

The case became an imbroglio. The government mounted an aggressive and persistent prosecution against Hans Haupt, for here they thought they had someone who actively participated in his son's preparation for sabotage. In the first trial, the government secured convictions against both parents for giving aid by harboring and sheltering their son. Hans was sentenced to death, but this conviction was overturned on appeal.[35] At the retrial the government concentrated its fire on Hans, but it added more charges than it needed. A conviction for the overt act of securing the job at the optical company would easily have passed constitutional muster, as would, most likely, a charge based solely on buying a car to help Herbert in his mission of sabotage. But the government added, as intended overkill, the overt act based on Hans's harboring and sheltering an enemy agent. A conviction followed, with a sentence of life imprisonment.

The intended overkill almost saved Hans. The conviction was based on three alleged overt acts of treason. The jury came in with a single verdict of guilty, which would hold up on appeal only if every possible theory of the jury's verdict were legally solid. The charge of treason based on providing room and board to his son was the weakest of the government's alleged overt acts, hardly more plausible than the argument that failed in *Cramer*. This time, however, the Supreme Court was ill disposed to reverse the conviction. With little discussion of what "aid and comfort" meant, eight Justices voted that what Hans did was enough and they affirmed the conviction.[36]

The most intriguing argument that Haupt made on appeal was that though he may have aided and sheltered his son, he did not do so for reasons of loyalty to the Third Reich. He was simply acting out of attachment to his own flesh and blood. It is perfectly natural for parents to provide shelter and meals for their visiting son. And even the acts of buying a car and getting the old job back are what any parent would do for a son. Treason, allegedly, was far from their minds.

Where the issue was the inner state of Haupt's sentiments, however, the Supreme Court was content to rely on the jury's assessment of his loyalty. They were instructed to vote not guilty if they found that the defendant's intention was merely to aid his son "as an individual, as [opposed to] to aiding the German Reich."[37] Though the case appears to pose a conflict of loyalties, between Haupt's attachment to his son and his duty of allegiance to the United States, that is not the way the Court's reasoning unfolded. Haupt would have been entitled in principle to remain loyal to his son, so long as that loyalty did not translate into his adopting as his own his son's mission of furthering the war effort against the United States.

Who Must Be Loyal and Why

Theft, murder, and other acts of aggression violate universal legal prohibitions. Absent diplomatic immunity, anyone who commits one of these crimes is subject to criminal prosecution for the deed. If Haupt the younger had stolen a car in Chicago, he would have had to stand trial in the local courts. No one would ask whether he was German or American, Christian or Jew, fascist or democrat. These questions of personal status are irrelevant to the obligations imposed by the criminal law. Though still suffering some exceptions, the criminal law strives to cover all crimes and to apply universally to all people within the jurisdiction of the court.[38]

Again treason differs. Not everyone present on American soil owes a duty of allegiance to the United States. If Hans Haupt had terminated the bond of citizenship with the United States, he would have been free to identify with the German cause, to adhere to a military enemy of his former country.

As a German saboteur, Herbert Haupt could not be expected to bear a commitment of loyalty to a military enemy. His wrong against the United States was defined by the laws of war: passing behind enemy lines in civilian clothes with the aim of engaging in hostile action.[39] Crimes against military enemies do not breach duties of loyalty. No one demands of alien belligerants that they be loyal to the United States, and it makes no difference whether they temporarily reside on American soil.[40]

From whom, then, can the U.S. government legitimately demand the kind of attachment and loyalty that is breached by "adhering to the enemy giving them aid and comfort?" From whom can the United States or any country exact loyalty, as a wife demands loyalty from her husband?

The constitutional framers skipped over this essential question. They took pains to limit treason to fewer cases than were found under the English statute of 1351, but they wrote the treason clause as though anyone who "wages war against the United States" or "adheres to the enemy" could be prosecuted and convicted of treason. Yet the United States cannot demand attachment and loyalty from the whole world. How should one go about delimiting the sphere of loyalty and possible treason?

The model of marriage carries us only so far. True, treason and adultery intersect at their foundations. Both stress internal commitment. Both are breached, arguably, by a shift of emotional attachment. Yet marriage is a voluntary commitment. One expects fidelity from a spouse because he or she undertakes to be faithful. There is no comparable commitment, voluntarily contracted, that grounds the duty to be loyal to one's country.

One might say that as a naturalized citizen, Hans Haupt took an oath of allegiance to the United States and that therefore he came under a duty of loyalty to his adopted country. He has taken a new country, and therefore he is obligated to be faithful to his bride. The concept of contract seems to solve our problem, for we understand the ethics of promising and making commitments. These ideas respond to the liberal, voluntaristic ethos of our time. People define themselves by their chosen commitments. Breaching a commitment, whether to spouse or country, is a wrong that fits well in the matrix of our moral assumptions.

But the model of contract, I submit, leads us astray. Contract is the quintessential liberal criterion of obligation. It moves us to parse particular words and phrases as the touchstone of the concrete self that commits itself. Does it really matter what Hans Haupt said when he took the oath of citizenship? Should we care whether there was anything in the oath about breaking off ties with his children? The key question is whether the United States was *his* country. Was it his home? If it was, he was capable of betraying it; those whom he left behind in Germany were outside the domain of loyalty and betrayal.

The process of naturalization may be conclusive on whether the United States had become Haupt's country. But there is no reason to think that everyone must go through this process of voluntary commitment in order to owe allegiance to a country. The problem is beautifully put in the postwar prosecution in England of William Joyce, a voice well known as the radio propagandist Lord Haw-Haw. After a long period of fascist activities, Joyce left England for Germany some time between late August and mid-September 1939, just as German armies were massing on the Polish border and claiming the first victims of their aggression. As early as September 18, 1939 Joyce appeared on German radio and began broadcasting in English to undermine his countrymen's commitment to the war.

At least it seemed that he was committing treason against his countrymen. He adhered to the German cause, with his body and voice as well as his mind. His broadcasts gave aid and comfort to the German cause. Yet an unexpected problem emerged at the trial in London's Old Bailey. It turned out that Joyce was not a British subject. He had been born in Brooklyn, New York, in 1906. Though born an Irishman and a British subject, his father became a naturalized American citizen. Therefore William was an American by birth, and though his family took him at the age of three back to Ireland (then under British sovereignty) and he grew up under the authority of the British crown, he never officially acquired British citizenship. He fraudulently acquired a British passport and used it for his travels abroad, including the one-way trip to Germany in 1939. He became a naturalized German citizen before the United States declared war in December 1941.

Joyce's case seemed almost too slippery for the heavy hands of the law. He did not commit treason against the United States, because by the time Germany became an enemy of the United States, Joyce had become a German citizen. He did not commit treason against the United Kingdom, because even though it was the culture that nurtured and brought him to maturity, he was not their subject and arguably owed them no allegiance. He declared himself to be of the enemy, but changing allegiances substitutes one loyalty for another. Joyce's shift of countries was arguably akin not to adultery but to divorce and remarriage.

The English courts responded with their own wiles. Joyce had acquired an English passport, and that expressed his willingness to receive the crown's protection abroad. Thus his case came close to fitting the model of consent and contract. If he chose to receive the crown's protection, he owed allegiance in return. This artificial argument worked for one count of the indictment, and in the end he was convicted, the House of Lords affirmed, and he was hanged for treason.

Joyce was not an alien in the United Kingdom, but he was alienated from the crown and his countrymen.[41] Aliens, total strangers, owe no allegiance, even if they temporarily pass through our countries. Someone is alienated when his experiences reach that vague point of intensity where we would normally expect attachment and loyalty. When someone is alienated, as Joyce was, why does he *owe* his country anything at all? If he does not feel an attachment, who should say that he must feel it?

The liberal idea of contract fails us here, for only by a wild leap of metaphor could one say that growing up in a country, failing to leave when one has the chance, constitutes a voluntary commitment to be faithful. But no one chooses his homeland, neither hero nor traitor. This is the problem that Socrates wrestles with after he is convicted of subversive teaching in Athens and must choose whether to escape with Crito or to submit to the death sentence rendered against him.

In an effort to explain why he should remain loyal to Athens and take the hemlock, Socrates imagines that if he were to flee with Crito, "the laws and Constitution of Athens would come and confront" them and demand an explanation why with his act of escaping he was trying to destroy them. They would argue:

> Socrates, we have substantial evidence that you are satisfied with us and with the State. You would not have been so exceptionally reluctant to cross the borders of your country if you had not been exceptionally attached to it. . . . You have definitely chosen us, and undertaken to observe us [i.e., the laws and Constitution] in all your activities as a citizen.[42]

If Socrates' remaining in Athens generated a contract to observe all the laws, then it was the type of coerced contract known in law as a contract of adhesion. He accepted the whole package or none of it. There was no room to negotiate; he could not have said: "I will accept this part of the Constitution, but not that." One hardly consents unless one has a plausible alternative. A buyer of goods can be said to consent only if he has options. For most people, leaving one's homeland obviously represents a deeper pain than forgoing a typical commercial contract.

The personified laws of Athens make a better argument why Socrates should be loyal to them, but as they make this argument the laws come to stand for the broader social structure that nurtured Socrates and made him who he was:

> Did we not give you life in the first place? Was it not through us that your father married your mother and begot you? . . . Have you any [complaint] against the laws which deal with children's upbringing and education, such as you had yourself? Are you not grateful . . .?[43]

This argument comes closer to explaining the foundations of national loyalty. The claim is not simply that Socrates is indebted to Athens because of the benefits he has received. These benefits were neither given nor received in the anticipation that fair recompense would be surrendering to a premature death.

Sometimes it is argued that obligations arise, regardless of contract, as a matter of fair play. If I accept the benefit that others have bestowed upon me, I become obligated to return the benefit in kind. Everyone else in the community takes a turn at guard duty; therefore an analogous duty falls on me. But the most that could be exacted from Socrates under this mode of reasoning is that he pass onto the next generation that which he received himself.

Socrates' argument should be read rather as the claim that because Athenian society had made him what he was, he would not disavow even a harsh judgment of that society. He could not leave and take up his life in Thessaly. "But of course you want to live for your children's sake," he admits to himself . . . [but not by] "taking them off to Thessaly and making foreigners of them." In the end, he submits to the laws of Athens because he recognizes that his honor and personality are rooted in Athens. By coming to realize who he is, he has no choice but to stay.

The models of consent and contract are but an overlay, a gloss, on the historical factors that generate personal identity. For ancients and moderns alike, the narrative of choosing elicits a sense of personal power and autonomy. It generates the sense, perhaps illusory, that we are the architects of our lives.

Our contemporary notions of national loyalty come to us from these diverse sources. The feudal model is the easiest to comprehend. The sovereign provides protection, and his people owe to him a reciprocal duty of fealty and service. But the last days of Socrates teach us that we find the duty of loyalty as well in the process of self-recognition, of recognizing the extent to which our personalities have become interwoven with those who have nurtured us. Even apart from his self-recognition, the laws argue, Socrates should be grateful for the protection afforded in his coming of age. In this way of reasoning, treason is a great crime precisely because it breaches the duty of gratitude.[44] These three arguments—protection, self-recognition, and gratitude—interweave in the grounding of the duty of loyalty to country.

Thus we can offer an answer to the question, From whom may the modern nation-state exact a duty of loyalty? It must limit the duty of loyalty to those who stand in relationship to the state as does the vassal to his protecting lord, as Socrates to Athens. The answer in conventional legal terms is that loyalty is due only from citizens and those like permanent residents of the state who stand in an ongoing relationship of interdependence and expected gratitude with the society the state represents. This, then, is the modern domain of loyalty. These are the people who are subject to prosecution for treason if they act disloyally toward their country.

Pluralism and Loyalty

Would that it were all this simple. If the nation-state today were organized as the perfect unity of state and society, one could readily justify the state's exacting penalties for disloyalty. It is not clear that this
perfect union ever existed, except perhaps in native villages isolated
from the rest of the world. In a world history of conquest, taking
slaves, free-flowing migration, and expelled refugees, the union of
state and society has long been a myth. The objects of our loyalty are
families, tribes, or communities that at best overlap haphazardly with
organized political authority. Think of an Israeli Arab loyal to the
Palestinian cause. His actions on behalf of the Palestinians could
make him guilty, in principle, of betraying his country, for technically
he owes a duty of loyalty to Israel, a state that he might not recognize
in his heart. Or consider Jonathan Pollard, who acted out of loyalty to
his people (the Jews), though undoubtedly he felt some conflicting
loyalty to the country in which he was born and educated.

Modern life is rife with these conflicts of loyalty, for we no longer
can fuse the communities that compel our loyalty with the authorities that collect our taxes, exact military service from us, and orga-
nize the economies that sustain our material existence. If we canvass
the globe for treason trials, both formal and informal, in the last
decade, we are more likely to find them in substate organizations
battling for political recognition. Militant groups in South Africa
exact loyalty from blacks and regularly execute those convicted,
admittedly by informal trial, of collaborating with the enemy. The
same is true of the way the PLO once disciplined Palestinians living
on the West Bank: For a time, the duty of loyalty to the cause had
displaced the right of Palestinians to choose whether they wished to
cooperate with the Israeli government.

The crime of treason to a nation-state can survive only if the principle "thou shalt not betray me" as applied to the state retains as
much moral coherence as the imperatives of interpersonal crime—
for example, "thou shalt not kill" and "thou shalt not steal." In a
world of dual and conflicting loyalties, the state's demand for exclusive loyalty is rapidly losing its grip.

The decline of treason is reflected both in unrealistic demands of
loyalty and in a trend toward eliminating the offense, either explicitly or in practice. In its pre-*perestroika* excesses, the Soviet Union

demanded a degree of loyalty from its national minorities that reflected fantasies of a single national community. The crime was committed, among other acts, by anyone who left the country or stayed abroad without permission, with the vague intention of harming the Soviet motherland. In 1970 a group of Jews were convicted of treason, and two were sentenced to death (later commuted) for attempting to commandeer a commercial airplane that would fly them from Leningrad to Helsinki. Natan Sharansky was convicted of treason on the basis of allegedly distributing readily available information about the location of computers to Western journalists. If these passionate Jews were guilty of a crime against the Soviet state, it was a crime that existed solely in the eyes of the authorities.

Excessive demands of loyalty mark the tyrannical state. Under the Third Reich Germans indulged in an expansive conception of treason that swept up every conceivable act of disloyalty, including unflattering comments about Hitler. It is not surprising that among the first reforms of every newly flourishing democratic society is a pruning back of treason. The reform of the notorious article 64 (betrayal of the motherland) of the old RSFSR Criminal Code is high on the list of necessary reforms in the new nation of Russia and its neighboring republics.[45] In reaction to their National Socialist perversions, the West Germans totally abolished the crime of treason as it is understood in this chapter. They have retained the label *Hochverrat* ("high treason") for another crime now covering acts committed by anyone, regardless of citizenship, that tend to undermine the constitutional order. The German crime of treason has merged with the distinct offense of sedition, a crime designed not to punish betrayal but to secure the institutions of constitutional democracy.

The United States has not prosecuted anyone for treason since World War II. The concept of "enemy" to whom the traitor must adhere, "giving them aid and comfort," is now so narrowly drawn that there are no enemies and no official traitors left. Governments seem no longer to care about actual sentiments of loyalty. Of concern today are the control and dissemination of information. The crime of espionage covers the selling of secrets, and it attaches regardless of the suspect's citizenship. The press as well as judges may describe the Rosenbergs, Walker, Pollard, Blunt, and Burgess as traitors, but they are prosecuted for their acts of conveying information, not for their emotional disloyalty and identification with a foreign power.

This is not to say that the sentiments of personal and group loyalty are less important. Indeed, they are of growing significance within the ethnic groups that once constituted the empires of the past—the Habsburg empire in Eastern Europe, the Soviet Union, and even smaller unions like Yugoslavia. The United States as well is encountering growing demands of loyalty within the ethnic communities of "hyphenated Americans." African-Americans are expected to stand by their embattled brothers, and indeed some black politicians are slow to criticize figures like Louis Farrakhan and Leonard Jeffries who made themselves anathema to the country as a whole.

We are witnessing, then, increasing demands for loyalty within smaller and smaller units of group identification. The intense need to belong, the craving for reciprocal attention and devotion, the quest for meaning in group action—all of these ever-present yearnings put pressure on our loyalties. And these pressures, in some contexts, move loyalty from the minimal condition of non-betrayal toward the opposite pole of maximum devotion.

CHAPTER 4

Maximum Loyalty: "Thou Shalt Be One with Me"

Loyalties invariably entail commitments that cannot be grounded in reasons others share. There comes a point at which logic runs dry and one must plant one's loyalty in the simple fact that it is *my* friend, *my* club, *my* alma mater, *my* nation. I could try to explain why I love her, why I adhere to this tradition rather than to that, but all these reasons will be partial. In the end, in explaining loyalties, I must tell you not only about the object of loyalty but about the agent who is loyal. Loyalty blurs the distance between subject and object. In loyalty, as in love, there is not even an illusion of scientific neutrality and intellectual impartiality.

This nonrational component of loyalty induces deep emotional attachments. The minimal condition of nonbetrayal slides readily into devotion, and the devotion comes to be demanded as a requirement of the relationship. Avoiding adultery is not enough for the loving spouse. Abstaining from treason hardly suffices for the patriotic citizen. And rejecting idolatry hardly constitutes the religious life. Yet what does one do to express the enthusiastic dimension of loyalty? What is the level of activity, beyond the minimal state of nonbetrayal, that will make one a loyal spouse, a patriotic citizen, a faithful believer?

There are many ways of showing devotion beyond the minimum required by *not* committing adultery, treason, or idolatry. We make sacrifices of our time and other resources to establish our commitments to others. Yet sometimes we deepen our bonds not by actually doing something of substance but by engaging in rituals that demonstrate our fidelity. This aspect of devotional loyalty, the dimension of ritual, requires our attention, for it is the least understood among the ways we are loyal to each other.

My claim is that ritual plays a key part in the unfolding of committed loyalties. The ritual, varying from incidental acts of gift giving to settled forms of religious worship, demonstrate the depth of the loyal bond. Bringing ritual and its relationship to loyalty into focus can help us fathom the deep and lasting appeal of patriotic, religious, and sexual rites.

Patriotism

The distinction setting patriotism apart from loyalty repays examination. The passive virtue of national loyalty stresses the dichotomy of being with or against the nation. As loyal or disloyal, the citizen is either in or out, here or there. Thus loyalty reveals its conceptual and etymological connections with law. As one can be only loyal or disloyal, one can act only lawfully or unlawfully. The root for "law" is the Latin *lex*, which has also generated the French terms *loi* (law) and *loyauté* (loyalty). A legitimate child was once known as a "loyal child," and good money was called "loyal money." Note that you can trust people more or less, love them more or less, be more or less patriotic, but you cannot be lawful or loyal sometimes more, sometimes less. When it comes to the dichotomies of law and loyalty, you are on one side or the other.

For Americans, the term "patriot" rings with greater resonance than does "loyalist."[1] At the battlefields of Concord and Yorktown, those fighting for independence were the patriots; those remaining with King George III were the loyalists. The British were the lawfully constituted authority in the colonies, and therefore those siding with them were appropriately called the "loyalists."

Patriotism expresses a romantic passion for the people and culture, the flora and fauna, of a particular polity. And significantly, patriots do put their country above established legal authority. Prior to 1983, the Argentine military had always sworn its allegiance to the *patria* rather than to any specific set of laws. President Raoul Alfonsin changed the oath to require a sworn commitment to the Constitution. Even a symbolic change in the focus of the military's sense of duty can reduce the risk of a patriotic coup d'état.

The crime of treason sanctions lapses of loyalty, not of patriotism. No one was ever required by law to be patriotic but only, more modestly, not to go over to the enemy. As a country devoted to law, as the nation with the single constitution longest in force, we should feel a stronger emotional attachment to the concept of loyalty, with its overtones of law, than we do to the connotations of lawlessness implicit in patriotism. Yet there appears to be a split in the American consciousness. We still identify, it seems, with our glorious moment of revolution and, by extension, with all romantic rebellion against established power. Paradoxically, our empathy with those who cast off authority may account for the strong liberal identification with those who express their alienation by burning the flag.[2] The American way of protest, still rooted in revolutionary exuberance, constitutes the deep structure of our constitutional values.

Though muted and perceived through the emotions darkly, this was the debate between George Bush and Michael Dukakis in 1988. Bush's appeal to the Pledge of Allegiance harked back to a prelegal moment of national assertion. If the Constitution had to be reinterpreted to conform to a growing urge to express love of country, well . . . that is the task of good lawyers. The issue was not *loyauté* and law, but *patria* and pride. Dukakis' response, his taking shelter in a few decisions interpreting the Constitution, missed the point.[3] A stronger response would have traded not on the law but on the deep American respect for individual choice and freedom of conscience. Love of country, and of the American way, is not cerebral. And it is not rule bound, it is not so readily subject to discipline that its romantic urges submit to the dictates of judges.

Perhaps the Constitution invites not patriotism but loyalty. Yet even this usage would be odd. How might one be disloyal to the Constitution? There is no alternative lurking in the wings. It would make no sense for an American judge to consider applying the German or the Canadian constitution. Nor would it have made sense in 1789, after the annulment of the Articles of Confederation and the adoption of the Constitution, for a judge to say that he was loyal to the Articles. What could this possibly mean? Either the 1789 Constitution was binding or it was not; the gears of loyalty simply do not engage the Constitution.[4]

A patriotic element often enters into constitutional judging. Judges are moved by their sense of identity, of being rooted in one tradition or another. For American judges, it often appears important to disavow European principles of criminal justice. For example, in the march of precedents leading to Miranda v. Arizona[5] (the famous case requiring that police read suspects "their rights"), the Supreme Court had to decide whether it was consistent with our tradition to allow police officers to dominate interrogation sessions without defense lawyers present. In the 1950s the prevailing view was that confessions generated by aggressive and coercive police interrogation were likely to be unreliable and therefore should be excluded.

In a pivotal case leading toward *Miranda*,[6] Justice Felix Frankfurter reasoned that these confessions are excluded not because they "are unlikely to be true, but because the methods used . . . offend an underlying principle in the enforcement of the criminal law."[7] Why? Because, as Justice Frankfurter expressed the identity of the American legal system, "ours is an accusatorial and not an inquisitorial system—a system in which the State must establish guilt by evidence independently and freely secured and may not by its own coercion prove its charge against an accused out of his own mouth."[8] The turning point in Frankfurter's reasoning is that we are not like *them*—those inquisitorially minded Europeans who are presumably willing to secure confessions at any cost. No, the Court, led by Frankfurter, would stay with the Anglo-American way of doing things.

The same way of thinking about law determined the current conservative posture toward abortion in the western part of united Germany. In 1975 the Federal Constitutional Court invalidated a liberal abortion law as a violation of the constitutional provision granting "everyone a right to life."[9] The judges interpreted the term "everyone" broadly to include fetuses because "the historical experience and the moral, humanistic confrontation with National Socialism" required them to bend over backwards to protect life. It did not matter to the Court that in fact the Third Reich had a conservative position on abortion: The stigma of the death camps required the Court to take a stand in favor of protecting the unborn. As the U.S.

Supreme Court sided with the American mode of trying criminals, the German Court identified itself with what it took to be a humanist, life-affirming current in German culture.

These preferences are, at once, rational and nonrational. The rational component consists in the reasons that the courts can advance for their position, namely, that the accusatorial mode of trial is superior to the inquisitorial mode, or that the fetus should be viewed as having a right to life. But, as we well know, convincing reasons are available to defend the opposing positions as well. Therefore, as the judges themselves concede, these decisions ultimately rest on a nonrational element. That element is the loyalty the judges express to a particular legal culture or strain within that culture.

Loyalty Oaths

Judging carries with it compelling rituals. Both before entering the legal profession and again before assuming the bench, novitiate judges must swear to uphold the law and the constitutional system. These oaths that judges take frame a solemn moment of transition, a change of status.[10] Swearing an oath reminds the novitiate that he or she is about to embark on a solemn enterprise. The oath of witnesses is of this sort, as are the oaths prescribed by the Constitution for the President[11] and others assuming government office.[12] At their naturalization ceremony, new citizens are required to swear allegiance to the Constitution and the laws of the United States and to renounce their allegiance to any "foreign prince, potentate, state or sovereignty." Like judges and government officers assuming their charge, new citizens taking this oath are likely to share the solemnity of the moment and regard the taking of the oath as an honor.

Unfortunately, these salutory oaths that frame a critical moment of transition have become confused with the use of oaths by embattled governments to probe and deepen the loyalty of their citizens. During the American Revolution, General George Washington exacted an oath of loyalty to the American cause, and after the Civil War Reconstruction state governments commonly used oaths as a way of isolating those who had been disloyal to the Union.[13]

Contemporary thinking about loyalty oaths cannot ignore the stigma left on the practice by the anti-Communist mania of the

1950s. The abuses of suspicion associated with the name of Senator Joseph McCarthy have left us with an easily triggered reaction against national breast-beating. Demanding that people sign oaths that they had never been members of the Communist Party or even—in the milder version—to uphold the Constitution, supposedly had the effect of ferreting out the enemies of the nation. It became common practice for government institutions to demand oaths of all new employees, in effect, that they had been loyal in the past and would be loyal in the future.

The most blatant forms of these anti-Communist oaths were declared unconstitutional.[14] But some watered-down versions survived. For example, in the early 1970s, a Boston hospital required all new employees, including staff researchers, to take an oath not only that they would uphold and defend federal and state constitutions but that they would oppose illegal efforts to overthrow the government. Why should a research sociologist employed by Boston State Hospital swear to defend and uphold the Constitution? Her work in the hospital had nothing to do with politics, law, or the nation's charter. Indeed, it is not clear what it would mean for her in the course of her duties to uphold or not uphold the Bill of Rights.

The point of the oath was obviously to weed out the disloyal from every form of government employment. It would be hard to imagine an effort more inane. There might have been a time prior to modern skepticism when even the disloyal were so infused with a sense of God's majesty and power that they would not have dared to take a false oath. But that was certainly not the case during the cold war, when there was no reason to think that Communist agents (if they were serious atheists) would have scruples about taking false oaths.

Remarkably, a slight majority of the Supreme Court upheld the authority of the hospital to demand the oath, even the second part that smacked of the anti-Communist fears of the 1950s.[15] The reasoning is simply that the second part of the oath concerning opposition to violent overthrow of the government is innocuous because it repeats, in negative language, the point of the first part. In general, the majority concluded, oaths to uphold the Constitution are unproblematic because that is what the Constitution demands of judges, legislators, and others assuming a public trust.

This casual assimilation of loyalty oaths to oaths taken by judges and other public officials reveals a deep confusion. Nothing could be more at odds with the honor of assuming office or adopting a new citizenship than suspicion of disloyalty to one's native land. The evil of loyalty oaths is not simply that they are of dubious efficacy in isolating potential traitors and that they inhibit the political activities of those required to take them. There is an independent wrong in demanding, without probable cause of disloyalty, that someone affirm his allegiance to the Constitution. The wrong is the insult of being treated, without grounds, as someone disloyal to his or her country.

These insulting practices, which represent a residue of the Communist scare of the 1950s, persist. For example, Columbia University, my employer, would like me to sign an oath that reads:

> I do hereby pledge and declare that I will support the Constitution of the United States of America and the Constitution of the State of New York and that I will faithfully discharge the duties of the position of [Professor of Law] to the best of my ability.

New York State Education Code §3002 makes it unlawful for me to teach at an institution that claims a tax exemption for its real property without signing this piece of paper and sending it to the administrator charged with keeping track of these things. It is also unlawful for Columbia University to employ me without having my "oath" on file. My thoughts about this so-called oath of allegiance are the same as those about the oath the research sociologist was expected to take as a condition of employment at the Boston State Hospital: It would be ludicrous if it were not so demeaning.

First, the statement that I will "support" the constitutions of the United States and of New York is hardly an oath. The relevant verb is watered down from "swear" to "affirm," for those squeamish about invoking God's presence, and thence, for the even more agnostic, to "pledge" and even the innocuous "declare." In its form as oath, it should be administered by the president of the university, but presumably the president had better things to do, and therefore he sent out a piece of paper that needed only be signed and put on file.

Second, it is hard for me to know what it means to "support" a constitution. Does that mean I will never argue in class that the Constitution was wrong in adopting the three-fifths compromise on the census of the black population, that the Second Amendment really and incorrectly recognizes an individual right to bear arms, and that the Fifth Amendment unsoundly grants every criminal defendant a right to a grand jury indictment? Obviously not. Academic freedom means nothing if I cannot criticize both the Constitution and its interpretation by the Supreme Court without fear of sanction. Also, at the extreme, since the Constitution incorporates its own procedures for unlimited amendment, support for the Constitution is compatible with a call for its repeal.

It is no defense to the state's demanding this so-called oath that other oaths are constitutionally mandated for government officers charged with interpreting and enforcing the Constitution. The appropriate oath for a university professor, if there needs be one, would be, in the words of Elie Wiesel, "to speak truth to power." The only way "faithfully [to] discharge the duties of professor to the best of my ability," therefore, is to refuse to take the oath. The Boston State Hospital sociologist was right, and the courts will eventually appreciate the distinctions expressed here and invalidate the demeaning institution of loyalty oaths.

If patriotic rituals, such as the Pledge and singing the national anthem, also expressed disrespect for the nation's citizens, one would have serious doubts about these routine rites of national attachment. There may be some aspects of the Pledge—particularly the affirmation of "with liberty and justice for all"—that may strike some people as meretricious and therefore demeaning. We take up this topic in greater detail in Chapter 6. For now it is worth underscoring the historical connotations of loyalty oaths as devices for weeding out the politically unreliable from positions of responsibility. This tainted ritual of meaningless oath taking, a survival from an infelicitous period of postwar American history, will disappear as soon as the practice is understood for what it is.

This is not to say that oaths do not fulfill an important function celebrating the assumption of an honored station such as judge, lawyer, or citizen. The oath should be designed to capture the true responsibilities of the role and assist the oath taker in assuming a new set of commitments. In this limited function, oaths bear some resemblance to the rituals of loyalty that attend sexual fidelity, patriotism, and religious practices. In all these cases the ritual not only communicates commitment but strengthens resolve to remain steadfast in one's duties of office or in secular or religious loyalties.

Ritual and Idolatry

The claim about the role of ritual in loyal relationships takes on even greater force in religious worship, where the nonrational attachment to a particular god and particular religion exacts a unique set of practices. Idolatry in the Jewish tradition is expressed, in part, by engaging in the rituals properly reserved for a "jealous" god. Because it so richly illustrates the relationship between ritual and loyalty, the theological taboo against idolatry warrants our attention.

Whether one is religious or secular, theological issues offer instruction in the theory of loyalty. The central commandment of the Jewish religion is the imperative of loyal and exclusive devotion to the historic God of Israel—the God of Abraham, Isaac, and Jacob, who led the Jews out of Egyptian bondage. The way this commandment of a "loving God" is discussed and explained in the meditations of Jewish thinkers reflects our understanding of marriage and other forms of human loyalty. To reach these teachings, however, we must first cover some basic ground.

While the first of the Ten Commandments requires us to believe in God,[16] the second and third demand loyalty to this God:

> Thou shalt have no other gods beside me. Thou shalt not make for thyself any carved idol, or any likeness of any thing that is in heaven above, or that is in the earth beneath, or that is in the water under the earth: thou shalt not bow down to them, nor serve them: for I the Lord am a jealous God.

This passage is rife with puzzles. How could there be a prohibition against "having other gods?"[17] Do these other gods exist or do they not? If they do exist, what is wrong with acknowledging their existence? If these gods do not exist, why does God need to command their nonrecognition? As we shall see, this uncertainty about the existence of competing gods—and what to do about them if they do exist—permeates the Jewish effort to ban idolatrous practices.

The second sentence refers to a "carved idol" (*pesel*) or, as sometimes translated, a "graven image." Though this biblical passage provides the foundation for the prohibition against idolatry, the term "carved idol" has no linguistic tie with the Hebrew expression for idol worship. The path to the ban on idolatry begins in the penultimate phrase, which prohibits "serving them." The Hebrew word could be rendered as "service," or "work" or better as "worship"; the essence of idolatry is service or worship that is misdirected—in Hebrew, *avodah zara*, or "weird worship." Although the root of the prohibition of misdirected worship is located in these words, the actual term "idolatry" or "weird worship" comes into its own only later in the talmudic discussion.

One last point about the passage from the Ten Commandments. An adequate account of idolatry would have to explain why God refers to himself as a *El Kanai*—a "jealous" or "zealous" God (the term *kanai* could be translated either way). The concluding clause describing the impact of God's zeal on succeeding generations is deleted,[18] for the important theological question is why God chooses to describe himself in these all too human terms. Why does he take on the attributes of a jealous lover? What is the theological work that is done by thinking of God in this way?

With this host of puzzles we should review what we can take to be solid ground. We can assume that idolatry consists in taking some physical object too seriously as a source of power in the universe. Its paradigmatic form, as Exodus suggests, is making a "likeness of [a] thing that is in heaven above, or that is in the earth beneath, or that is in the water under the earth" and bowing down to or otherwise worshiping it. The problem is fathoming why idolatry constitutes *the* basic sin in Western, and particularly Jewish, religious thought.[19]

To make headway on the problem, I suggest two distinct ways of thinking about idolatry, each approach associated with a different view of Jewish origins. One story derives from Abraham's responding to a call from a single, abstract, transcendental God; the other story is from Moses' leading his people from bondage into a relationship and a covenant with this same God known by the tetragrammaton (YHVH).[20] All the Bible tells us about why Avram, later Abraham, left the city of Ur is that God told him to leave and to found a great nation in Canaan. Elaborating on this version of Judaism's birth as a religion, the legends (*Midrash*) have treated Abraham as history's first iconoclast. He smashed the idols he saw around him and committed himself to following a power beyond time and physical space.

As Maimonides explains the root of idolatry,

In the days of Enosh, the people fell into the great error of believing that because God had created the stars, put them in an honored position in the heavens to direct the course of events on Earth, the people should also honor and worship them.[21]

They erected temples to worship particular stars, depending on which false teaching they followed about the ultimate power of the universe. They forgot the unifying power behind these particular emanations and eventually could not see beyond the supposed divinity of their favored image.

Abraham reflected on these practices and perceived irrationality in these attachments to particular sources of power. He began to teach that there must be a single power beyond all the particular emanations, and it should be only this power, called God, that all people should worship. Worshiping an idol comes into focus, then, as a species of irrationality, akin to superstition. It is analogous to being disturbed about a black cat crossing one's path or being fearful of bad events on Friday the thirteenth. It is misdirected faith, a misguided effort to understand the nature of the universe. As Einstein had faith in a unified field theory behind particular forms of energy, Abraham began to preach that a single power, a single creator, is presupposed in the existence of particular items of creation.

The Moses story generates a different conception of Jewish origins and a corresponding view of idolatry. With Moses as his instrument, God leads the Jewish people out of the land of Egypt so that they may serve him in the desert. When, according to the text, God appears to Moses at Mount Sinai, he identifies himself to the Jews by signaling this event: "I am the Lord the God who brought thee out of the Land of Egypt, out of the House of Bondage."[22] The people of Israel are bound to their God not because they have chosen Him but because the Exodus is the constitutive event in Jewish history. It is the event without which Jews would not exist as a people, and therefore they are bound by history in a relationship beyond rationality, beyond human choice. This covenant, lying at the center of Western religious thought, bespeaks a duty of loyalty.

It would be a mistake to think that this covenant, by which Jews are obligated to conform to God's commands, resembles the modern notion of voluntary contract. The covenant is binding because God offered it, not because the Jews freely accepted it. To fend off the arrogant illusion of voluntary choice, the Talmud teaches that God "inclined the mountain over them like a tilted tub and that he said: if you accept the Torah, all is well, if not here will be your grave." It is commonly taught that the element of coercion—which the Talmud reads into the historical situation[23]—rendered the original covenant defective. The defect was supposedly cured after the Jews are saved from destruction under the reign of Ahasuerus in Persia (as described in the Book of Esther), for then the Jews supposedly "acknowledged and accepted" the law, the Torah as given at Sinai. This event, of dubious historicity,[24] hardly renders the covenant freely chosen: first, because the text refers only to a commitment to keep a holiday called Purim as a remembrance of the military victory; and second, so far as there is a broader acceptance of God's rule, it responds to a sense of indebtedness engendered by that victory. Rather than confirming the voluntariness of the covenant, the Book of Esther confirms Israel's duty of loyalty based on the divine protection and guidance that has enabled the people of Israel to survive in history.

When God appears to Moses on Mount Sinai and speaks the Ten Commandments and the other laws that govern Jewish life, his prime concern is that Israel remain loyal to him. The Second Commandment prohibits worshiping other gods, not because it would be irrational to do so but, I submit, because it would be a betrayal of the Jew's historical God to worship a competitive deity.

These two themes—irrationality and disloyalty—interweave in our thinking about idolatry. Though the theme of irrationality may in fact underlie Abraham's iconoclasm, the claims of idolatry as disloyalty gain the upper hand in the biblical narrative. The prophets Hosea, Ezekiel, and Jeremiah repeatedly draw the analogy between Israel and an unfaithful wife. As Jeremiah laments in the voice of God: "Surely as a wife betrays her husband, you [the people of Israel] have betrayed me."[25] The marriage relationship captures the personal bond between God and the people he drafted to follow his law. Significantly, God is portrayed as the jealous husband, and Israel as his wife.[26]

For the prophets, the disloyalty, the breach of the covenant, consisted not, as Jesus later taught,[27] in just lusting after other gods. The betrayal consists in actually consummating the act by engaging in the "weird worship" of foreign gods such as Baal, Mercury, and Peor. Again, the troubling question recurs. Do these other gods actually exist? If they are not real, if worshiping them has no point, why should it be treated as a violation of the marital covenant with God?

If they do exist, another theological paradox arises. Surely these other gods would have to be of lesser power. Why could God not destroy them rather than subject his people to constant temptation? And if for some reason he chooses not to destroy them, why should he be jealous of these petty competitors?

I pose these questions not just as theological conundrums but as questions that run to the heart of loyalty as a moral virtue. We are driven to understand loyalty at the theological level so that by turning the analogies around, we can better grasp loyalty and jealousy in human relationships.

In an effort to resolve the paradoxes posed above, the rabbinic teachers pondered the questions of jealousy and God's tolerance of petty competitors. A philosopher queried Rabbi Gamaliel why God did not simply destroy an idol in the form of a dog. Rabbi Gamaliel replied:

> If it was something unnecessary to the world that was worshipped, He would destroy it, but people worship the sun and moon, stars and constellations, streams and valleys. Should he destroy His world because of fools?[28]

The response of Rabbi Gamaliel on the question of God's jealousy informs us on the nature of jealousy in loving relationships. In response to the suggestion that jealousy honors the competitors, for "Is a wise man jealous of anyone but a wise man, a warrior of anyone but a warrior, a rich man of anyone but a rich man?" Rabbi Gamaliel parries:

> I will give you a parable. [God's jealousy] may be compared to that of a man's first wife after he takes an additional wife. If the second wife is her superior, the first will not be jealous of her, but if she is her inferior, the first wife will be jealous of her.[29]

The claim is that jealousy runs only toward those who are regarded as inferior and therefore an improper object of the husband's affections.[30] If the second wife were superior, the appropriate sentiment would be envy rather than jealousy. A more salient contemporary example might be the attitude of one divorced parent, say the father, toward his child's preferring the influence and tutelage of the mother. If the father regards the mother's care, concern, and competence as superior to his own, he has no reason to be jealous of her, for he knows that the choice is in the interests of the child he loves. But if the mother is an inferior influence and the child nonetheless favors her, he has reason to be jealous, both for his own loss and the suffering of his child.

The "jealousy" or "zealousness" of God (recall the ambiguity of the Hebrew *kanai*) expresses God's devotion to the relationship. Though analogized to the suffering jealous husband, he remains ever open to their return. The prophet Ezekiel bespeaks God's rage to shame and punish Israel for playing the harlot but then reveals God's promise to forgive the wayward wife and renew the covenant.[31] Though technically under Jewish law a husband cannot take back a wayward wife who has remarried and then divorced, the rabbis understood the metaphor of the marital relationship in the covenant more broadly. In the postbiblical legends they cite Hosea "For I am God, not man"[32] to recognize that reconciliation must be possible, even after the betrayal of whoring after other gods.[33]

As the talmudic sages turned to the problem of idolatry, the focus shifted from the nature of the sin as betrayal to a detailed working out of the ways in which the betrayal occurs. The general thrust of the discussion was to limit human liability and human sanctions for what others perceived to be acts of idolatry. In a critical limitation, the *Mishna*, codified at the end of the second century, makes it clear that citizens could not use self-help to prevent and punish idolatry on the spot.[34] Also, however grave the betrayal of God, human courts could not effectively prosecute and punish the offense. In theory, the offense was punishable by stoning to death. But the talmudic procedural requirements undercut the possibility of enforcement: Witnesses had to be present, observe the idolatry, and give the would-be idolater a prescribed warning, which he then disregarded.

Even within this restrictive procedural framework liability was further limited. As Maimonides summarizes the legal development, the only clear cases of punishable idolatry (provided that witnesses gave the required warning) were engaging in certain paradigmatic overt acts of worship. The act could consist in misappropriating one of the forms of worship reserved for God, such as prostrating oneself before or bringing a sacrifice in honor of another god. Or it could consist in engaging in a paradigmatic form of worship constitutive of the idolatrous religion, such as exposing oneself to Peor or throwing stones at Mercury, as one apparently did in worshiping these gods.

For Maimonides, however, the external act was never enough to determine whether idolatry actually transpired. As it evolved, Jewish law permitted the apparent idolater to take refuge in a broad doctrine of error. The wayward worshiper could argue, for example, that it only appeared that he was worshiping Peor when in fact he was contemptuously mocking the ritual. Or he could argue that he was simply inclined out of general "love or fear" to worship the idol. If he did not, in some act of inner conviction, actually accept the idol as a god, there was no act of idolatrous worship.

Intriguingly, Maimonides holds that in the case of error, as when the idol is worshiped contemptuously, there is no prosecutable offense; nonetheless, the responsible party must bring a sin offering to atone for the act. For generations, commentators have been puzzled by the difference between this case and worship out of a general "love or fear," for in the latter case no sin offering need be brought. The best account probably is that if purely aesthetic impulses impel the worshiper toward the idol, these nonrational forces make it clear that the worshiper does not stand in a personal relationship with the false god. He is neither mocking it nor submitting to it. His senses are distracted, but his spirit does not enter into a disloyal relationship.

Religious worship, with its own semantics of bringing sacrifices or prostrating oneself, expresses ultimate respect, submission, and honor. The concern in Maimonides' analysis of idolatry is, in part, to ensure that acts of respect toward God not be misappropriated and diluted by being directed toward false gods. Similarly, in the rituals of patriotism, we have traditionally sought to maintain a language of respect toward the flag as a symbol of the nation. As religious rituals express and confirm loyalty to God, treating the flag with respect and pledging allegiance to the "republic for which it stands" confirm and intensify loyalty to country. The problem that remains is whether the same rituals of respect and devotion enable us to comprehend the ethics of sexual fidelity.

Sexual Loyalty

Any attempt to assess sexual mores treads on uncertain factual ground. Whatever one says risks refutation by those with different experiences, who passionately affirm the opposite. The most that I say about the following claims is that they make sense to numerous men and women with whom I have discussed them. In this context the only thing that matters is whether they also make sense to you, the reader.

Discussions of sexual fidelity typically begin with the recognition that historically married women were expected to be monogamous, men less so. There may well have been economic and social reasons for the male interest in securing their blood line and being assured of an heir of their body. Of greater concern is the attitudes of women toward men that have crystallized in the course of their emancipation in Western societies. There have been recurrent, short-lived outbursts of a free love ethic, in which women sought to emulate the sexual freedom that they perceived men enjoying. The more typical response, and the dominant attitude today, at least in the United States, is that in stable, ongoing relationships women readily commit and expect a reciprocal male commitment of fidelity. The institution of marriage may be in long-term decline, but the demands of sexual fidelity are gaining ground as a moral imperative. To the extent that this is true, we have a puzzle. What is the point of this sexual loyalty?

Of course, there are functional explanations of sexual fidelity—avoiding disease and unplanned children. But these practical considerations hardly account for the pain that lovers feel upon learning that their partners share sexual intimacy with others. There is no way to know for sure why we make these demands on others, and therefore my speculative hypothesis merits a sympathetic hearing. My suggestion is that sexual acts serve as ritualist confirmation of the underlying relationship of emotional devotion. The sexual act is a way of saying to the other: "You and only you matter to me. And I demonstrate this commitment by sharing this profound pleasure exclusively with you." Monogamous sexuality is a rite of pleasure that overcomes each partner's recurrent doubts whether the other is fully there. Not surprisingly, then, in a world of generally easy sexual contact, fidelity becomes a relatively greater need. Because disloyalty is so easy and so tempting, constant reassurance becomes mandatory.

If this view is right, we are in a position to perceive the unity in the rituals underlying the devotional dimension of loyalty. Loyalty without devotion, or minimum loyalty, is satisfied by the condition of nonbetrayal. Citizenship (or permanent residence) without adhering to the enemy satisfies the conditions of national loyalty. And avoiding idolatry satisfies the requirements of loyal religious faith.

Thus a marriage (love affair) without adultery means that each spouse is faithful and loyal.

The devotional dimension of loyalty requires more than avoidance of betrayal. This additional condition is expressed in part in the rituals of attachment and devotion, as in patriotic observances, religious worship, and the rites of sex and love that sustain and deepen personal relationships.

* * *

In these first four chapters I have put forward a conceptual theory of loyalty. The key elements of this account are: First, loyalty is an expression of the historical self. Second, loyalty is more than a habit of attachment; it is based on a recognition of duty. Third, loyalty sometimes implies merely the avoidance of betrayal and sometimes a deeper, romantic unity sustained by rituals expressed in patriotism, religious devotion, and erotic love. The loyalty of the historical self is realized on different levels—to persons, to groups, and to God—and these dimensions of loyalty often conflict with each other. This grammar of loyalty permits us now to speak to some nagging concrete questions, high on the agenda of American and European politics.

In Chapter 5, we rely upon the concept of loyalty to refine our understanding of the proper relationship between the state and the individual. I broaden the notion of the private sphere, secure against state interference, to include relationships expressing personal and religious loyalties. These are "horizontal" loyalties that the state must respect. Yet the state—in particular, the Unites States—can claim "vertical" loyalty to itself and to its democratic, constitutional foundations. These bonds to the state are nurtured, as I suggest in Chapter 4, by rituals, and the center of these rituals in American culture is the flag. Thus in Chapter 6, we address the controversy about the Pledge of Allegiance, and, in Chapter 7, we locate the debate about flag burning as free speech in the broader context of sustaining national loyalty with due respect for individual liberty. In Chapter 8, we turn finally to the moral limits on loyalty, to the task ensuring that loyalty be not a vice but a virtue.

CHAPTER 5

Loyalty as Privacy

Few ideas have grasped the imagination of twentieth-century lawyers more firmly than the now pervasive principle of privacy. If we cast a glance at the state of the law in 1900, both here and abroad, we can hardly find an explicit reference to the principle that individuals should be left alone. The idea is not found in the great codifications of nineteenth-century Europe. It was not then known in Oriental legal cultures, and it had yet to find elaboration in Anglo-American law.

In the course of this century, the idea of privacy has taken hold both as a basis for tort recovery and as a principle of constitutional law that commends itself to diverse lines of thought in Western jurisprudence. The common law tort, breach of privacy, traces its roots to the classic article by Brandeis and Warren, published just before the dawn of the century.[1] Although the German Civil Code, which came into force in 1900, does not contain a provision on privacy or related concepts, the German courts interpreted the open-ended tort provision of the Code to include a "right to personality." This is the phrase that has come to be the Continental equivalent to our notion of privacy.

At the constitutional level, the right to privacy (or personality) has become a standard figure in the pantheon of basic human rights. The 1949 German Constitution recognizes that "everyone has a right to the flourishing of his or her personality." The European Convention on Human Rights, adopted in the same year, recognizes the right to a "private life." And as is well known, the U.S. Supreme Court has found a right to privacy embedded in constitutional provisions that recognize the right of the individual to be left alone.

The methodology for recognizing new rights, at the level either of tort law or of the Constitution, is to elaborate the patterns with which the law is already instinct. Brandeis and Warren found a pattern supporting a right to privacy in the laws of defamation and of copyright. In its path-breaking *Griswold* decision, the Supreme Court found a pattern of privacy in clauses of the Constitution protecting not only freedom of association but the sanctity of the home and of private papers as well as of private space.[2]

Perceiving a pattern in existing rules of law requires at least two components. First, there must be some data that could invite the perception of a pattern. Second, there must be a normative impulse, stimulated by the values of the time, to infer the pattern for the fragmented data.

In this chapter I intend to make a similar argument about relationships expressing loyalty. The claim is that relationships of loyalty should be entitled to be free of the state's intrusive hand, precisely as privacy has come to enjoy this principle of freedom from interference. The state should not force people to betray their commitments to their friends, lovers, family, community, or God. The thesis is both descriptive and normative. It is descriptive so far as the data elicited from American law do in fact support a pattern of relational privacy-based commitments of loyalty. The thesis is also normative. It asserts a claim about the way the law ought to be, for the claims about existing practice are too scant to support the generalization without our inclining favorably toward the data.

The argument begins with examples drawn from legally respected loyalties within the family and then expands to suggest that tightly drawn religious and ethnic groups are entitled to be treated with the kind of deference accorded families. The argument has implications for the current debate about multiculturalism in the United States. The implication of the argument that emerges here is that, within the limits to be explored, it is sound education to rear children with a sense of loyalty to the group that defines their ethnic and religious origins.

Testimonial Privileges

In this seemingly technical area of the law, we encounter strong sympathies for the principle that the law should not interfere with significant relationships of loyalty. The professional loyalties of attorneys to their clients and physicians and psychotherapists to their patients are secured in the sense that the clients and patients can prevent the disclosure in a legal dispute of material transmitted to the professional in confidence. Of greater relevance to us are the privileges of family members not to testify against each other.

In an illustrative case that arose during the McCarthy period, a woman named Blau tried to avoid Congressional interrogation about her political activities; she went into hiding and told her husband of her whereabouts. When he was called to the stand and required to testify under oath, could he refuse to disclose where she was?[3] The answer is yes. The husband need not betray his wife on the stand. He can stand loyal, guarding the confidences of their intimate relationship.

This privilege obviously takes a toll on legal procedures. Less information is available in the proceeding. Mistakes might be made in determining the facts on which the criminal or civil trial turns. Yet this sacrifice is thought necessary in order to protect one of the bonds of loyalty at the foundation of our social life. This much seems clear. Yet commentators disagree whether the privilege not to testify expresses utilitarian values or respect for family autonomy as an end in itself.

The conventional utilitarian view advanced by John Wigmore, a leading scholar in the field, is that encouraging confidential communication between husband and wife and strengthening the institution of the family justifies the loss of useful evidence to the courts.[4] The test is utilitarian, for it requires a balancing and weighing of the family against the state's interest in securing evidence. If it turned out, therefore, that the cost of forgoing evidence is greater than the benefit to the witness's family, the utilitarian should be willing to override the privilege.

Even if one concedes the importance of strengthening the family, the utilitarian grounding of the privilege is dubious. If one spouse is forced to testify against the other, it is not at all clear that the required testimony damages a healthy relationship. The presence of legal coercion should enable people to accept the damaging disclosure as the doing not of the spouse but of the legal system. And regardless of the minimal likelihood that one spouse might have to testify against the other, intimate lovers will continue to confide and trust in each other.

The better explanation of the privilege between husband and wife is that if a relationship is intimate and entrenched in a legal bond of loyalty, then demanding that Blau harm his wife on the stand is like asking him to harm himself, to incriminate himself. Significantly, the Fifth Amendment sanctifies each individual's right to remain silent and thus to escape the sense of being trapped between "a rock and a hard place": between harming oneself on the witness stand and committing perjury to protect oneself. It is a minor extension of this principle to recognize an analogous right to remain silent where the choice is between harming a spouse and committing perjury.

The marital privilege has come under attack recently in the Supreme Court, but the essential core, as explained here, remains intact.[5] Originally, married defendants could invoke the privilege to prevent their spouses from testifying. This meant that if a wife witnessed her husband commit child abuse, the husband could prevent her from testifying against him. This version of the privilege went too far; it could be explained only on the grounds of a fictional union between husband and wife. Jeremy Bentham aptly quipped that this version of the privilege goes beyond making every man's house his castle and permits a criminal to convert his house into "a den of thieves."[6] It "secures, to every man, one safe and unquestionable and ever ready accomplice for every imaginable crime."[7] Sensibly, the Supreme Court affirmed a conviction on federal drug charges based on the willing testimony of the defendant's wife.[8] If the thought of harming her legal spouse were unconscionable, she could have invoked the privilege and remained silent.[9]

The rationale for the privilege informs its reach. The issue debated today is whether the principle of family autonomy should extend to the relationship between parents and children. So far as the driving rationale is the promotion of family solidarity, the extension is probably not necessary. Parents and younger children need no stimulus from the law to remain loyal to one another; older parents will often be dependent on their grown children regardless of what the law does. But if the rationale is recognition that in some situations a witness's testifying against a loved one is akin to harming himself or herself, then the privilege should apply exactly as it does between husband and wife.

A few state legislatures have begun to more in this direction.[10] The New York courts have recognized a privilege of the parents not to testify against minor children.[11] In an important federal case, a lower court held that a son could not be required to testify against his father in a grand jury proceeding.[12] Extending the privilege in this way is strongly encouraged in the scholarly literature.[13] There is no important difference in principle between protecting the relationship between spouses and protecting the parent-child relationship. Accordingly, we should expect continuing expansion of the principle that no one should be required to be a witness against himself or herself, or against those with whom he or she stands in a close bond of loyalty.

If carried to its logical conclusion, the principle would insulate witnesses from the duty to testify any time the person affected was "part of oneself." This would suggest that even close friends should not be required to testify against each other. Consider Norma Kopp, the friend of the defendant Cramer, who was called to the stand to testify about the depth of Cramer's adhering to the German enemy.[14] According to her admissions, Cramer knew that the German agents who suddenly surfaced had come by submarine and that they were on a mission on behalf of the Third Reich. Kopp was only Cramer's friend, not his wife, and therefore she did not have the option of remaining silent.

That friends must testify against each other may come as a surprise. An English judge conceded in 1792, "It is indeed hard in many cases to compel a friend to disclose a confidential conversation; and I should be glad if by law such evidence could be excluded."[15] Sanford Levinson argues today that as a matter of principle friends should be included within the privilege to remain silent.[16] But on the way from principle to workable rule, the point often gets lost. The law is a rough instrument, and despite these sentiments repeatedly voiced, the rules of privilege cover only some relationships of loyalty.

Surrogate Motherhood

The deference to familial relationships in the law of privileges suggests an approach to the moral and legal problems of surrogacy contracts. In this innovation in childbearing, a woman commits herself, for a fee, to let herself be artificially inseminated, to carry a child to term, and then to surrender the child to the other contracting party, thereby forfeiting all her parental rights. The problems that attend these contracts are well illustrated by the agony of Mary Beth Whitehead.

Ms. Whitehead, a mother of two and homemaker of uncertain income, responded to an ad in a local New Jersey newspaper and learned, upon contact with a fertility center in Manhattan, that she could earn $10,000 by acting as a surrogate, giving birth to a healthy child without deformities, and surrendering the child to the child's biological father and his wife. If she did not deliver the goods—a healthy child—she would receive only one thousand dollars for her time and trouble.[17] The parties with whom she eventually contracted were William and Elizabeth Stern, both with advanced university degrees, and with an income in the upper few per cent of American society.

People who believe strongly in contract see nothing wrong with arrangements of this sort. They give full vent to the parties' autonomy and capacity for rational self-governance. Contracts represent the ideal of impartial morality. Every concrete individual in the world, both real and corporate, qualifies as a partner, and we each bear within us the capacity to make a binding commitment. Promises and contracts are binding because we all assume that competent adults can commit their personalities to an agreement and thus sacrifice the freedom to change their minds.[18]

Though contracts are a vehicle of economic development and stable cooperation, it is extraordinary that one can sacrifice one's future freedom for the sake of present advantage. This is the basis of the recurrent Faustian metaphor of pacts with the devil; for the sake of present fame or fortune, one commits oneself to a price that one hopes will never come due. Contracts glorify the capacity for individual commitment, but they also represent the means by which individuals sell themselves into slavery. Philosophers like John Stuart Mill, who revere contract as an expression of freedom, also recognize the overweening importance of preserving freedom in the future.[19] No one should be able to go too far in selling his or her future for the sake of present compensation. And how far is "too" far? Mill thought that contracts of slavery went too far. Though he regarded the commitments of women who entered into polygamous marriages as immoral, he would not have forced them to be "civilized." In the law today, we say that unconscionable arrangements are void, as violations of "public policy."

In the arrangement between Whitehead and the Sterns, something was bound to go wrong, for no one told the hospital about the plan to surrender the child.[20] The sensible way to execute an adoption from birth is to have the baby removed immediately, without coming into contact with the mother. But after giving birth in late March 1986 to the little girl Sarah, later known as Baby M, Mary Beth received her child in her arms, and like any other mother in the ward she nursed her, ogled her, and began to love her. She left the hospital a few days later with the child she naturally and predictably came to regard as her own. The transfer to the Sterns was supposed to take place three days after birth, away from public view, at the Whiteheads' home.

The arrangement was clearly designed with some concern for what other people would think. There may have been an element of shame, for the suspicion came easily that the Whiteheads, the Sterns, and the lawyers had devised a scheme that reduced babies to a commodity, to be bought and sold. More likely they were concerned about possible criminal prosecution[21] and whether the contract to deliver a healthy child in return for $10,000 would hold up in court.

The Whiteheads did deliver the child as promised, despite Mary Beth's feeling that as a result of giving up her child her life "wasn't worth anything . . . [she] was no longer worthy of being [a] mother [to her other two children].[22] But there followed over a year of extraordinary pulling and tearing at the child the Whiteheads called Sarah and the Sterns, Melissa (whence the name Baby M).[23] The day after giving up the child, Mary Beth walked into the Sterns' home and managed, somehow, to walk out with her Sarah.[24] The Sterns tried legal remedies to get their Melissa back, but the Whiteheads fled with the child to Florida. A court order, secured in Florida,[25] put the Sterns back in custody, and the Whiteheads were reduced to fighting in the New Jersey courts to eke out whatever rights might be left to them. As the dust was settling, the child was adapting to life with the Sterns, and this fact in itself tended to strengthen their case that they could provide a better home for Baby M.

If the contract turned out to be valid, however, there would be no discussion in court about who had a superior moral claim to Baby M and who could provide a better home for the child. The contract would terminate the mother's claims forever. Therefore the judges of

New Jersey had first to ponder how far people should be able to go in trading their future lives and the fate of children in return for present advantage. It is not hard to imagine arrangements close to the Whitehead-Stern contract that would be obviously void as a violation of public policy. Suppose that the Sterns had wanted a son and therefore introduced a term in the surrogacy contract requiring Whitehead to have an abortion if the fetus tested female. This condition would be void on several grounds. The courts would not countenance an agreement that discriminated against the birth of girls, and further, the notion that a woman would be compelled to abort a fetus would be so clearly unconscionable that the discussion would have been brief. Yet there is not much difference between requiring a woman to abort a fetus and mandating that she abandon her child. It is indeed more difficult to contemplate the loss of the born child, particularly if it is provided that the mother will possess and nurture the infant for a few days after birth.

Nonetheless, the New Jersey trial court came to the surprising conclusion that indeed contract ruled the matter: The mother's rights were to be terminated forever. The judge carried out a hasty adoption ceremony in chambers; Elizabeth Stern replaced Mary Beth Whitehead as the legal mother of the child. The New Jersey Supreme Court brought the state to its senses. The seven justices unanimously reversed the trial court and held that the agreement violated the basic principles of law and justice in the state.[26] Conceiving children and determining custody is not within the autonomy of contracting parties.

In the court's characterization of the surrogacy agreement, the natural parents had determined the custody of the child even before it was conceived. If a contract for this purpose were valid, it would usurp the judicial function of deciding whether custody with the natural mother or the natural father better serves the best interests of the child. There are other problems as well. The contract seeks to terminate a mother's rights even before the child comes into existence. It violates the premise that wherever possible children should grow up nurtured by both their natural parents. "Worst of all, however," the court continues, "is the contract's total disregard for the best interests of the child."[27] Where the parents do not live together, as was the case with William Stern and Mary Beth Whitehead, the courts must intervene to make this decision about the child's welfare.

In the first days of a child's life, it is fanciful for a court to try to determine whether she would flourish more in one family or another. There is no way to project alternative lives into the future without the intrusion of the crassest forms of social and economic bias. How could a court balance the love and devotion of the natural mother against the wealth, education, and worldly sophistication of the father? Should it matter that the Sterns had divergent ethnic and religious backgrounds? that the Whiteheads' finances were in difficulty at the time of trial? that Mary Beth Whitehead had already successfully (whatever that means) reared two children?

Better courts have thoughtfully distanced themselves from attempting in this way to divine the advantages and disadvantages of alternative modes of life. In the end, there is no more sure guide to the child's welfare than the commitment felt by the natural mother. The mother's loyalty sustains the child more deeply than the supposedly objective factors of wealth, opportunity, and lifestyle.[28]

The New Jersey Supreme Court adopted a peculiar way of talking about a mother's claim to care for her own child. The question was supposedly one of the mother's "right to the companionship of her child."[29] American lawyers and judges commonly phrase every issue as an expression of individual rights, but I take it that the dominant thought motivating mothers like Mary Beth Whitehead is not the notion of right but of duty. The mother of Baby M felt compelled to care for her offspring. Her attachment, her sense of loyalty, to the child that she brought to term defined the course she had to take. To speak of a "right to the companionship of her child" is to treat a mother's most basic impulse as little more than an interest in being amused.

The father's donating his sperm does not generate a duty of comparable force. It would be ludicrous for a father to sue a sperm bank to force disclosure of the identity of a child born of his sperm used in artificial insemination. He could not plausibly claim a loyalty to the child solely on the basis of his genetic transmission. The mother's loyalty is grounded not just in biology but in the experiential connection of carrying the child to term and nurturing it after birth.[30]

The evil of the surrogacy contract is aptly formulated in the language of loyalty. The contract to bear a child for another family requires a mother to act disloyally toward her own offspring. And it is an act of disloyalty that has permanent consequences of estrangement and self-alienation. It is indeed comparable to a contract prior to conception that if the fetus is not of a particular gender, the mother will terminate the pregnancy. As it would be unconscionable to force a woman to go through with an abortion, it would be equally wrong to force a woman to carry out an agreement made before she has held the child in her arms. Contracts are no more than useful instruments for furthering human designs. Where they rivet people in arrangements with consequences disastrous to their self-esteem, they are to be disregarded.

Gift Giving and Inheritance

There are good arguments, based on the principle of equality, for prohibiting gift giving and inheritance.[31] It is not fair for some people to have an advantage over others just because they happen to have been born of wealthy circumstances. They invariably have an advantage in their access to education and cultural influences, but why should inequality be compounded by inheritance? A high regard for justice for all, on equal terms, would lead us to recognize not only that the recipient of a gift or inheritance has no moral claim to it but that allowing the individual to keep it would perpetuate inequalities of wealth and opportunity.

Those who receive gifts without working for them appear to gain a windfall. In defense of gift giving, one might say that those who own property should have the right to give it away. Yes, they should, but it does not follow that the recipients have a moral right to keep their unearned gains. At least the moral desert of the recipient is not as clear as that of someone who invests his labor in generating an asset of value—raising crops, taking possession of a wild animal, or working raw material into a usable commodity. Nor does the recipient of a gift have the kind of claim that an injured person has for compensation to correct the wrong he or she has suffered.[32]

Despite these sound objections to gift giving and inheritance, both are routinely endorsed in the legal systems of industrialized societies, including those of the formerly Communist countries. If the practice is so clearly unjust, if it entrenches the social position of wealthy families, why should it be allowed? There are at least two distinct ways to justify gift giving across the generations as an expression of family solidarity.

The first argument derives from the thesis of this chapter: Sharing wealth reflects a duty of loyalty, and the law should not inhibit people from acting on their loyalties. Testamentary power provides a means for individuals to express their love and loyalty to children, relatives, and friends as well as to social causes outside the family. The institution of giving and bequeathing enables the individual to make himself present, even after his demise, with the people and projects that carry his spirit. It is a way to realize one's loyalty to those in the next generation. The imperative of loyalty, then, might be strong enough to convert an act that seems like a gratuitous give-away into an act compelled by duty. The recipient has no moral claim to the wealth bestowed upon him, but nonetheless the law should not stand in the way of those expressing their loyalty by bestowing gifts.

Expected loyalties also circumscribe the effective range of testamentary freedom, for these expected loyalties shape deliberations about the validity of wills. When the testators' expressed wishes deviate too far from the expected, as when they leave their money to strangers or pets, a fight often ensues over whether the decedent's actions were sane and free of undue outside influence. For example, when Alice Curtis Desmond died in 1990, the trustees of a community library expected a large bequest. Ms. Desmond had gone on record as firmly committed to the library, yet in the end most of her money went to her lawyer and her nurse. It was not too difficult for the library to convince a local judge that the lawyer and nurse had exercised "undue influence" on the dying Ms. Desmond and that their shares should be reduced in order to generate a more ample bequest for the library, the expected object of Ms. Desmond's loyalty.[33]

The second mode of justifying inheritance casts doubt on the supposedly undeserved and gratuitous nature of receiving property as a bequest from a family member. No one earns money and accumulates property solely for himself or herself. Husbands, wives, children, and parents provide some of the incentive for the testator's earning what he or she has to will at death. From a moral point of view, they are already partial owners of the estate. They have entered into the testator's historical self and thus, at least metaphorically, continue as owners when they receive their formal bequest. To be sure, the scope of those with this "moral right" is ill defined. Just as it is difficult to circumscribe the friends against whom one should not be compelled to testify,[34] so the range of those who constitute a significant part of one's biography remains murky.

Curiously, under this approach it is easier in principle to justify giving every close relative a prescribed statutory share than it is to vindicate the power of the testator to direct his estate from the grave. Many European and Latin American codes already follow this system of recognizing the rights of the *legitime*.[35] Under this plausible way of conceiving property rights across the generations, the testator cannot disown a member of his or her family who may claim a statutory share of the estate. Testamentary power fills in the gaps left in the statutory scheme for transferring wealth at death.

There are two distinct ways, then, that the imperatives of loyalty ease our qualms about the inequalities and undeserved windfalls generated by the system of inheritance. Transferring property across the generations enables us to express our love, concern, and loyalty to children. The legal system may tax our estates, but it could not properly prevent us from acting on these intergenerational loyalties. Alternatively, the system of inheritance merely recognizes and validates a broader conception of ownership by the family as a whole.

We have canvassed three areas of the law that testify to the power of loyalty within the family. The law of testimonial privileges, the invalidity of surrogacy contracts, and the power to transfer property at death all trace the common theme of insulating family loyalties from the power of the state. The challenge at this stage of the argument is whether we can broaden the base of protected loyalties from the family to larger social groupings.

The Free Exercise of Religion

One of the enduring mysteries of constitutional law is why the exercise of religion should be entitled to greater protection than other expressions of human belief and commitment. The First Amendment provides that "Congress shall make no law . . . prohibiting the free exercise [of religion]." There is no dispute about the core meaning of the provision. There has never been a court fight (so far as I know) about the right of groups of people to withdraw to a private place and engage in whatever traditional rites and rituals they wish under the name of religious worship. Nor has there ever been an effort by Congress or the states to impose criminal penalties on people for their opinions and beliefs, no matter how heretical their views about God, creation, and salvation may seem to others.

The problem begins when religious beliefs find their expression, as they invariably do, in actions affecting people outside the religion. If a group of fundamentalists seeks to bring back animal sacrifice or the institution of temple prostitution, they most likely could not avoid criminal prosecution by invoking their religious commitments. If slaughtering sheep is generally prohibited, alleging a purpose of religious worship would probably not generate an exemption from the statute.[36] Timothy Leary tried, unsuccessfully, to secure an exemption from the prohibition against the use of marijuana with claims that his usage was spiritual and religious.[37]

When religious practices offend conventional moral principles or affect outsiders, however, the community claims a proper interest in resolving these conflicts between differing communities of belief. This problem of accommodation did not reach the Supreme Court until the late nineteenth century, and then the Justices reasoned, as they upheld a federal prohibition of polygamy, that the state could prohibit any conduct that was "in violation of social duties or subversive of good order."[38] It did not matter that the appellants before the court were Mormons and that their polygamous practices were sanctioned and even commanded as a community responsibility by their church. If the regulation was neutral on its face, it did not matter whether the burden fell harder on Mormons than on Christians and Jews who had no interest in polygamy.

It appeared in this and other cases decided prior to World War II that the free exercise clause gave no special protection at all to religious minorities. So long as the statute did not intrude upon a group's right to believe what it wanted and worship privately as it wanted, the statute could regulate all forms of behavior that appeared to the majority to be offensive or harmful. It is not surprising, then, that eight Justices on the Court voted in 1940 that all pupils in state schools could be required, on pain of expulsion, to salute the flag and recite the Pledge of Allegiance.[39] It did not matter that the dissenting pupils, expelled from school for their refusal to participate in these rituals, were Jehovah's Witnesses whose parents and ministers taught them that saluting the flag constitutes "worshiping a graven image" in violation of the Third Commandment.[40]

This "neutral" approach to religion draws support from the structure of the First Amendment, which prohibits both laws "respecting an establishment of religion" and those "prohibiting the free exercise thereof." As the argument goes, the principle of neutrality represents the only way to avoid bending too far in favor of or against religious practices. In particular, granting an exemption to a religiously motivated claimant favors those who are religious and therefore arguably constitutes an establishment of religion. If, for example, only Mormons were allowed to practice polygamy, this exception to the rule might seem like a gratuitous award for being Mormon. The state's giving grants-in-aid to Mormon schools would "establish" religion in violation of the Constitution; therefore it seems that favoring Mormons by other means would do the same.

The policy of neutrality prevailed in the Supreme Court prior to World War II, and it has recently renewed its position of supremacy among a strong majority on the currently conservative Court.[41] Yet between 1943 and 1990, the Court adopted a distinctly different approach to the free exercise of religion that warrants our attention. It illustrates the general principle that the law should not interfere with existing loyalties and force people to act disloyally. The Court's thinking between 1943 and 1990 exemplifies this deferential attitude toward compelling loyalties as an expression of respect for the religious and ethnic minorities that constitute a multicultural America.

The beginning of the new policy crystallized in the Court's dramatic reversal, in 1943, of its decision permitting state schools to expel Jehovah's Witness children who refused to salute the flag.[42] The proper interpretation of this decision in the *Barnette* case remains a matter of controversy, and we will examine the opinions of the Justices in detail in Chapter 6. It is fair to say, however, that the majority of the Court signaled in 1943 that they would begin to take a more tolerant and indulgent attitude toward religious groups that dissented from the common practices of American society. The Court would not allow the legal system—neutral laws or not—to compel members of these groups to act disloyally toward their fellow members and, in a way yet to be explained, to betray the external authority to which they had subjected themselves.

The tolerance for deviant groups has expressed itself in three prominent areas. First, Jehovah's Witnesses are treated as exempt from statutes that they, as a group, regard as pushing them too far toward idolatrous practices. They need not salute the flag.[43] They need not stand for the national anthem.[44] They need not carry patriotic messages on their license plates.[45] Second, Sabbatarians—those who refuse to work on Saturdays—do not forfeit their claim to unemployment compensation if they refuse to accept jobs that require work on Saturdays.[46] The same policy applies to Christians who refuse to work on Sundays[47] and presumably would extend to Moslems who refuse to work on Fridays.

Third, and most significant, the Court held in the early 1970s that parents in an Amish community in Wisconsin could refuse to send their children to a public high school that, parents feared, would educate them in ways foreign to the community's traditional religious culture.[48] The children were attending public school until the age of fourteen, but state law demanded education until the age of sixteen. The Amish wanted their children not only to avoid the secular influences of a public high school but to settle down in early adolescence into the adult roles of farming and homemaking prescribed for them in the community's traditional way of life.

Like the Jehovah's Witnesses in the flag salute controversy, the Amish relied upon their own interpretation of Scripture. Though all Christians share the passage in Paul's Epistle to the Romans, "be not conformed to this world,"[49] the Amish insist on a literal reading that requires them to separate themselves from the surrounding American culture and devote themselves to a simple agricultural life suffused with religious thought and devotion.[50]

These, then, are the categories in which complainants have received religious exemptions from neutral laws. It is worth noting that all three of these sects that have fared well in the Supreme Court are splinter Protestant groups. They are minorities within the dominant Protestant religious culture of the United States. Quakers and other Protestant pacifists have not had to litigate claims of conscientious objection to military service, for the Selective Service Act itself recognizes an exemption.[51] Yet there is evidence that if the statute had not provided the exemption, the Court would have[52]—at least during the period 1943–1990.

Despite this favorable treatment of Protestant sects, other religious groups have not received the same deferential recognition. Jews and Moslems have fared badly before the Court.[53] The treatment of Native Americans has been less than respectful.[54] Scientologists received short shrift.[55] Oddly, we do not know whether Catholics would have benefited from the transiently tolerant attitude of the Court, for cases posing special burdens on Catholics have not come to the attention of the Justices. Yet a principle of recognizing exemptions only for Protestants was never articulated or even hinted at by the Court. The very idea would be shocking to the legal community and general public. There would be no way to defend a constitutional clause that, in the end, inured to the benefit of only one denomination in American life.

Though the period of tolerance and deference has passed, the Court's present policy of strict neutrality is likely also to be temporary. Therefore, it is worth thinking about the best possible case for recognizing exemptions from neutral statutes on the basis of religious commitments. Pondering this problem may lead us to appreciate why the Court—even during the period of its tolerance—appeared to discriminate against some non-Christian religions.

There are two basic sources of anxiety in recognizing religious exemptions from seemingly neutral statutes. First, why, in principle, should religious people be preferred to their nonreligious neighbors? Why should a Sabbatarian receive better treatment than someone who prefers, for sound secular reasons, to take Wednesdays off? If the Amish can keep their children out of high school, can hippies living in Big Sur do the same? Second, what do we mean by a religious claim? If someone claims his religion requires him to smoke pot, we are not likely to believe him.[56] Why not? The philosophical essence of religion eludes us, for there is no single criterion for classifying group activities as religious or not. A number of practices invoke religious associations: belief in God, acceptance of a revealed text, a regular form of worship, a quest for the ultimate truth about the origin and purpose of human existence. Yet committing ourselves to a list like this one only introduces the bias of our historical situation. These are the factors that characterise Judaism, Christianity, and Islam, and therefore we are inclined to think that they are constitutive of the religious life.

There is no way to make headway on the constitutional concept of religion without first developing a theory about why the Constitu-

tion should wish to defer to religious commitments. The present
tendency on the Court and among scholars is to think that the psychological intensity of religious beliefs requires us to accord these
beliefs special protection. Forcing people to act contrary to their religious beliefs imposes a certain sort of harm, and this harm must be
balanced against the state's interest in securing universal compliance,
say, with a law prohibiting polygamy, requiring attendance in school,
or imposing military or prison discipline. The conventional mode of
analyzing free exercise claims in the period of tolerance, 1943–1990,
required that the Court first establish whether the claimant sincerely
held the religious view asserted and then, on the other side of the
ledger, whether the state had a "compelling interest" that over-
weighed the religious claim.

This way of thinking was deeply flawed. First, intensity of belief
could not provide the relevant test for religious beliefs, for there are
many beliefs as strongly held as those characteristic of the great religions. The Court in *Yoder* captured the problem in this example:

> Thus, if the Amish asserted their claims because of their subjective
> evaluation and rejection of the contemporary secular values accepted
> by the majority, much as Thoreau rejected the social values of his
> time and isolated himself at Walden Pond, their claims would not
> rest on a religious basis. Thoreau's choice was philosophical and per-
> sonal rather than religious, and such belief does not rise to the
> demands of the Religion Clauses.[57]

The analogy is strained, for Thoreau had no reason to seek refuge
in the Constitution; there was nothing illegal about his return to
nature. But let us suppose, if we can, that we have a case of someone
holding personal commitments as deep as Thoreau's that require
deviation not only from social but from legal norms. It would be difficult to say that, as a psychological matter, these commitments
would be less strong than those imposed by the recognized religions. Nor could one claim that humanistic objections to war or a
particular war might not be as strong as objections based on religious belief. Yet the Constitution protects only religious beliefs, and
therefore there must be some account of these beliefs that is both
plausible and adequate to explain why religiously motivated conduct
is singled out for preferred treatment.

The second flaw in the conventional way of thinking about free exercise exemptions is that if the claimant really could make out a claim of religious commitment and we understood why these commitments should prevail over secular legal obligations, it is hard to imagine why an interest of the state—compelling or otherwise—should outweigh the religious commitment. Imagine Creon arguing with Antigone about whether the community's interest in civic solidarity should prevail over her loyalties to her dead brother and to Hades. Creon could well argue that the state's interest was compelling, to which Antigone would properly respond, in the contemporary idiom: "Creon, you just don't get it." Hades' law required her to bury her dead brother. There was no room in her mental calculus for balancing competing interests.

We need an account of religious commitment that goes beyond the recognition of the psychological weight of these commitments and an explanation of why these commitments should prevail over secular law. My account invokes the general theme of this chapter: The legal system should not intrude upon relationships of loyalty. The religious life, as we know it in the West, is based on the individual's having loyalties to a transcendental authority, and these loyalties preclude giving wholehearted allegiance to a secular authority. He must "render unto Caesar the things which are Caesar's and unto God the things which are God's."[58] Antigone must render unto Creon that which is Creon's and under Hades that which belongs to Hades.

These loyalties are directed toward the divine voice, but they cannot simply express a vision that God exists and has spoken to the believer. These aberrant claims about communication with God are more likely to be taken as a sign of mental illness than as an expression of an orientation worthy of constitutional protection.[59] In order for a claim of higher loyalty to be plausible, it must be embedded in a community practice. There must be others who hear the same voice, and there must be, in recited legends or in a written text, some objective manifestation of what the higher power demands of loyal followers. The loyalty to God then becomes interwoven with loyalty to a community and fidelity to a tradition. It is not an accident that in those cases in which the Court has recognized a religious exemption, the claimant always rested his or her claim on a biblical passage, most of them in the Ten Commandments. The relevant passages instruct believers not to worship a graven image, to keep the sabbath, not to kill, and from the New Testament, the injunction not to "conform to this world." Where the religious belief or practice had no biblical foundation, like Leary's claim to use drugs or an Amish claim not to pay taxes, the Court found one reason or another for dismissing the claim as ill founded.

A suit illustrating the problem was brought by a Native American, Steven Roy, for welfare benefits on behalf of his two-year-old child, Little Bird of Snow.[60] Though the applicable statute required that Roy submit a Social Security number on behalf of the child, he refused, citing the opinion of his chief in the Abenaki tribe that technology was "robbing the spirit of man" and that Social Security numbers had something to do with technology. The Justices seemed perfectly willing to concede that Roy believed, heart and soul, that using a Social Security number for Little Bird of Snow would rob her of her spiritual power. Why, then, did Roy receive only one unequivocal vote among the Justices?[61] Is the prevention of welfare fraud by using Social Security numbers so compelling a state interest that it should override Roy's deep religious commitment? It is hard to see why.

Although the Justices were hardly forthright about their skepticism, they did not take Roy's claim as seriously as they would take a claim based on the Ten Commandments. Read these dismissive words written by Chief Justice Warren Burger:

> Roy may no more prevail on his religious objection to the Government's use of a Social Security number for his daughter than he could on a sincere religious objection to the size or color of the Government's filing cabinets.[62]

Could you imagine the Court writing in that contemptuous tone about the Commandment to observe the sabbath or the Commandment not to kill or even about the peculiar readings given by the Amish, the Witnesses, or the Adventists to the biblical clauses that shape their culture? Yet the Court failed to address the question whether Roy had a religious view worth taking seriously. To do so would put the Court in the embarrassing position of assessing whether a particular religious view was theologically sound.

Whether the Court admitted it or not, the Justices simply could not allow the opinion of one chief, as interpreted by one man, to prevail over a federal statute. There was no tradition, so far as we can tell, in the Abenaki tribe supporting this eccentric view; the claims about spiritual power had not been tested by community debate. They had not passed from one generation to the next as the wisdom the Abenaki live by. To accept this claim as the basis of a free exercise exemption would have made federal law hostage to every chief and indeed to every Native American with an idiosyncratic view about maintaining spiritual power.

Roy's request for an exemption was an easy case. There was no way he could have won. Yet the Court decided against him without confronting the real question, namely, whether he had in fact made out a claim that he was subject to a conflicting loyalty, whether he had a strong rooting in his community for the claim that he had to render unto the gods of the Abenaki that which belonged to the gods of the Abenaki. The remarks of one chief, as interpreted by one man, do not a religion make. Yet because the Justices are fearful of becoming the "arbiters of scriptural interpretation,"[63] they would not offend Roy directly by saying that his deeply held view was eccentric and chimerical. They offended him only indirectly by devising an ill-fitting argument to explain why they could not honor his concern about Little Bird of the Snow's spiritual power. The rationale of Chief Justice Burger's opinion takes off from the dismissive remark equating Roy's belief to "a sincere religious objection to the size or color of the Government's filing cabinets."[64] The point of the metaphor is that however sincere and committed the religious belief, the free exercise clause "does not afford an individual a right to dictate the conduct of the Government's internal procedures."[65]

Hard cases—as the saying goes—often make bad law, but it is not so often that easy cases make bad law. Yet the doctrine spawned in this case would live on to do great mischief. The next time it was applied in the Supreme Court, Native Americans protested the federal government's plan to build a road on government land in a national forest.[66] For over 200 years "the Yurok, Karok, and Tolowa Indians [had] held sacred an approximately 25 square-mile area of land" through which the road would run.[67] According to the finding of an independent study, building the road "would cause serious and irreparable damage to the sacred areas which are an integral and necessary part of the belief systems and lifeway of Northwest California Indian peoples."[68] For over 200 years the Native Americans had carried out their land-based rituals in "privacy, silence, and an

undisturbed natural setting."[69] All of that would be compromised by
the government's road.

The devastating impact of this road-building plan on religious
practices entrenched in a community for generations had little to do
with Roy's highly personal claim about the spiritual power of his
child. Yet, with remarkable insensitivity to the religious life, the
majority of the Court could not see the difference:

> The building of a road or the harvesting of timber on publicly owned
> land cannot meaningfully be distinguished from the use of a Social
> Security number in *Roy*. In both cases, the challenged government
> action would interfere significantly with private persons' ability to
> pursue spiritual fulfillment according to their own religious beliefs.
> In neither case, however, would the affected individuals be coerced
> by the Government's action into violating their religious beliefs.[70]

For the Justices of the Court, all beliefs are the same.[71] It does not
matter whether they are prompted by the occasional comment of a
single chief or whether they are refined and cultivated over generations by hundreds and thousands of believers. It does not matter
whether they are merely tentative views about spiritual power or
whether they are rituals and practices that have been executed over
and over again.

The fundamental error, I submit, is the assumption that religious
belief can be reduced to the intense and sincerely held beliefs that
believers label religious. Religious beliefs, so far as they are to be
taken seriously, arise in congregations or communities of believers.
They represent a submission to an external authority that commands
obedience. They are expressed not only in views about the world
but in shared, interdependent rituals based on the those views.
Prophets calling in the wilderness may indeed hear the voice of God,
but standing alone, they cannot expect to be honored in their own
land.[72] Abraham may indeed have been privately commanded by
God to sacrifice his son,[73] but if he had, he should not have
expected his homicide to be treated as the free exercise of religion.

There are at least two reasons for understanding religion as the
outgrowth of communitarian practices. The competing loyalty that
religious commitments represent is a loyalty to the group as well as
to the divine voice. The congregation's understanding of the voice
disciplines our tendencies to accept every mystical moment as a true

religious command. The foundation of the religious life is the acceptance of a higher power in the universe, and that acceptance, in turn, entails humility as a condition of the religious life. Humility requires that one hear the voice of God not as a self-proclaimed prophet but as one member of a congregation that tests its visions over time.

Further, and more significantly, a congregational conception of religion mediates against the excesses of individuals who think they hear the voice of God. Whether Abraham (or Agamemnon) received a divine command or not, the practice of child sacrifice could not survive over generations as an institutionalized ritual. Only those practices survive that contribute to the flourishing of the community and its members. The Amish may prosper over generations by keeping their children at home and rearing them in opposition to their host culture, but they cannot expect to flourish as a minority in a host country if they categorically refuse to pay taxes to a lawful government.[74] The issue is not only one of maintaining good relations with the host country but of supporting the framework that makes their autonomy as a community possible. In the long run, the only views that tend to be accepted as divinely commanded are those that serve the welfare of the group as a community living among and with other communities.

The correct interpretation of the free exercise clause, then, would defer to religious loyalties only if they are founded on a system of beliefs embedded in community practices and tested and refined within a community of believers. The best way to establish these features of a belief—and the mode that has typically worked in the Supreme Court—is to ground the belief in a biblical passage or its equivalent. The 200-year practice of land-based ritual by the North American Yurok, Karok, and Tolowa tribes is a clear equivalent. The personal views of one Abenaki chief and one follower are not the equivalent of a holy book.

There is little doubt that a communitarian approach to the free exercise clause may require the Court to assess whether a particular community really grounds its views in the Bible or whether these views are the product of independently motivated customs and convictions. Yet the inquiry may not be as difficult as it seems. I have little difficulty identifying the view that mothers with preschool children should not work outside their homes as a customary conviction shared by some Christian fundamentalist groups, but that is not enough to classify the view as religious.[75] Firing a pregnant teacher on these grounds can hardly be defended as submitting to the command of God.[76] I also find it hard to understand how a Christian community could derive racial prejudice from a careful reading of Scripture. A Christian college's prohibiting interracial dating may express the college's innermost convictions, but these convictions are not necessarily responsive to God's word.[77] These views about women and racial exclusiveness may often be tendered by the devoutly religious, but they are no more than biases that have become entrenched as the custom of the community. The purpose of the free exercise clause is not furthered by recognizing transient customs as equivalent to Scripture. Enthroning these customs and biases as "religious" is to cheapen the convictions of those who must act on their loyalty to a higher power.

There are obviously limits to how far one can go in deferring to the values that crystallize within the subcultures of a multicultural society like the United States. As there are limits to personal privacy, there are limits to society's capacity to defer to the intragroup loyalties of families and religious communities. A woman's right to an abortion is grounded in the principle of reproductive privacy, but that principle yields, at the point of viability, to the interests of the fetus. Similarly, the autonomy of private groups, whether religious or not, must yield to society's commitments to racial and gender justice, at least where the behavior of the group affects outsiders. My only claim is that the state—the organ of society as a whole—should defer in principle to the loyalties that constitute friendships, families, and religious subcultures. The starting point for the debate should be the principle of deference to existing loyalties. These are loyalties that play themselves out between friends and lovers, between parents and children, and, in the religious context, between individuals and the divine voice as understood in a community of believers.

CHAPTER 6

Teaching Loyalty

The schoolroom is where loyalties first collide. In the seemingly neutral activities of learning literature, history, and biology, deep tensions between the home and the dominant society come to the fore. Secular education offers pupils from religious homes an alternative to the authority of divine revelation. Religious practices at school challenge pupils from nonobservant homes to adopt new values. Parental roles at home may conform to traditional male-female stereotypes. But the school may convey a different ethic about the way men and women should relate to each other. In these fissures among home, mass culture, and school, young people begin to see that they must find their own way. Their flourishing depends on their assessing the merits of conflicting influences.

In immigrant countries like the United States, with a diversity of religious and linguistic heritages, schools have traditionally been the crucible for casting a single national community. At the turn of the century, when immigration flowed primarily from the old world to the new, the United States had a special concern in using the schools as a medium for generating loyalty to a new country and culture. Today there is hardly a prosperous country in the industrialized West that has not faced the challenge of absorbing immigrants. The schoolroom remains the primary means for melding the new with the old.

The teaching of literature, history, and civics provides the primary vehicle for casting this common identity. Pupils must not only speak the same language, they must come to rehearse the same books and poems, cherish the same national heroes and villains, and develop common sentiments toward their shared institutions. This is what it means to live in a common culture.

In the last five years we have witnessed a major challenge to the traditional view that the schools should inculcate a common identity and unified nationhood. The buzzword of the 1990s is "multiculturalism." We have suddenly awakened to increasing diversity in the ethnic backgrounds of elementary school classes. Growing Hispanic and Asian immigration has brought about a shift in the ethnic composition of elementary school classes. Over the last decade, the percentage of so-called minority children in the total school age population has increased 5 percent. Many people are prompted, therefore, to rethink the orientation of the grade school curriculum, particularly the teaching of history and of patriotic attachment to the United States.

Unfortunately, the call for multicultural education frequently gets confused with a not so subtle anti-European and anti-American bias. In some circles it has become chic to label the "white man's" conquest of the new world as a crime against the native peoples. The five hundredth anniversary of Columbus's stumbling upon an unknown continent has generated self-doubts in the culture that came in its wake. There is no doubt that it would be desirable to expose schoolchildren to a serious study of Islam and Judaism as well as Christianity. And nothing would be lost by communicating greater respect for Mexican and indigenous cultures than was once the wont in the schools of the Southwest. Nor is there any reason why all children, both black and white, should not be exposed to the cultural contribution of Africans as well as mixed-race Europeans.

Yet we should not forget that whatever happens at home, virtually all of our schoolchildren (if they have been in the United States for a few years) speak the same language, play the same games, watch the same television programs, and cheer for the same athletic heroes. Of course, there are exceptions in the case of children who are zealously kept separate from the dominant culture. But it is hard to find an American child who has not heard of Ninja Turtles or who is not up on the latest fashions in running shoes. Cultural differences in the United States cannot even begin to compare with the religious and ethnic hostilities that have led to the disintegration of the Soviet Union and Yugoslavia.

It would be a great tragedy if the political agenda of some angry adults forced children into cultural models that accentuate their differences. Though we still have one nation, the sense of common commitment could easily get lost in the process of teaching children that their histories diverge, and though they in fact share a culture, they are not supposed to think of themselves as a single nation. Because the schools now have as great a responsibility as ever to foster a commitment of nationhood, it is worth looking back a century to when the country responded to the four hundredth anniversary of Columbus's discovery by spontaneously adopting the Pledge of Allegiance.

Proposed in a magazine called *The Youth's Companion*, the ritual of the Pledge caught on quickly. Even before government got involved,[1] millions of pupils were reciting the original version, which read "I pledge allegiance to my flag and the Republic for which it stands, one nation indivisible, with liberty and justice for all."[2] The Pledge was hardly poetic, but it obviously filled a need in an immigrant nation for a rite of national identity.

The language of the Pledge has changed frequently in the last century. In 1923, the First National Flag Conference proposed a change in the wording from "my flag" to "the flag of the United States." The delegates to the conference feared that when immigrants said "my flag," they would get confused as to whether they were paying homage to the flag of their old country or to the stars and stripes.[3] In 1954, in a questionable move encroaching upon the separation of church and state, President Dwight D. Eisenhower endorsed a House Joint Resolution adding the words "under God" after the phrase, "one Nation."[4] The last phrase "liberty and justice for all," generated protests from politically committed students in the late 1960s and early 1970s who read it as a hypocritical claim of fact rather than as an aspiration.

Despite the flare-up between Michael Dukakis and George Bush in 1988, there was not then and there has not since been any serious discussion about the merits of patriotic education for children. For that reason I wish to offer the best account for using the classroom as a vehicle for instilling sentiments of loyalty and patriotism. The objections to patriotism should be taken seriously. At the very least, the course of the discussion will bring into focus basic issues of pedagogic philosophy. To make the best possible case for the Pledge, we should revise its wording in order to eliminate controversial and divisive passages. Consider, therefore, the following version:

I pledge allegiance to the flag of the United States of America and to the Republic for which it stands, one nation, united in diversity, committed to liberty and justice for all.

Eisenhower's addition "under God" should be deleted in order to maintain the Pledge as a ritual that unites all children, regardless of their religious background. The phrase "united in diversity" harks back to E pluribus unum, an original American motto, now adapted to capture ethnic, racial, and religious diversity as the bedrock of American culture. The change in the final clause brings home the point that "liberty and justice for all" remains an aspiration rather than a documented fact.

The point of the Pledge is surely not to test the loyalty of the young but rather, by a process of ritualized expression of respect, to instill an emotional attachment to their country. The mind becomes more receptive to facts and analytic arguments as the spirit becomes attached to the object of study As physical education requires more than reading and analysis, the teaching of loyalty requires more than intellectual persuasion. Of course, ritual cannot provide a substitute for instruction in American history, its heroes and villains (of all races and constituent cultures), as well as the principles of our constitutional democracy and the Bill of Rights. The Constitution should be studied more deeply than it is. The great rhetorical moments of our history, from Lincoln's Gettysburg Address to the "I Have a Dream" speech of Martin Luther King, Jr., should be allowed to move and inspire the young. But ritual also has its place in opening the hearts of children to a greater commitment to the common ground of our history.

Of course, there is no way to prove that intensified patriotic practices in our schools would bring about the desired effect of giving our young people a shared sense of purpose in building a pluralistic and caring America. Apart from skepticism about the positive value of the Pledge, at least two types of principled objection are often raised against patriotic rituals in the schools. First, it might seem questionable to try to instill moral values in the impressionable minds of the young. Moral education may appear to be a form of indoctrination. The question is whether schools, both primary and secondary, should undertake to communicate values (as well as facts and methods) to our pupils. Put in these terms, the question answers itself. Schools do not work unless they communicate at least some values, namely, the values of learning, the importance of hard work and individual achievement, the desirability of cooperation as well as competition, and the indispensability of honesty and integrity. In addition, a sound educational effort teaches respect for evidence and reasoned argument. Of course, there may be some disagreement in educational circles about the relative merits of discipline and creativity, but this and similar disputes take place within a framework of shared pedagogic values.[5]

The question, therefore, is not *whether* schools should teach values but rather *which* values they should teach. The school obviously communicates by example as well as by articulation. The allocation of power between men and women over teaching and administration communicates a message about gender roles. The practices of grading and imposing discipline impart messages about just rewards and fair procedures.

If treating people fairly is a message worth communicating to pupils, then so is the value of loyalty. In conducting their classes and relating to pupils and students, teachers should respect prevailing bonds of friendship. Consider the way in which the "honor system" for taking examinations exacts disloyalty from students: Those witnessing cheating, whether by friend or stranger, must report the breach to the responsible authorities. As it functions in American military academies, the honor system is ideally suited to breaking down intragroup loyalties and inculcating a strong sense of obedience and loyalty to military superiors. But if intragroup bonds are an important value, disciplinary systems should respect existing patterns of loyalty among students.[6]

In light of our schools' bringing together blacks, whites, Christians, Jews, atheists, Asians, and Hispanics in a single enterprise, forging unity in the classroom serves an educational as well as a larger social function. Generating a sense of common ground and shared national identity are as central to the educational mission as teaching the virtues of fair play and disciplined learning. The objection against just this form of moral education hardly proves convincing.

A second and deeper objection to the Pledge builds on the shared American commitment to respecting dissent and freedom of conscience. The problem is always, what if either parents or children object to being indoctrinated as patriotic Americans, of being absorbed, by the covert force of ritual and song, into feeling that the

United States has a special place in their hearts? Another way of putting the same question is whether there should be room in this context for respecting antipatriotic sentiments as a matter of conscience. Some people might feel that patriotism poses "a constant moral danger"[7] of prejudice and even of aggressive war, and therefore that it might be better for children not to be exposed at all to this sentiment that allegedly has brought so much suffering in its train.

The question of conscience requires us to focus on the central conflict between the interests of the group and the dignity of the dissenting individual. To begin our understanding of when we should honor this dissent, let us turn first to a significant recent debate in France on the same question.

The French Analogue to the Pledge Dispute

Pledging allegiance to a flag may seem antiquated in a burgeoning economic community that plans at the end of 1992 to dismantle its internal borders. Yet if one looks closely at educational policy decisions in European societies, one finds the same concern for national solidarity and unity that has erupted in the American dispute about patriotic observances in school. In the fall of 1989, for example, a dispute broke out in France that posed the question whether the religious conscience of parents and children should prevail over the efforts of the schools to generate a single French national community. For the French, the question that divided both the left and the right was whether Moslem girls should be allowed to wear the hijab, a partial veil, in the classroom.

The dispute began in early November 1989 when three teenage girls in the town of Creil, a suburb of Paris, came to school with scarves wrapped around their heads. Though these scarves did not cover the girls' faces, they had a distinctive Moslem look. Politicians referred to the head covering as the veil. This piece of cloth symbolized to everyone an intrusion of Moslem fundamentalism into the classroom. It invoked in the popular mind Khomeini's fanaticism and the condemnation of and homicidal search for the author Salman Rushdie. On the heads of these schoolgirls, the hijab represents, it is said, a particularly virulent effort to subjugate women. Because of these charged issues, a handful of Moslem girls could bring the French political system to a moment of wrenching reappraisal.

The dispute took a course peculiar to French politics. The battle lines were drawn in Paris. With the entire system of education centralized in the capital, it fell upon the national Minister of Education Lionel Jospin to decide whether the three girls in Creil should be allowed to go to class. He decided that tolerance was the better policy and let them in, scarves and all. The symbol of Khomeinism in the classroom provoked a French reaction that hints at the American struggle, long since settled, for tolerance of religious diversity in the classroom. Five leading Parisian intellectuals published an open letter, with front page billing, in the leading weekly magazine *Nouvel Observateur*.[8] The title ("Profs, We Won't Surrender") and the first line ("The future will reveal that this year of the Bicentennial became the 'Munich' in the history of the republican school") left no doubt about their passions.

The letter, ending with an appeal to teachers to demonstrate their solidarity, enjoyed a political impact that no Op-Ed piece in the *New York Times* could claim. Though the causal connection with ensuing events is unclear, teachers in Poissy went on strike until a Moslem student removed her veil. And within a few days Jospin backed down and submitted the dispute to the *Conseil d'État*.[9]

The significance of the French dispute is that it occurred on the left, not on the right. Tolerance for diversity is generally a hallmark of secular politics on the left. It is true that the French right is generally more intolerant of Moslem immigrants than is the left. Before the impact of the open letter could have been gauged, a survey revealed that only 30 percent of those who saw themselves on the right approved Jospin's policy of tolerance, while after some initial hesitation his supporters on the left grew to 57 percent.[10] Nonetheless, on the whole, more French would have excluded the girls from school than would have let them in with their semiveils. It is worth noting, however, that among those polled, people under forty favored tolerance of the veil by a margin of two to one.

The appeal of the five leftist intellectuals fell on receptive ears not only because there might be transient political advantage in excluding the symbols of religious fundamentalism from the classroom; the letter also raised serious problems of principle that the Socialist Party could not ignore. An examination of the arguments repays attention, for the dispute takes us back to the mood that prevailed in the United States in the late 1930s, before our policy of religious tolerance in the schools became the accepted norm.

The five intellectuals speak with a passion and commitment about the nature of public education that is wanting in the United States. The monotone media critique of American schools is that we do not adequately teach basic skills. Admittedly, we do not, but there are more basic questions in education. Do we have a vision of the kind of person we expect to emerge from the schools and become a citizen of a democratic society? French Socialists have that vision, and it is expressed in a notion of schooling that, as the five intellectuals maintain, offers all children an opportunity to liberate themselves from their communities of origin and enter civil society on an equal footing. The basic principle of equality requires that the mode of education be based exclusively, as they put it, on the "authority of reason and experience, accessible to all." The governing principle of education should be freedom of inquiry and reasoned argument.

Symbolic religious loyalties preclude open dialogue and free inquiry because the symbolism testifies to an attachment that transcends reason and evidence. In a subsequent interview, one of the five, Alain Finkelkraut, spoke of the classroom as an "abstract place that one may not transform into a juxtaposition of different communities."[11]

The five on the left do not conceal their contempt for Islamic fundamentalism. The effect of permitting girls to wear the hijab in class would be to open the control of the classroom to the fathers and brothers, who represent, in their words, "the most recalcitrant patriarchy in the world." The veil symbolizes female submission, and for that reason it is unacceptable in a world committed to human rights. But the issue, they say, is not discrimination but rather the discipline of an egalitarian school. Though Finkelkraut maintains a high Jewish profile, he conceded that if Moslem girls could not retreat behind the hijab, orthodox Jewish boys should not be able to sport their yarmulkes in class.[12]

Leftists are inclined to favor strong schools that offer pupils an opportunity for emancipation and that bind the pupils together in a single community. The French Republic, the open letter asserts, is not "a mosaic of ghettos"; it aims to create a people that share universal criteria of argument and reason. The school that is "republican" in this sense, they maintain, is the "foundation of the Republic."

The *cris de coeur* of the French intellectuals stands for a positive philosophical commitment to secular education. Americans also hold fast to keeping religion out of the schools, but seemingly only in the negative sense of prohibiting religious education. The Supreme Court steadfastly opposes prayer and other religious rites, even a nominally neutral minute of meditative silence, on school property.[13] But other forms of religious intrusion, such as including "under God" in the Pledge of Allegiance, are accepted as a matter of course.[14]

Whatever American protestations about walling off church and synagogue, we in fact lack a strong commitment to either a secular state or a secular school system. We tolerate "In God we trust" on our coins, on our paper money, and on the front wall of every courtroom.[15] From the perspective of any rigorous secular philosophy, such as one finds in contemporary European society or even in the supposedly theocratic state of Israel, these incursions of religiosity would be intolerable. Europeans have nothing comparable to courtroom witnesses swearing on the Bible "to tell the truth, the whole truth and nothing but the truth." And in Israel, any effort to inscribe religious symbolism on the state's money would upset the delicate balance in that country between the devoutly religious and the devoutly secular.

But Americans appear to be less committed to secularism as a surrogate for the religious worldview. We are not appalled by the casual invocations of a nondenominational deity in daily life. And we have no serious anticlerical movement or philosophical school that could serve as a focal point for secular education. Our notion of secular education seems to connote, above all, the absence of orthodoxy. And this opposition seems to imply tolerance for all points of view. Though the Supreme Court struck down efforts to put "creationism" on an equal footing with Darwin's theory of evolution,[16] textbooks are now backing away from presenting factual validation in the sciences as undisputed fact. In guidelines adopted by the standard-setting California Board of Education, the appropriate tone in textbooks should be to the effect: "some people reject the theory of evolution purely on the basis of religious faith; [these] beliefs should be respected and not demeaned."[17]

French secularists, in contrast, press unabashedly for their own vision of reasoned emancipation in education. Their rigorous secular approach to education requires more than a rejection of religious instruction. It requires a commitment to shared criteria of argument and validation. The appeal of the scientific method is that it strives to base validation on evidence available to all, regardless of parochial loyalties and sacred texts.

To appreciate the position of the French secularists, think of the use of religious symbolism in the courtroom. Imagine a religious judge wearing a veil or a yarmulke and being called upon to decide a point of law—say on the inheritance rights of women—on which her or his religious tradition clearly departed from the philosophy of American law. The litigants might plausibly fear that they would not receive an impartial judgment under the law of the jurisdiction. More seriously, a symbolic declaration of being bound by God's law might compromise the judge's commitment to apply the law of the land.

In the end one might affirm the right to wear the sign of subservience to God's word even on the bench of a secular court. In the *Goetz* trial, a nun wearing the habit of her Episcopal order reported for jury duty. The trial judge decided, correctly I believe, that the nun could not be disqualified for cause merely because she wished to wear her habit in the jury room.[18] But the point remains: A declaration of religious loyalty conflicts with the shared commitment to reason that should prevail in legal deliberations.

Moving from the courthouse to the schoolroom admittedly lowers the stakes of the dispute, but the principle is the same. Should individuals in a secular setting be permitted to declare their loyalty to an external power and thereby endanger the neutrality of intellectual discourse? This may be a rather sophisticated way of putting the case for opposing the veil in the classroom, particularly as the policy is applied to children. In reality the value at stake is the imposition of a single culture on all children with a view to creating one society, one republic.

This is the sense in which the ambitions of the French Socialists dovetail with the effort to instill a shared sense of identity in a diverse society like the United States. Admittedly, the Pledge and patriotic rituals achieve their intended effect by inducing an emotional response. The French leftists adhere to a community of reasoned discourse, undistorted by symbolic declarations of religious commitments. But I take this difference to be minor relative to the aim of generating a common culture and identity at the foundation of national political life.

The French Socialists seem to have lost the fight in principle, but they have won in practice. In late November 1989 the *Conseil d'État* upheld the Moslem girls' right of free expression and freedom of conscience, provided their wearing of religious symbols in class did not prove to be disruptive.[19] The question whether their dress was disruptive was left to the judgment of each headmaster, and it seems that in practice the girls have been required to leave the hijab in the cloakroom.

As French educators confronted this problem in 1989, Americans wrestled with the issue of religious diversity in the schools a half century ago. In 1935 two grade school pupils named Lillian and William Gobitis refused to salute the flag in a rural Pennsylvania schoolhouse.[20] Like their counterparts in Creil, these young Americans grounded their differences in their family's religious teachings. The case posed by the Gobitis children became the starting point for a long debate about conformity and diversity in American society. This debate generated the controversy between Bush and Dukakis in 1988 and, as we shall see, it has yet to find a definitive resolution.

From Neutrality to Respecting Differences

The commitments of children can call our basic premises into question, as did the constitutional crisis caused by the Jehovah's Witness children in *Gobitis*. Their claim of conscience was that saluting the flag constituted worshiping a graven image in violation of the Third Commandment in Exodus.[21] The Gobitis children were obviously subject to a crisis of loyalty. Either they could conform to the practice of the school or they could remain loyal to their religious community and, so far as they had internalized these teachings, to God as the supreme authority in their lives. One cannot but respect their choice to stand firm against secular authority. They paid the price of expulsion from school. And the courts failed to protect them.

Though supposedly overruled in *Barnette*, the *Gobitis* decision has yet to lose its force as constitutional precedent. Scorned as a nadir of tolerance in American constitutional law, the case has nevertheless recently risen from the dust of decaying court reports. In 1990 a majority of five on the Supreme Court, led by Justice Antonin Scalia, upheld an Oregon regulation that denied unemployment benefits to Indians fired for smoking peyote, even though their use of the "controlled substance" was exclusively for religious purposes.[22] The Court perceived the general prohibition against using drugs as religiously neutral; it was not aimed at any particular religion, any more than the prohibition against polygamy was aimed at Mormons.[23] For the time being, a majority of the Court regards this kind of neutrality as sufficient to uphold a statute that impinges on some religious practices more than on others.

In the United States as well as in France, strong voices insist that all religious groups conform to neutral laws designed to promote the general good. As Justice Scalia argues, relying on Justice Felix Frankfurter's words in *Gobitis*:

> Conscientious scruples have not, in the course of the long struggle for religious toleration, relieved the individual from obedience to a general law not aimed at the promotion or restriction of religious beliefs.[24]

In other words, if you are a Jehovah's Witness, do not expect an exemption from the Pledge just because it violates your religious scruples. Or if you are a Moslem girl in France, do not expect an exemption from the general prohibition against wearing religious symbols in class. Neutral laws "not aimed at promotion or restriction of religious belief" must be observed by everyone.

That *Gobitis* has this enduring appeal should only make us appreciate more deeply the profound struggle that engaged the Supreme Court as it made the wrenching transition from *Gobitis* to *Barnette*[25] in the years 1940–1943. With the revival of *Gobitis* in Justice Scalia's recent opinion, the question has more than historical interest. We may have to recreate the transition that occurred fifty years ago when, beginning with Chief Justice Harlan Fisk Stone's lone dissent expressing solicitous concern for "small and helpless minorities,"[26] the Court gradually abandoned the principle of neutrality in *Gobitis* and moved in *Barnette* toward a position of greater respect for differences among diverse American communities.

If *Gobitis* is still alive, then the case that appeared to slay it (but did not), namely *Barnette*, has nonetheless acquired something like precedential sainthood. There are few opinions more often cited and more revered than Justice Robert Jackson's opinion supporting the schoolchildren in *Barnette*. The only problem is that no one is entirely sure about the rationale for commanding the local school board to let the Barnette children back into school.

On the one hand, if the case is read primarily in its historical context, then it stands for a principle of religious freedom. A majority of six voted to uphold the right of the children to abstain from the Pledge, which means that their right to the free exercise of their religion prevails over a neutral law. On the other hand, if Justice Jackson's opinion for the Court is read carefully, it appears that the guiding rationale is not freedom of religion but freedom of speech. According to this rationale, freedom of speech includes the right not to speak, in particular the right not to participate in a patriotic ritual.

This contest of conflicting interpretations pits two distinct clauses of the First Amendment against each other. The narrow reading limits the impact of *Barnette* to those who have a religious objection to the Pledge; the broader reading based on free speech extends the case to anyone who objects to reciting the Pledge. The Court refers to the importance of protecting freedom of conscience, but if the argument of free speech is taken seriously, then the same principle should apply on behalf of anyone who objects to the Pledge, whether for reasons of conscience, politics, or convenience.[27]

The historical shift from *Gobitis* to *Barnette* is one of the more dramatic turnabouts in Supreme Court history. A shift of personnel tells only part of the story.[28] Three Justices, Black, Douglas, and Murphy, underwent a major conversion in their thinking about the rights that should be enjoyed by "small and helpless minorities."[29] All three abandoned Frankfurter's theory of neutrality and moved to recognize the legitimacy of the Witnesses' conflicting loyalty. All three felt called upon to submit concurring opinions in *Barnette* in order to explain their change of heart and vote.

For Black and Douglas, in particular, the shift represents their emergence as "activist" judges, more willing to impose their vision of constitutional rights on the states. They had initially adopted a position of holding back, of deferring to the states. They were reluctant

> to make the Federal Constitution a rigid bar against state regulation of conduct thought inimical to the public welfare. . . . . Long reflection convinced us that although the principle is sound, its application in [*Gobitis*] was wrong.[30]

Though destined to become two leading judicial activists on the Warren Court, Justices Black and Douglas were still smarting in these years from the fight over the constitutionality of New Deal legislation. In the mid-1930s the Court struck down several statutes enacted to "regulate conduct thought inimical to the public welfare."[31] Intervening in the name of principle can impede as well as further social progress, and it took Black and Douglas a few years on the Court to refine the distinction between the economic liberties of the free market and the political and civil rights elaborated in the first eight amendments. As the distinction took hold, it made more and more sense to limit the principle of deference solely to legislative programs that interfered with economic liberties.

In his separate concurrence, Justice Murphy also nods to the "reluctance to interfere with considered state action";[32] but the change seems to derive more from his conception of religious liberty. He conveys sympathy for the plight of those caught in a conflict between national and religious loyalties:

> But there is before us the right of freedom to believe, freedom to worship one's Maker according to the dictates of one's conscience, a right which the Constitution specifically shelters. Reflection has convinced me that as a judge I have no loftier duty or responsibility than to uphold that spiritual freedom to its farthest reaches.[33]

There are no similar words of passion in the concurrence of Justices Black and Douglas.[34] Their move from one side of the activist divide to the other reflects rather their concern about hostile discrimination against Jehovah's Witnesses. Witnesses and civil authorities had in fact reached the point of open combat in which virtually every means seemed permissible. As Justice Jackson reports in a separate opinion,[35] the Witnesses, under the zealous leadership of Joseph Franklin Rutherford,[36] engaged in evangelic solicitation that can only be called provocative. They would designate a target city like Jeannette, Pennsylvania, ring every doorbell, and play a record of their leader's voice condemning other religions, particularly the Catholic Church, as frauds and rackets. When the local mayor protested, they brought in an additional hundred canvassers from neighboring towns. They exploited the peace of a Palm Sunday afternoon for a major confrontation with the local residents.

The Jehovah's Witnesses, therefore, were no more popular in the rural America of the 1940s than are Moslem fundamentalists in France fifty years later or drug users, even ceremonial peyote smokers, in the America of the 1990s. The Witnesses' tactics, particularly their confrontational evangelism, triggered various municipal efforts to keep them in check. Typically, the local authorities invoked ordinances designed to control door-to-door peddling. In Jeannette, Pennsylvania, the complaint was that the Witnesses did not have the required peddling license. In Struthers, Ohio, the argument was that they violated an ordinance forbidding the distribution of handbills door to door.

Even though these ordinances seemed neutral on their face, it was clear in the context that they were being used to impede the field work of the Witnesses. To use the language of *Gobitis*, they were not nominally "aimed at the . . . restriction of religious belief," but in practice they were being invoked to contain and control the Witnesses evangelical zeal. In May 1943, as the Court was preparing to decide *Barnette*, a trilogy of Witness evangelism cases was framed for high court resolution. It was clear that Douglas, Black, and Murphy were going to shift sides on the general question whether the Court should intervene to protect the Witnesses against harassment.[37] These door-to-to-door solicitation cases gave them their first opportunity to emerge as part of a new majority.

In the Jeannette, Pennsylvania case[38] the new majority of five[39] decided that the Witnesses had a constitutional right to "preach the Gospel through the distribution of religious literature and through personal visitations."[40] In the majority's view, this was an "age-old type of evangelism."[41] The local authorities could not tax this right by demanding a license to solicit door to door. "The power to tax the exercise of a privilege," they concluded, "is the power to control or suppress its enjoyment."

In the Struthers, Ohio case the same majority of five again upheld the rights of the Witnesses, but this time, in the opinion of Justice Black, the argument shifts from the protection of religious liberty to the more general claim of free speech.[42] What were these Witnesses doing but trying to *speak* to the homeowners? It is true that their purpose was evangelical, but would their efforts at communication be any less important if they were labor or political organizers? Soliciting door to door, Black reasons, is "one of the most accepted techniques of seeking popular support."[43] Suppressing it violates the right not only of evangelical religious groups but of everyone who seeks contact with others.

The tension between the freedoms of speech and religion strikes at the foundations of the First Amendment. Why should communicative activity receive greater protection if it is called religion rather than speech? The religion clause should be understood, as I argue in the Chapter 5, as a recognition of the commanding importance of religious loyalties. The protection of free speech is a recognition of a personal right to communicate, to be heard, and to listen to others, however unpopular the opinions may be. Religion is exercised in a community of believers; speech, by individuals of diverse opinion. The conflicting interpretations of the Witnesses' constitutional challenge reduce, therefore, to a choice between thinking of them as acting in a community with a distinct set of internal and religious loyalties and thinking of them as individuals seeking to express their personal opinions.

Of all the Justices, Robert Jackson was the most skeptical of privileging religion over speech and dubious in particular about protecting the rights of the Witnesses as a community.[44] In the May 1943 cases, he would not join the new majority that sought to protect the Witnesses from harassment, some on the grounds of religion, some on the grounds of speech.[45] Indeed, in his dissent, Jackson took pains to describe the provocations of the Witnesses against those they were trying to convert.[46]

The Barnette Opinion

One can only guess about the negotiations that induced Jackson to come over to the side of the Witnesses by June 1943. In view of his strong anti-Witness sentiments expressed in May of the same spring, it is likely that he would join the five already in place only if the majority's opinion were written so that the case turned out not to be about the religious rights of Witnesses at all. The price for his joining the majority may have been his assuming charge of drafting the opinion.

Whatever the political background, there is no doubt that Jackson's eloquent opinion in Barnette turns on the relationship between religion and speech. It is no longer religion that appears to be the privileged clause of the First Amendment: Free speech becomes primary. Gobitis warranted overruling precisely because in 1940 the Court assumed "that power exists in the State to impose the flag salute discipline upon school children in general."[47] Jackson set out to show that the more basic principles of free speech precluded imposing the Pledge as obligatory ritual in the schools; there was no need, therefore, even to reach the question whether the state's interest in teaching patriotism should prevail over religious freedom.[48]

As the opinion reads, Jackson downplays the status of the complainants as the children of Jehovah's Witnesses who arguably suffered harassment and discrimination. After the first few pages, he writes as though the parties complaining were not children in school but adults forced to take a public oath in violation of their consciences. The long opinion takes the high ground, ignoring both the religion and the youth of the people affected by the Pledge requirement.

On the basis of a few assumptions, Jackson's opinion for the Court glides to his conclusion that the Barnette children should be protected, regardless whether they were believers or nonbelievers, regardless whether they were children or adults. The first assumption is that children in school have full rights under the free speech clause of the First Amendment. This is a radical claim that, if taken seriously, would eliminate the notion of "school." It implies, first, that schools have no legitimate interest in grading students according to what they write on exams or even in requiring pupils to use polite speech in class. If school adolescents enjoy the rights of dissidents on the hustings, where do teachers get the authority to censure students for bad grammar or limited vocabulary? Imagine the pupil's defense of using "ain't": "It's a free country, ain't it?"

The second assumption, as controversial as the first, is that sitting or standing silently while others are reciting the Pledge is itself an act of speech and therefore warrants protection under the First Amendment. This proposition comes in two different variations. The first is that silence in the midst of speech communicates something, and therefore it must come under the protective umbrella of the First Amendment. This is a strange thing to say about the Witness children abstaining from the Pledge, for they were not trying to communicate anything (except to God). They simply did not want to "worship" the flag.[49]

The second variation of the silence-is-speech argument is that no one, as a matter of basic constitutional principle, should be compelled to utter words that he does not believe in. Freedom of speech should include, therefore, the freedom of nonspeech, the freedom to abstain from joining in the words that come easily to the lips of others. This second variation appears to be dominant in Justice Jackson's thinking. The gist of his case against the Pledge is that it is wrong for public authorities to "compel [an individual] to utter what is not in his mind."[50]

Admittedly, there is something degrading about forcing individuals to subscribe to partisan political slogans. A good example came to the Court some years later when Jehovah's Witnesses (once again testing the Constitution) objected to New Hampshire's stamping on license plates the slogan "Live Free or Die."[51] Though the vote was close, the Court invoked the teachings of *Barnette* and concluded that being forced to advertise these words ran afoul of a general right to abstain from propagating opinions and ideas that offended the speaker's sensibilities. The New Hampshire slogan was obviously partisan; it reflected one end of the political spectrum. I doubt if the same result would be reached if the license plate merely proclaimed "New Hampshire the Great State" and a complaining motorist happened to think ill of the area.

In the final analysis, it is hard to tender sympathy for the practice of expelling Jehovah's Witness children from school for failure to recite the Pledge of Allegiance. Yet it is not clear whether the rationale for the decision in *Barnette* was, or should be, narrow or broad. Is the decisive factor the freedom of this particular religious minority to abstain from the Pledge, or more broadly, is it the right of all children to refuse to utter what is not in their minds? Is the decision based upon deference to the children's loyalty to their families, their community, and their God, or is it based on the right of all individuals to dissent from a message they do not believe in? The Court was torn about the issue in the 1940s and successive generations of judges have remained conflicted about the question. Though Jackson's opinion endorses a sweeping principle of free speech, there is ample evidence that the majority of the Justices then took the rationale of religious liberty to be the more telling ground of decision.

Six Justices signed Jackson's opinion grounding the decision in freedom of speech. Yet two of the six, Justices Black and Douglas, explicitly indicate in their separate opinion that they only "substantially" agree with Jackson's opinion,[52] and they proceed to develop their own argument based exclusively on the narrow grounds of religious liberty. At the most, then, a minority of four Justices wholeheartedly supported Jackson's theory of free speech.[53]

Six months after the *Barnette* decision, the attitude of the Court toward speech and religion came into clearer focus, once again in a constitutional challenge posed by Jehovah's Witnesses. Massachusetts sought to enforce a child labor law against Witness children who were selling their publication *Watchtower* on street corners.[54] The right to disseminate one's publications is surely included in freedom of speech and the press, and therefore if *Barnette* had seriously vested in children full rights under the speech and press clause of the First Amendment, this should have been an easy case.

But the state's interest in enforcing social welfare appeared stronger to the Justices than an interest in instilling patriotic sentiments in schoolchildren. Justices Douglas and Black, it will be recalled, initially voted for the state in *Gobitis* because they were reluctant "to make the Federal Constitution a rigid bar against state regulation of conduct thought inimical to the public welfare."[55] Now with Witnesses challenging social welfare legislation as applied to one of their children, the *Barnette* majority fractures and disintegrates.[56] Six months after *Barnette* eight votes tallied to support state legislation that encroached both upon freedom of religion and freedom of speech.

In the course of their opinions in this child welfare case, six of the Justices describe *Barnette* as a decision primarily about religious liberty. The dominant view is that *Barnette* supports the "right of children to exercise their religion and of parents to give them religious training."[57] The understanding of the Court, at least immediately after the *Barnette* decision, was that it had upheld not the rights of children to speak their minds, but rather the rights of children and parents to hold to their religious commitments. This narrow reading of *Barnette* prevailed until the 1960s and the challenges posed by the outpouring of student protest. In 1948 even Justice Jackson referred to the decision in *Barnette* as a defense of religious liberty.[58]

If the consensus of the Court for a quarter of a century was that *Barnette* spoke to the issue of religious liberty, why did Justice Jackson's opinion speak so passionately about the dangers to free speech of enforcing the Pledge? He likens the *Gobitis* approach to

the Roman drive to stamp out Christianity . . . the Inquisition, as a means to religious and dynastic unity, the Siberian exiles as a means to Russian unity, down to the fast failing efforts of our present totalitarian enemies.[59]

Jackson's argument against the Pledge turns heavily on associating it with obviously objectionable practices of thought control that lead, ultimately, to "exterminating dissenters." His most eloquent passage has been often repeated:

> If there is any fixed star in our constitutional constellation, it is that no official, high or petty, can prescribe what shall be orthodox in politics, nationalism, religion, or other matters of opinion or force citizens to confess by word or act their faith therein. If there are any circumstances which permit an exception, they do not now occur to us.[60]

"No official orthodoxy," Jackson insists. It is not permissible, therefore, to inculcate a love of country in the nation's schoolchildren. Any teaching of values is tantamount, supposedly, to indoctrination and the suppression of dissent. As I argued earlier in this chapter, this view is untenable: The educational mission itself entails a commitment to certain values.[61]

At first blush it seem courageous, in the midst of a world war, for the nation's highest judges to rule in favor of diversity and freedom of conscience.[62] Yet it was precisely the engagement against the fascist enemy that best explains that radical stand against "orthodoxy in politics, nationalism, religion or other matter of opinion." The case for the Pledge was undoubtedly compromised by the resemblance between the original flag salute and the posture of the German masses paying homage to their *Führer.* Children were supposed to stand with their right hand raised toward the flag and their palms turned upward, almost as though they were preparing to shout "*Heil Amerika.*"

Congress had already changed the salute to placing the right hand over the heart,[63] but this made no difference. The entire ritual smacked of the enemy's style of inculcating and expressing loyalty. The United States would, in Jackson's view, achieve national unity only if it could be fostered by "persuasion and example."[64] Coercive rituals, he reasoned, should be unacceptable in a free country.[65]

Rereading Barnette in the 1960s

Understanding the evolution of *Barnette* during the quarter century between 1943 and 1968 requires, then, a certain flexibility of mind.

At one level, the case stands for undercutting (but not necessarily overruling)[66] the philosophy of *Gobitis* and an affirmation of the rights of a religious minority to abstain from the ritual that they take, rightly or wrongly, to be an act of idolatry and disloyalty to their God. At another level, the case—particularly the opinion of Justice Jackson—stands for a sweeping affirmation of passive dissent as free speech, whether by adults or by children in school. In the long run it does not matter much what Justice Jackson and his colleagues intended in 1943. The meaning of *Barnette* and every other Supreme Court decision depends not on authorial intent but on the way the case is read and understood long after it is decided.

As a practical matter the former, narrow reading remained dominant during the quiescent years of the fifties and early sixties. Then, as the civil rights movement and protest against the Vietnam War gained vigor, *Barnette's* universal affirmation of dissent emerged from the shadows of dormant precedent. The decision that crystallized the new reading of *Barnette* was Tinker v. Des Moines School District, a controversy triggered by three public school pupils, ages thirteen, fifteen, and sixteen, who wore black arm bands to class to protest the war in Vietnam. Refusing to remove the arm bands when commanded to do so by school officials, they were suspended. The children eventually prevailed in a 1968 decision of the Supreme Court; the First Amendment protected their right to wear the symbols of protest as an act of symbolic speech.[67] It is hard to know how much attitudes toward the Vietnam War influenced the decision, but there undoubtedly would have been less sympathy for pupils wearing symbols of support for the Ku Klux Klan.[68]

In reasoning parallel to the French *Conseil d'État* in the veil dispute, the Court ruled that speech in the classroom should be permitted so long as it does not "substantially interfere with the work of the school or impinge upon the rights of other students."[69] Arm bands proclaiming a racist message would presumably have been more provocative and have disrupted the class's tranquility. The view gestating in Jackson's *Barnette* opinion—namely, that children have rights of free speech—now comes to term.[70] In Justice Abe Fortas' often quoted line:

> It can hardly be said that either students or teachers shed their constitutional rights to freedom of speech or expression at the schoolhouse gate.[71]

The Court has since distanced itself from any argument that children enjoy full rights of speech in school and ruled that a school can censor student newspapers in a way that would be unthinkable in adult society.[72] The prevailing view now is that "A school need not tolerate student speech that is inconsistent with its 'basic educational mission.'"[73]

Even to broach the question of free speech in the *Tinker* case, however, the Court had to assume that wearing an arm band qualified as an act of speech.[74] Whether certain forms of communicative conduct should be treated as "symbolic speech" and therefore receive the special constitutional protection reserved for speech will concern us later when we turn to the topic of flag burning. For now, it is important to note simply that the Court in *Tinker* reinterprets *Barnette* to be a precedent protecting symbolic speech—not about religious liberty and not about the distinct question whether individuals may be forced to recite words they do not believe in.[75]

Justice Black was not convinced. A quarter of a century after staking out his position in *Barnette*, he finds himself in the minority of a Court now willing to take the precedent he helped to generate to new frontiers of student rights. Dissenting in *Tinker*, he confines *Barnette* to its narrow holding: All the Court did there, he claims, is "forbid a state to *compel* little schoolchildren to salute the United States flag when they had religious scruples against doing so."[76]

In the late 1960s a new wave of secular protests against the Pledge zeroed in on the words "liberty and justice for all." For those committed to the struggle for civil rights, these words, seemingly full of self-righteous pretense, could not pass their lips. Also, it was a time when the targets for possible protest—particularly against the war in Vietnam—remained elusive. We wanted to go on strike, but against whom? High school administrators who insisted on the Pledge became a welcome surrogate for undefined powers who would not show their face.

In case after case brought in the years 1968–1972, the courts vindicated the position of students and teachers who protested the Pledge. The leading authority was always *Barnette*, as interpreted by *Tinker*. The notion that *Barnette* was a limited holding about religious liberty disappeared in the trend to uphold the rights of the protesting students. Witness the opinion in a case brought by Susan Russo, a teacher in a small New York town whose probationary appointment was not renewed because she refused to do more than stand respectfully while her students recited the Pledge.[77] The second circuit decided in her favor, reading *Barnette* as teaching that "school children may not be compelled to utter the Pledge of Allegiance when it offends their conscientiously held beliefs to do so."[78] Thus all pupils, presumably of any age, may abstain from the Pledge if their nascent consciences so dictate. Since teachers have no fewer rights than students, they too may object to patriotic rituals on the same grounds of conscience.

Freedom of conscience provides a bridge from the narrow to the broad reading of *Barnette*. "The freedom to worship one's Maker according to the dictates of one's conscience," as Justice Murphy put it in *Barnette*, collapses readily into the freedom to do anything according to one's political conscience. Yet the constitutional scheme accords privileged status to one form of conscientious conviction, the kind of conviction that drove Luther to declare that he could do no other. For good or for ill, loyalty to an external authority, namely, to the perceived word of God, as interpreted in a religious community, is respected in the constitutional scheme; fidelity to one's inner convictions is not so respected. Unless the distinction between these two types of conscience is rigorously maintained, the free exercise of religion catapults into a right to disobey any law that runs afoul of one's political commitments.

Further Misreading?

If Justice Scalia can revive the scorned *Gobitis* decision in his opinion for the Court denying special treatment for the peyote-smoking Native American Church, then surely the constitutional ledger should never be regarded as closed. If *Tinker* and *Barnette* were reread one way in the post-Vietnam mood of skepticism toward patriotic rituals in the school, they surely are open to another reading as our sentiments of loyalty recover and we rediscover the importance of national solidarity.

A statute mandating the Pledge could be written in the following form: "Teachers *shall* lead their students in the Pledge of Allegiance every morning." There is no need (but also no reason not) to provide an exception for religious dissenters, for that is unquestionably implied by the Constitution. It is critical, however, that the statute remain silent about sanctions against teachers and students who object in principle to patriotic observances. It is not clear whether participation in the ceremony could be treated by analogy to participation in physical education, where abstaining students presumably suffer a lower grade for rejecting the pedagogic practices of the school. But so long as no one is dismissed from school or from his or her post, a statute directing the use of the Pledge would be upheld by the current Supreme Court.[79]

The future of this area of law depends, in large part, on how we understand the phrase read into the First Amendment, "freedom of conscience" and, in particular, whether this notion, understood either as speech or as religion, accords students the power to influence school decisions about patriotic observances. Another controversy, about the flag burning decisions of 1989 and 1990, requires us to penetrate to the heart of conscience and understand whether respect for individual opinions runs so far as to prevent the state from asserting its punitive hand in the face of those who attack its symbols.

CHAPTER 7

Rights, Duties, and the Flag

The recent political and cultural history of the United States, particularly the years 1988–1991, revolves, to a surprising degree, around the stars and stripes. In 1988 presidential politics, the Pledge of Allegiance became an unexpectedly central issue. In the summer of 1989, a constitutional debate about punishing flag burning brought to the surface deep sentiments about individual liberty in an American civil culture searching for symbols of stability and unity.

A political radical from Brooklyn, Gregory Lee Johnson, became a leftist hero because he set fire to a flag during a Dallas protest march in August 1984. As the renomination of President Ronald Reagan was taking place at the Convention Center nearby, the flag burned and the protestors chanted, "America, the red, white and blue, we spit on you." At his trial for violating a Texas criminal statute, Johnson explained the point of burning the flag:

> And a more powerful statement of symbolic speech, whether you agree with it or not, couldn't have been made at that time. It's quite a just position [juxtaposition]. We had new patriotism and no patriotism.[1]

In the heyday of protests against the Vietnam War, the Supreme Court decided a number of important cases on the question of whether the state could threaten criminal punishment as a means of securing respect for the flag.[2] These precedents left the question open whether burning the flag as an act of protest should be protected under the First Amendment prescribing that Congress (and by interpretation, the states) should "pass no law abridging the freedom of speech." Some of the most "liberal" Justices in the twentieth century, including Hugo Black and Abe Fortas and Chief Justice Earl Warren,[3] committed themselves to the view that prohibiting flag burning was compatible with the First Amendment. It might have been expected that with a new "conservative" majority on the Court, the assumption that the flag was a protectible interest would have held firm.

Yet on this issue, political rules of thumb do not hold. In Johnson's case, the only significant decision of the Court's 1989 term to uphold individual rights against the state, a bare majority of five votes, including those of two new "conservative" Justices, Antonin Scalia and Anthony Kennedy, held that the right of free expression protected those who would burn the flag in public. The Court's decision produced an immediate reaction in Congress. By the early fall, the House and Senate, sensing the public mood,[4] passed the "Flag Protection Act of 1989,"[5] providing:

> Whoever knowingly mutilates, defaces, physically defiles, burns, maintains on the floor or ground, or tramples upon any flag of the United States shall be fined under this title or imprisoned for not more than one year, or both.

This statute produced a new round of constitutional challenges. In the first judicial response to the new statute, a federal judge in Seattle ruled that four protestors charged with burning a flag owned by the government were engaged in an act of political self-expression; their mistreatment of the flag was therefore protected by the First Amendment. Under the name *United States v. Eichman*, this case went to the Supreme Court on expedited appeal. In May 1990, a few months before Iraq's invasion of Kuwait, the same majority affirmed the ruling in *Johnson*, opining that there was no essential difference between the new Congressional statute and the Texas statute already declared unconstitutional.[6]

In the aftermath of these decisions there might then have been reason to worry about the consequences of the Court's failure to defend the flag. Justice John Paul Stevens despaired in dissent about the decline of the flag's symbolic value: "A formerly dramatic expression of protest is now rather commonplace."[7] It did indeed appear that, for want of resolute legal protection, the flag might loose its grip on American sentiment. These fears fueled an unsuccessful

White House initiative to amend the Constitution to protect the flag. In the end, however, Congress's reverence for the canonized words of the First Amendment prevailed over patriotic sentiments.

Subsequent events have dramatized how ill-founded were these fears that the flag would lose its hold on the American imagination. Iraq's invasion of Kuwait and our build-up in Saudi Arabia united the country in a cause long yearned for. In the fall of 1990, flags suddenly sprouted on poles, in shop windows, on car antennas, and even affixed to basketball jerseys. Not only did the flag survive but the exuberance of its display reminds us of Alasdair MacIntyre's comment that patriotism poses a "constant moral danger."[8] In a small town in upstate New York, a prosecutor wore a tiny flag in his lapel as he addressed the jury. Defense counsel protested on the ground that the flag might unduly influence the jury. A local judge, however, sided with the prosecutor and ordered sanctions against the lawyer who had the temerity to criticize "another citizen of this country [for] wearing a flag pin."[9] In another incident, the fans responded with so much hostility when a pacifist Slovenian refused to wear the flag on his Seton Hall basketball uniform that the player left school and went back to his home in Trieste, Italy.[10]

A new symbol for supporting our troops, the yellow ribbon, caught on spontaneously. Americans who had been shy about their patriotism suddenly declared, with stars and stripes, yellow ribbons, and bumper stickers, that they were behind the war effort. Even those opposed to war as a matter of principle thought it important to support the troops; a not-so-random sample of law students claimed, to my surprise, that the generation protesting the Vietnam War had betrayed that war's innocent veterans when they returned home.[11] Even more significantly, the protest movement in the early weeks of the bombing campaign expressed itself in marches and slogans against spilling blood for the sake of oil, but flag burning was not on the protest agenda. As events turned out, the Supreme Court's rulings on the flag had virtually no impact either on popular attitudes toward the flag or on the disposition to burn it as an act of protest.

The recurrent role of the flag in contemporary national politics feeds, undoubtedly, on many needs. Media pundits faulted President Bush for pressing the Pledge issue when so many domestic problems ached for attention. The campaign for a constitutional amendment to protect the flag was treated as an effort to undermine the Bill of Rights. Rarely has there been an issue so popular with the people and so steadily scorned by academics and media commentators.

Our preoccupation with the flag reflects an ongoing search for a means to express our identity and unity as a people. Unlike the English, we have no royalty to regard as our link with the past and future. Unlike the French, we do not treat our language as secular liturgy. Unlike religious Jews and Moslems, we have no holy book that captures our history and constitutes us as a single nation. Of course, we are committed to the Constitution and the Bill of Rights, but the abstract ideas of our basic charter do not lend themselves to ritualistic expressions of loyalty and national unity.

The debate about respecting the flag captures, in pointed legal form, the more general question whether inculcating and protecting sentiments of national loyalty is a worthy national project. If educating the young to respect the flag is proper, does it follow that the government must have the means to back up its message to children by punishing adults who flagrantly disavow this teaching? And if the vast majority of the people regard flag burning as a criminal offense worthy of punishment, is this an area in which the majority should be permitted to rule? Or does punishing flag burners so clearly encroach on freedom of speech that the majority will should be disregarded? These and other questions posed by the controversy require us to clarify both the relationship of the flag to our feelings of national loyalty and the values at stake in tolerating expressions of disloyalty.

The flag is hardly the property of the conventionally patriotic. Of the many ways the flag can be portrayed, the most evocative I have seen is a 1977 photograph by Robert Mapplethorpe. The photo renders a tattered and frayed flag, in desolate black and white, the surroundings barren. The sun shines against the field of stars. The edges of the stripes curl in the wind. It is a touching image that evokes an America that has not realized its promise.

There is much to be learned from the controversy over Mapplethorpe's photography, generated, of course, not by his treatment of the flag but by his bold choice of homoerotic themes. Many people were shocked by his photographs of muscular men in the nude and by one of a little girl sitting with her dress up, her genitals visible. They were "offended" simply by seeing things they do not ordinarily see. There was little support for the argument that these works were obscene and therefore subject to prohibition,[12] but for many lay people and politicians, notably Jesse Helms, it was intolerable that the National Endowment for the Arts provided financial support for Mapplethorpe's work.

The intriguing point for our purposes is that both people who witness flag burning and those who see Mapplethorpe's photographs claim to be "offended" by what they see. Also, significantly, both flag burning and Mapplethorpe's shots are considered communicative activities or "speech" under the First Amendment.[13] Thus the question is raised whether being offended is either relevant or controlling in thinking about prohibiting either provocative works of art or acts disrespectful toward the symbols of the state.

A parallel question arises in contemplating the prohibition of sexual behavior that many people regard as "offensive"—not when they witness it but when they even think about other people doing it. The widespread practice of prohibiting sodomy illustrates the point. In 1985 a close "conservative" majority on the Supreme Court held that the states could prohibit and punish homosexual conduct in private.[14] In his opinion for the Court, Justice Byron White implied that the public's being offended by the thought of what goes on behind other people's closed bedroom doors could justify prohibition under the criminal law; the "majority sentiments about the morality of homosexuality should [not] be declared inadequate."[15] Before turning to the question whether any or all three of these "offensive" actions should be protected as speech under the First Amendment, we should try initially to fathom why a state would wish to punish flag burning, obscenity, or homosexual conduct.

The Problem of Criminal Punishment

The threat of criminal punishment is typically deployed to prevent some people from aggressing against the interests of others. The standard felonies—homicide, theft, rape, arson, burglary—are designed to protect specific human interests against attack. But there are occasional offenses, in the borderland of the criminal law, that are meant to punish conduct simply because it is wrong in itself, wrong regardless of its impact on tangible human interests.

The prohibitions against sodomy, obscenity, and flag desecration arguably fall into this latter category of intrinsic wrongs. The former has its roots in the biblical prohibition against "lying with a man, as one lies with a woman."[16] And obscenity is wrong, some people argue, because it is intrinsically degrading to women. There are some who argue, of course, that neither of these offenses is wrong in itself. Homosexual sodomy was sometimes said to be wrong because it undermines the traditional family, and obscenity is sometimes charged with triggering violence toward women.

Flag desecration is paradigmatically perceived as conduct wrong in itself. The terminology of "desecration" and "defilement" derives from our quasi-religious attitude toward the flag. We drape the flag on coffins of fallen soldiers and national heroes, we fly the flag at half mast as a gesture of mourning—these are rituals that express an attitude of reverence comparable to the use of specially designated artifacts in churches and synagogues. The flag is not merely a symbol of the nation, as an evergreen tree is a symbol of Christmas or the star of David of Judaism. No one quite says that the flag is holy in the way the Eucharist is holy, but our language of "desecration" or "de-sacralization" reflects a yearning to treat the flag like a holy object.[17] In view of this language, which suggests deification of the nation, one has greater sympathy for the Jehovah's Witnesses who regard our patriotic practices as akin to idolatry. These rituals of loyalty, they maintain, should be reserved for God.

In its original statutory use at the turn of the twentieth century,[18] the expression "flag desecration" targets promotional and advertising activities as the primary mode of desecration. The offense was committed not by burning or trampling upon the flag but by "placing some unauthorized mark or symbol on the flag" or by explicitly using it for purposes of decoration or advertising. According to this understanding, the proper attitude of respect toward the flag required that one treat it with a certain distance, as an object to be admired but not to be appropriated for private purposes. In the flag ethic of the time, it would presumably have been questionable, if not criminal, to wear the flag on the front of a basketball jersey.[19]

In the first case that came to the Supreme Court testing these statutes,[20] the question was whether the state of Nebraska could fine a beer manufacturer $50 for having marketed his product with a picture of the flag on the label.[21] The Court notes that about half the states had then adopted statutes of similar language; and in Illinois[22] and New York[23] local courts had held the statutes unconstitutional. Yet the Supreme Court had no difficulty affirming the power of the states to pass statutes of this sort, which the Justices perceived as a rational effort to promote the "common good."[24] The flag was so central a symbol of national pride and loyalty that it seemed to be in everyone's interests to protect it against commercial "secularization."

The constitutional problem, as it was posed at the time of this 1907 decision, was whether the restriction on the use of the flag violated some basic liberty or privilege of citizenship. In the Justices' view, there was no countervailing right that protected the beer manufacturer against the perceived demands of the common good. Significantly, the Supreme Court had not yet interpreted the First Amendment's protection of freedom of speech to be a direct federal restraint on the authority of state legislatures.[25]

In this original understanding of the crime of flag abuse, the act of flag burning was seen not as desecration but as an instance of another quasi-religious form of abuse: defilement. In a distinct clause, the Nebraska statute declared anyone guilty of a misdemeanor

> who shall publicly mutilate, deface, defile, or defy, trample upon or cast contempt, either by words, or act, upon any such flag, standard, color or ensign, shall be deemed guilty of a misdemeanor.

Note that "burning" is not specifically mentioned as a prohibited act, nor is it included in the Uniform Flag Statute of 1906.[26] If for some reason "burning" is not considered defilement, Johnson's torching the flag would readily have fit under the catch-all phrase prohibiting any act of publicly casting contempt upon the flag. In this earlier understanding of flag desecration, there was clearly a sharp distinction between acts that reduce the flag to an everyday secular object, for example, the use of the flag on a beer label, and hostile acts directed against the flag "and the Republic for which it stands." The beer manufacturer punished in Nebraska had no desire to express contempt for the flag, but his appropriation of the flag for commercial purposes was nonetheless considered a form of impermissible desecration of the national symbol.

As the offense of flag desecration evolved over the following half century, two pivotal changes took place. First, the distinction between commercial desecration and contemptuous defilement gradually disappeared. Indeed, the original sense of desecration—that is, reducing the flag to an everyday object—gradually faded out of the law; all that remained was a broadened notion of desecration meant to include variations on the theme of defilement.[27] In the late 1950s, the American Law Institute proposed a new model statute that encompassed the desecration not only of flags but of all "venerated objects."[28] This is the proposal on which the revised Texas statute is based and which eventually came under constitutional scrutiny in *Johnson*. This version of the offense treats "a public monument" and "a place of worship or burial" the same way it treats the national flag.

More importantly, the notion of flag abuse as a wrong in itself began to give way to an act that is wrong because it offends people who are present and observe that act. When there was a clear consensus about what it meant to cast contempt on the flag, there was no need to specify the beholder in whose eyes the contempt was expressed. Presumably everyone would agree that certain acts, such as writing on the flag or dragging it through the mud, expressed the kind of disrespect called "contempt."

In more self-consciously pluralistic times, we are less certain that everyone knows contempt when they see it, and therefore in the late 1950s the American Law Institute defined the offense of desecrating a venerated object to require that the actor know that his act "will outrage the sensibilities of persons likely to observe or discover his action."[29] When Texas adopted this model provision, the legislature substituted the phrase "seriously offend" for "outrage the sensibilities."[30] Thus the notion of "casting contempt" became transformed into a complex process that requires (1) an observer (or person likely to discover the act) who is "seriously offended" and (2) knowledge by the actor that his action will cause this offense.

This may not seem like a great transformation. But in fact the crime assumes a new direction. There is no longer a shared understanding of an intrinsic wrong in abusing the flag, but only a wrong that inheres in causing offenses to observers. In 1907 the Supreme Court did not have to inquire whether affixing the flag to a beer bottle offended people who saw it, but in 1989 when the *Johnson* case reached the Court, the question of causing offense was at the forefront of the Justices' attention. It was almost as though the concepts of idolatry and adultery became transformed from sins of disloyalty and betrayal to sins of offending others.

This transformation of flag burning brings the crime into line with contemporary thinking about defining criminal offenses. One always wants to know what interest a crime violates. Punishing homosexual conduct between consenting adults is dubious precisely because one does not know who is harmed by private conduct between consenting adults. Because the impact on others is so elusive, it is called a "victimless offense."

Many sexual prohibitions would hardly make sense unless they found grounding in the Bible.[31] This means they are to be understood as crimes not against secular interests but solely against the divine will. Interestingly, one can decipher the prohibition against homosexuality not just as a wrong in itself but as an offense against a higher order (called God or Nature). Yet no one would seriously maintain that flag desecration violates a duty of loyalty to some higher spirit, such as the metaphysical spirit of the American nation.

In a secular society, based on principles of mutual respect for conflicting conceptions of God and ultimate reality, one can only be embarrassed by the survival of crimes that have no direct impact on human interests. Therefore, it is understandable that the American Law Institute (ALI) would advocate redefining flag desecration so that the crime consists in causing mental anguish to those whose sensibilities are outraged by the act.

There is, alas, a problem with this line of thought—one that the reformers at the ALI apparently did not anticipate. The more one treats a crime as an assault upon sensibilities, the more it comes into focus as equivalent to speech acts prohibited because they are offensive to some group in the society. The idiom of "causing offense" itself undermines the legitimacy of the legislative prohibition. In deliberating about the permissibility of punishing flag burning, the majority of the Court took their cue from

> the bedrock principle underlying the First Amendment . . . that the Government may not prohibit the expression of an idea simply because society finds the idea itself offensive or disagreeable.[32]

In brief, when defending a statute against a First Amendment attack, the worst thing you can say is that the conduct "causes offense." That admission brings the statute squarely into conflict

with the "bedrock principle" that causing offense can never be sufficient to justify prohibiting the expression of an idea. Offense to
observers was not enough to uphold a conviction for disturbing the
peace against a protestor who wrote the message "Fuck the Draft" on
his jacket as he walked the halls of the Los Angeles Court House.[33]
And offending many people was not enough to justify a civil remedy
against a magazine that published a "scurrilous caricature" of Jerry
Falwell's mother.[34] If conduct is the realm of communicative behavior, pointing out that it causes offenses serves only to undercut its
legitimacy.

Johnson turned out to be an easy case, at least for the five-vote
majority, because the statute in question conditioned flag desecration on the likelihood that the act would cause "serious offense" to
an hypothetical observer. In the angry wake of the decision, with
many members of Congress urging a constitutional amendment to
protect the flag, several law professors promoted the idea that a
statutory remedy would be preferable; a statute would supposedly
pass constitutional scrutiny if it scrupulously avoided referring to
the offense that flag burning might cause. Thus they urged, implicitly, that we return to the notion of flag desecration as an intrinsic
wrong. *Plus ça change, plus c'est la même chose.* The drafters of the
1989 Flag Protection Act revived an idea whose time had already
come and gone. The statute was supposedly designed not to protect
the sensibilities of witnesses but exclusively to protect the "physical
integrity of the flag." The logic of this position drove Congress to
prohibit private as well as public acts of assaulting any physical
object that met the statute's definition of a flag.

But the drafters forgot the quasi-religious roots of the original prohibition against de-sacralizing the means by which the United States
engages in its rituals of loyalty, remembrance, and devotion. In all
those situations where the criminal law seeks to protect "the physical
integrity" of concrete persons or things, a cultural matrix enables us
to understand the point of the prohibition. It makes sense to protect
persons against crimes of violence, houses against arson, and unique
objects of art against destruction. But absent this cultural foundation,
a general prohibition against destroying a mass-produced flag imprint
"on any substance, or of any size"[35] can only make one wonder.

It is not surprising, then, that Justice William Brennan, speaking
for the majority in *Eichman,* was perplexed by why Congress would

prohibit, as an end in itself, "the secret destruction of the flag in one's own basement."[36] No one sensibly prohibits assaults against privately owned mass-produced objects. Making sense of the prohibition, therefore, required the Court to read back into the statute the hostile communication that Congress tried to excise from the formula of desecration.

And that was not difficult to do. The array of verbs used in the statute—"mutilates, defaces, physically defiles, burns, maintains on the floor or ground, or tramples upon any flag"—zeroed in on disrespectful actions against the flag. If there was a good reason to engage in one of these acts, for example, if the flag accidentally caught fire and one "trampled" on it in order to extinguish the fire, one would hardly expect a criminal prosecution. Indeed, the statute itself distinguishes between good and bad reasons for burning by explicitly exempting "disposal [by any means] of a flag when it has become worn or soiled."[37]

Once the crime's definition reverted to the familiar focus of an act punishable because it was offensive, the majority encountered little difficulty declaring it unconstitutional. The drafters were caught between the Scylla of an arbitrary statute and the Charybdis of a speech act punishable because of its offensive content. The question that remains unanswered is whether there might be a way to steer a course between these shoals. Is there some way to conceptualize the relationship between the criminal prohibition and the First Amendment so that the statute founders neither as arbitrary legislation nor as an attempt to prohibit offensive speech? Answering that question requires that we review and re-examine strategies for defending a flag-burning statute against constitutional attack.

The Arguments against Protecting the Flag

There seems to be little doubt among those who teach and write about the First Amendment that the Court's decisions on flag burning were correct. Their argument typically goes something like this: Johnson and other protestors have a political point in mind when they burn the flag. Because others understand them to be making a political statement, their action constitutes speech, a type of communicative action conventionally called "symbolic speech." Further, the purpose of the flag-desecration statutes is precisely to suppress this type of speech. The third and clinching step in the argument is that flag burning does not fall within any of the recognized exceptions to the First Amendment's nearly absolute protection of expressive behavior.[38]

Does this seemingly airtight argument imply that those who are deeply affected by attacks on the flag must simply stomach the expressive acts of others? I confess that I have my doubts whether the First Amendment, if sensibly interpreted, entails this result. Undoubtedly, the project of explicating the value of loyalty makes me more amenable than most to the value of preserving the flag as an expression of the country's historical identity. Yet I begin this exploration of the issue with an unequivocal commitment to the principle of personal autonomy implied in the First Amendment. If the question were one of actual speech—say, a dirty ditty about the flag—I would have no doubts about the protective reach of the First Amendment. The government's duty to treat its citizens with respect precludes censorship.[39]

The problem is whether the prohibition of the kind of communicative action at stake in flag burning constitutes the suppression of controversial speech. Alternatively, it could be seen as prohibiting not communication but the action of flag burning, pure and simple. If treated as the suppression of speech, the statute would be tantamount to censorship; if seen as the prohibition of action, it would be like any other criminal statute designed to regulate human behavior. The question, therefore, is whether the statute impinges on the message that the would-be flag burner wishes to convey or merely the action of setting flame to a certain piece of cloth.

The question is hard to fathom and harder to answer. For how does one determine the way in which a statute impacts on the interwoven phenomenon of communicating a message *by* setting fire to a flag? How does one know what a state is trying to do when its legislature passes a statute, its police arrest a flag burner, and its courts render a conviction? As lawyers deal with these imponderables, the question is usually understood as an inquiry about the legislative purpose. Unfortunately, the quest for the purpose of a collective body is likely to produce contradictory results.

A good illustration of the problem is another controversial speech-by-torching case, decided at the height of the protest movement against the Vietnam War. In United States v. O'Brien,[40] the question was whether burning draft cards as a war protest should be protected under the First Amendment. On the face of it, it would seem that burning draft cards would be a much easier case for free speech than burning the flag. First, the collective investment of value in draft cards is nil compared to the deep historical ties to the flag. And second, as "symbolic speech," burning a draft card expresses a close fit between the act and its message. O'Brien chose an apt way of expressing his opposition to the Vietnam War, while desecrating the flag expresses, at most, a vague alienation and opposition to the United States. Also, the prohibition against destroying draft cards was new, enacted in 1965, in conscious response to those perceived as disloyal to the country's war effort; in the words of the Congressional committee, the statute was aimed at the "defiant destruction and mutilation of draft cards by dissident persons."[41]

To seven Justices on the Court,[42] this appeared to be an easy case for suppression, for treating the statute as falling outside the First Amendment. Congress supposedly had a legislative program of ensuring the "smooth and efficient function of the Selective Service System."[43] Apparently, the draft card contained obvious information, such as the registrant's address, Selective Service number, and draft status. The System could not function well unless each potential draftee carried his card with him. Losing or destroying the card meant that he could not readily establish his draft status.

It is hard to believe, even before the widespread use of computers, that the only way local draft boards could keep track of potential draftees and their status was by forcing them personally to carry their records around with them. The Court does not even claim that this fanciful interest in record keeping actually motivated Congress. The point is that the interest in "smooth and efficient" functioning of the System *could* have motivated a rational Congress.[44] That hypothetical purpose weighed more in the Court's thinking than the evidence that the Congress, by adopting the antiburning amendment in 1965, was actually trying to suppress a new and threatening form of protest. The fanciful interest in making the System work was apparently enough to convince the Court that the prohibition against destroying draft cards was "unrelated to the suppression of free expression."[45] The prohibition was limited to the "noncommunicative aspect of O'Brien's conduct."[46]

This conflict in the *O'Brien* decision between the actual purpose and the hypothetical purpose of a rational Congress reveals how easily these ideas can be manipulated, how difficult it is to know whether legislation curtailing symbolic speech is really censorship or not. The problem is always to figure out whether the legislation is directed at the message or merely the noxious conduct by which the message is communicated. If it is directed at the message, the regulation is called "content-based"; if at the means of communication, it is called "content-neutral." Of course, using these words of art does not move us closer to a principled solution of the problem.[47]

The government can usually vindicate a statute by arguing, as it did in *O'Brien*, that the "efficient operation" of some program like the draft requires the suppression of symbolic speech. Thus, the need to keep city parks clean and their natural beauty intact can justify suppressing a protest of sleeping in the park to demonstrate the plight of the homeless.[48] When the government can articulate a goal of this sort, it may strike at speech by treating the speech as a phenomenon, an event suppressed simply because it stands in the way of the government objective.

Now the question looms: Why is it not an acceptable goal of the government to develop and protect a set of rituals designed to express our loyalty and commitment to the country? Indeed, the government seeks to do precisely that by codifying an array of patriotic customs, including detailed rules on displaying, raising and lowering the flag.[49] The regulations exact respect for the flag. Significantly, the majority in Johnson conceded that "the Government has a legitimate interest in making efforts to 'preserv[e] the national flag as an unalloyed symbol of our country.'"[50] Why should it not be part of this legislative and regulatory package to enforce this program with a sanction, even a symbolic fine, imposed against those who dramatically express disrespect for the flag?

It is not an adequate answer to say that it is because the disrespectful are "expressing" something, for the issue is not whether the sanction is directed toward an expressive act but whether the program of developing patriotic customs is the kind of neutral interest that renders a statute content-neutral and therefore non-censorial. Admittedly, the flag has communicative significance, but if we recall that the point of content-neutrality is to determine whether the motive of the government action is censorial or not,[51] the communicative impact of the flag should not matter. At first blush there seems no good reason why furthering a program that has communicative significance is not just as neutral as trying to protect draft cards or keeping the parks clean.

Yet a contrary line of thought holds that the state's promoting a message of national solidarity comes dangerously close to the warning Justice Jackson issued in *Barnette:*

> If there is any fixed star in our constellation, it is that no official, high or petty, can prescribe what shall be orthodox in politics, nationalism, religion, or other matters of opinion.[52]

There is something "un-American" about orthodoxy of any stripe. Whenever any set of ideas becomes "politically correct," the individualist spirit of every thinking person rebels. No one should tell us what to think, and particularly not about matters such as "politics, nationalism and religion" that lend themselves to doctrinaire thinking. Is this the issue at stake in the flag-burning dispute?

The majority in *Johnson* invokes Justice Robert Jackson's memorable warning by arguing the government would be engaged in "prescrib[ing] what is orthodox" if it could prohibit actions that "endanger the flag's representation of nationhood and national unity."[53] If the state permitted the ceremonial burning of dirty flags and prohibited hostile burnings, it would apparently be engaged in prescribing an orthodoxy of respect for state symbols.

This is a remarkably confused argument. First, Jackson's famous warning in *Barnette* is directed only to the systematic inculcation of orthodox beliefs. The passage quoted above concludes: "or force citizens to confess by word or act their faith therein."[54] The emphasis is on forcing the recitation of the orthodox opinions both as a means of testing the faith of the citizenry and inducing them to hold the correct beliefs. His warning made sense (even if wrong) in the context of the Pledge dispute because the Pledge appears to be a confession of politically correct beliefs about the United States. The clearest application of Jackson's antiorthodoxy imperative is the Court's holding that citizens could not be required to display automobile license plates carrying partisan political slogans.[55] It would also make sense to invoke Jackson in developing a stronger line of attack against the routine use of loyalty oaths.[56] But it is difficult to perceive the "orthodoxy" implicit in requiring citizens to abstain from acting disrespectfully toward the flag.

The orthodoxy could not be the conventional fact of our culture that a certain red, white, and blue flag of fifty stars and thirteen stripes stands for the United States. There is nothing doctrinaire about recognizing that the flag is a "representation of nationhood and national unity." Johnson's and Eichman's attacks on the flag presuppose that this is true. In order for their protest to have a point, they must accept the flag in the full symbolic significance it has acquired in history.[57] The point of punishing flag burning, therefore, is not to protect the flag as an expression of the United States' presence. Both sides to the dispute agree that the flag already has that meaning in our culture.

The question, put more precisely, is whether the government should be allowed to use an existing idea—our shared understanding of what the flag means—as a way of developing a positive and patriotic attitude toward the United States. Encouraging a respectful and ritualistic attitude toward the flag may well increase sentiments of affection and devotion toward the United States. The question is whether promoting a "flag culture" is a legitimate aim of government.

Promoting constitutionalism is undoubtedly a proper aim of government. Federal and state governments may legitimately take steps, in prescribing school curricula or in sponsoring media presentations, to develop pride and commitment to their respective constitutions. No one would argue that these actions would constitute an illegitimate move toward a national orthodoxy in politics. Yet inducing a positive emotional attitude toward a state or nation still seems to be questionable.

Some supporters of the *Johnson* and *Eichman* decisions see loyalty to country as the kind of orthodoxy the state should not be allowed to further. But recall that patriotism is not a belief that could be true or false but an attitude of sentiment and devotion. The corresponding belief would be of the form: It is good to love one's country and, in particular, the United States. Yet the point of a flag culture is not to induce citizens to confess an American catechism. The point of rituals of respect is neither cognitive nor analytic; it serves directly to express and to intensify an attitude of devotion to the country and its people, all of its people.

Perhaps some supporters of the Court's decisions sense in loyalty and patriotism toward the United States a connection to a certain set of political beliefs. Patriotism might be thought to be connected to brutal mistakes such as the Vietnam War. But the continuity of the flag over history belies this claim. There is no particular doctrine, be it military adventurism or pacifism, that can claim the flag as its own. Patriotism could express itself in adventures such as the Gulf War, but it could also express itself in country-serving ventures, such as the Peace Corps, a "Teach-America" campaign to educate children in the inner cities, or a committed national effort to provide jobs for the unemployed and housing for the homeless.

The context of this discussion, it will be recalled, is whether the Congress has a sufficiently clear interest in promoting national loyalty to interpret the crime of flag burning as a sanction aimed not at the message of protest, but at the act, regardless of its political slant. Whether Congress and the country possess this interest depends, of course, on what one thinks of loyalty and devotion to country as a value. A high regard for patriotism, for sharing a common purpose in cherishing our people and seeking to solve our problems, leads one easily to perceive the expression of our unity as a value important in itself. The flag is at least as important—to go from the sublime to the ridiculous—as protecting draft cards so that the Selective Service System can function efficiently.

There is no doubt that if a case like *Johnson* or *Eichman* came to the Supreme Court in 1992, the outcome would be the opposite: The prohibition would be upheld as compatible with the First Amendment. What makes the prediction relatively safe, alas, is the shift in the Court's personnel.[58] One would like to think, however, that the Court would reconsider its reasoning and be convinced, for the right reasons, that protecting the flag was not an act of censorship. One way to support that result would be to recognize that promoting the flag culture was not a matter of trying to establish an orthodox opinion but a legitimate effort to promote a neutral interest in national solidarity.

There are at least three other ways that a newly constituted Supreme Court might reconsider the ideas that shaped its immediate predecessors' thinking. These ideas are worth pondering because they illuminate the kind of legal culture that would give greater voice to the values of loyalty and national solidarity.

Three Strategies for Protecting the Flag

Symbolic Speech. It is too late in the history of the First Amendment to argue that symbolic speech, that is, communication by actions rather than words, should not qualify as the kind of speech protected under the Constitution. Sometimes the most important political messages are conveyed by gestures in context. Thus, the Supreme Court held relatively early in the brief history of these matters that picketing was protected speech.[59] It reached a similar conclusion about the acts of activists unfurling a red flag at a Communist youth camp,[60] black protestors sitting-in silently in a segregated library,[61] and students wearing black arm bands to protest the Vietnam War.[62] In all of these cases, the symbolic speakers conveyed a message of political dissent, and the Supreme Court, by broadly interpreting the First Amendment, invested its prestige in insulating these oppositional groups from suppression.

It does not make much sense to insist that speech be limited to the articulation of phonemes. Yet a loosely defined category of speech-by-expressive-action could absorb virtually the entire range of human behavior, including nude dancing, wearing long hair, and expressing homosexual desire. It goes too far to argue, as did Melville Nimmer, that any act is speech "by which one intends to communicate and does in fact communicate to at least one observer."[63] A better test would focus on the shared understanding of the gesture in context, but this test too wants precision.

Because the category of "symbolic speech" has ill-defined and expansive borders, the Court recognizes vaguely that "the government generally has a freer hand in restricting expressive conduct than it has in restricting the written or spoken word."[64] Yet the extent to which "expressive conduct" should receive lesser protection is a theoretical problem of the first order, and it has yet to attract adequate scholarly attention. Think about what it would mean to interpret the notion of symbolic speech broadly or narrowly. A broad interpretation brings to bear the protection of the First Amendment in more cases, thus resulting in privileging speechlike acts and exempting them from the general prohibitions of neutral laws enacted in the public interest. A broad interpretation finds its grounding in a view of free speech that celebrates individual expression and creativity. We should recognize Johnson's flag burning as protected speech, a constitutionally privileged act, if we think that there is something important, something essential to his dignity as a person, about his expressing his antipatriotic sentiments in this way.

The argument for a narrow interpretation of symbolic speech (or recognizing it as speech but giving it less protection) is that Johnson could easily have made his point without burning the flag. He could have stood on a soapbox and denounced the United States as long as his lungs held out. He could have written and distributed flyers in front of the Republican convention hall. He could have "gone around" the prohibition on flag burning without sacrificing the point he wanted to make. This is the argument that informs Justice Stevens' dissent in the *Eichman* case.[65]

The reply is that you cannot separate the medium from the message. If Eichman had to make her point by using language, she might have been more articulate, but the message would have been qualitatively different from that of burning a flag on the post office steps. This may be true, but whether the loss would be great depends, in large part, on whose perspective we assume on the act of communication. From her point of view, the shortcoming would have been great. She could not express herself in another fiery way that seemed right to her. From the point of view of her audience, however, it is not clear that anything at all is lost. It is not hard to get the point that she hates the United States (if that is what she is trying to say by burning the flag). The more we shift our focus from the speaker to the audience, therefore, the more likely we are to insist on a doctrine of "effective alternative means" of communicating one's message.[66]

Whether a theory of free speech focuses on the speaker or on the audience depends in large part on the larger question that runs through this book. Do we see the isolated individual and his self-realization as the central value of moral theory? Or should the individual be understood as flourishing in a matrix of relationships? The latter perspective leads us to say that what is important about speech is not the thrill of self-expression, but the use of speech as a medium of communication to shape political, artistic, and commercial relationships with others. On this communitarian view of free speech, then, there is little doubt that the doctrine of "effective alternative means" should have required Johnson and Eichman to "go around" the prohibition against flag burning and rely upon the English language as their means of making their anti-patriotic statement.

Criminal Harm? When Shawn Eichman stood on the post office steps in Seattle and burned an American flag, it turned out that she had not burned just any flag. That particular piece of cloth belonged to the post office. That was serious. Not only did the government charge her with violating the 1989 Flag Protection Act but it also lodged an additional complaint for her willfully destroying government property. No one questions this charge. It is just assumed that the government has the right to prosecute Eichman for destroying government property.[67]

This is an amusing contortion of the law. So far as I can tell, no one has sought to argue that the First Amendment should prevail over the government's right to its property. Suppose that Eichman's point was to protest the existence of the post office, or the existence of private property. All the arguments about the medium being part of the message would come into play. There would no better way to protest the existence of government property than to destroy government property. Yet no one is inclined to think about letting free speech intrude upon the supposedly sacred domain of private property.

If we took free speech seriously, however, we would insist that it prevail over a property interest in a $25 piece of cloth. When the First Amendment collides with the flag as an emblem of national loyalty, liberal individualists assume that free speech must prevail. If the same constitutional claim collides with the flag as a privately (or publicly) owned red, white, and blue design, well, of course, the right of property trumps the First Amendment.

This is paradoxical. Typically, where a more valuable right comes into conflict with property, the other more valuable right prevails, provided that the right-holder is prepared to pay compensation to the person whose property is sacrificed.[68] Yet not even this standard mode of accommodating conflicting rights is seriously considered. Constitutional lawyers assume that where property is at stake, the would-be speaker must "go around"; she must rely on other means (whether equally effective or not) to make her point.

This quirk in the law is amusing because whether Eichman is burning a flag or burning a *state-owned* flag, her action is exactly the same. Under both descriptions, she seeks to express herself. If the lighting falls on her conflict with the flag, she wins; if the shadows reveal her to be using aggression against private property, she loses. Is the law just an ass, or is there is some sense to this reverence for private property? The most that can be said for this shadow splitting is that, as a general matter, when speech acts violate certain conventionally protected interests—like property—speech must give way.

No one would argue that assault or homicide should be permitted just because the aggressor is trying to make a political point. Accordingly, the argument goes, we should not permit speech acts to violate the interests protected under the criminal law.[69]

Several historically entrenched exceptions to the First Amendment illustrate this general thesis. Using words to defame another invades the right to a good name. Publicizing intimate details of another person's life without permission violates a right to privacy. Making copies of another's artistic or literary creation trenches upon copyright, the author's property right in her work. Under certain circumstances, verbal insults constitute the intentional infliction of emotional distress, entailing a duty to pay compensation for the injury. All of these actions for compensation represent traditional exceptions to the First Amendment's protecting the right to say and print whatever we want.

The pattern underlying these exceptions is always the same. The use of speech engenders a certain harm, and the law responds by insisting that the speech "go around" the harm—that is, that it find a channel of expression that does not result in the harm. Some harms, such as injury to reputation, copyright, and obscenity, are sufficient in themselves to bar the use of the harm-causing language. Symbolic speech differs from regular speech, for it triggers different kinds of harms. Ordinary speech cannot damage tangible interests in property, but symbolic speech can. Sometimes the invasion entailed by symbolic speech is no more serious than the unwanted presence of protestors on someone else's property. Sometimes the invasion of the physical realm leaves an irreversible mark—for example, a flag reduced to ashes.

Sustained, intricate discussions of the First Amendment have worked out, more or less, the catalogue of harms that bar the use of articulated or printed words. Yet the analysis of symbolic speech is a relatively recent development, and no one is entirely sure what kinds of harms should be sufficient for limiting symbolic speech. Whatever they are, they are surely likely to include many harms that do not come under discussion of a First Amendment designed to cover the communication of audible or written morphemes.

Two traditional examples suffice to make the point. We have no hesitation today prohibiting public fornication or even public nudity. It hardly makes a difference whether these acts have a communicative

point and are characterized as symbolic speech. Lady Godiva under-
took her legendary ride across Coventry, with her long flowing hair
her only uniform, in order to protest high taxation.[70] The act could
still be properly prohibited and sanctioned, even though it is by no
means easy to articulate the individual interest at stake. As a further
example, we would unhesitatingly design a criminal offense (if none
were now applicable) to cover a sudden upsurge in selling of human
stew made from the corpses of unclaimed bodies in the morgue.
Again it would not matter if the point of selling the stew was to
protest war or high taxes. These are instances of conduct in which
the relevant harm is not only to individuals but to a collective sense
of minimally decent behavior necessary to sustain group living.

There might be a temptation to define the harm in cases of public
fornication and disrespect for the dead by relying on the response of
most observers that these acts are disgusting and "offensive." Yet
relying, in American law, on individual offense veers too close to the
bedrock principle of the First Amendment that "the Government
may not prohibit the expression of an idea simply because society
finds the idea itself offensive or disagreeable."[71] It might simply be
more forthright to recognize a general public interest in maintaining
minimum standards of decent behavior.

The question then comes into focus whether abusive and disrespectful treatment of the flag can be understood, by analogy to these
cases, as public indecency. Surely not every crumpling of paper flags
would be indecent, and asking observers at an art museum to walk
over the flag and record their sentiments would probably be no
more indecent than nudity on stage. But there may come a point
where our collective sensibilities need not suffer further assault. As
in the cases of sexuality in public and the mistreatment of cadavers,
criteria of public decency begin to inform our conceptions of wrongs
that we need not tolerate.

This is not to say that either *Johnson* or *Eichman* might have been
decided on the ground that flag burning was a violation of public
decency. The statute in *Johnson* was based on causing offense to others; the statute in *Eichman*, on protecting the physical integrity of the
flag, in private as well as in public. At this stage in our legal thinking, the notion of violating public decency rarely enters into conversations about what we should prohibit and why. The foundations of
the criminal law need reconstructing to recognize that we should

express certain wrongs not as offensive conduct to individuals but as a violation of our collective sense of what is permissible in our public space.

The impact of liberal individualism in the criminal law is to think all relevant harm must occur to individuals. We no longer recognize that the notions of public space and the concept of public decency are fit subjects for politics. Working out our collective sense of what should be tolerated in public requires a commitment to the life of the community as well as to the welfare of individuals.

There is no doubt that the criterion of public decency, once articulated and accepted in core cases, could easily be manipulated and used in borderline situations for repressive purposes. It might be acceptable to rely upon this rationale as a justification for prohibiting obscenity,[72] but one would be loathe to see it invoked to support current prohibitions against polygamy and homosexual sodomy. Among the factors that would have to be considered in assessing public decency would be the degree and depth of a consensus supporting the prohibition and, in addition, whether the dissenting view expresses a particular mode of deepening loyal bonds within a distinctive subculture. Dissident Mormons and gays assert their sexual bonds as foundational in their respective ways of life. There is nothing comparable in the furtive, secretive world of incest. And acts of disrespect toward the dead and the flag express deviant value systems, but the values in question do not bring into being bonds of loyalty.

It is worth recalling the claims of Chapter 5 that the law should restrain its repressive hand in deference to relationships of friendship and loyalty. However valuable it might be to cultivate a standard of public decency to explain prohibitions against public fornication, disrespectful acts toward the dead, incest, and even flag burning, nothing in this approach should justify interfering in the internal affairs of groups seeking to assert their cultural autonomy.

Reciprocal Duties of Respect.   The discussion of flag burning has followed the contours of American constitutional discourse. The focus has been on the interests that governments may assert in regulating speech and the opposing rights of individuals and groups to express their opinions and maintain distinctive value systems. The model of analysis is conflicting rights: the state's rights, interests, or power *ver-*

sus the individual's rights. Supporters of the Court's decisions in *Johnson* and *Eichman* proceed both by denigrating the interests and rights of the states ("no official, high or petty, can prescribe what shall be orthodox in politics, nationalism . . .") and by promoting the individual's right of self-expression.

Yet there is a totally distinct conceptual mold in which these issues can be formulated. The question might be assayed not as a matter of conflicting rights but of conflicting duties of respect. The state's duty to respect its citizens comes into conflict with the citizens' duty to respect the flag, the Constitution, and the other institutions that sustain the life of the community.

The best account of the anti-censorship principle underlying the First Amendment invokes the state's duty of respect toward its citizens. No official can arrogate to himself or herself the authority to decide that some ideas are too dangerous to be spoken or heard. The potential censor is, after all, just another citizen, with no particular claim to moral authority. In a society without priests, without a cast that claims special insight into matters of ultimate truth, there is no reason to take a putative censor seriously.

Yet citizens should be treated as bearers of duties as well as rights. The language of rights separates us into warring islands, each person autonomous and defensive in his or her private space. The language of duties draws on our common commitments, on our parallel position relative to each other and to the life we share. According to article I of the German *Grundgesetz* (Basic Law or Constitution), as interpreted, every citizen is obligated to respect human dignity. This duty extends even toward entities that have no rights. A good example is the German recognition of a duty to respect the dead.[73]

Although German constitutional theory is silent on the duty to respect the emblems of national unity and solidarity, this duty is profiled in numerous provisions of the criminal code. Everyone subject to the criminal law is expected to act with respect not only for the flag but for the various other symbols of the Bundesrepublic as well—including its colors, its coat of arms, and its national hymn.[74] This duty is violated not just by symbolic speech but also by using words, by writing and distributing documents, or by speaking in a public gathering in a way that demeans or makes contemptible (*verächtlich macht*) any of these protected objects. Significantly, the special provision protecting the flag is limited to "officially displayed" flags.[75]

Admittedly, thinking about citizens' duties as well as rights is foreign to the American legal mind, with its liberal orientation toward protecting the sphere of individual freedom. Yet the communitarian orientation toward civic duties is found not only in German constitutional thought but in many traditional legal systems, notably in Jewish law.[76] Moral duties of self-restraint may indeed be the best way of rendering the idea of public decency. The forms of behavior that pose questions of decency, sexual modesty, and respecting the dead are better understood as duties to the society as a whole. There is no corresponding right-holder who is injured by sexual immodesty or desecration of the dead. The notion of a collective right or interest in public decency simply restates the duty of respect that we attribute to others in these sensitive areas.

Thus one is led to the idea that working out duties of respect may be a productive and sensible way of drawing limits to the traditional right-based conception of free speech. The most hotly debated areas today pose precisely the problems of respect for others. Obscenity raises the issue of respecting the dignity of women. Civil remedies for racial insults build on our duty to respect the humanity and the sensibilities of minority groups. A move toward penalizing disrespectful actions toward the flag trades on the same underlying idea, applied not to women or minorities but to the community's shared interest in cultivating the values of reciprocal loyalty and solidarity.

A jurisprudence of respect would raise many problems that we have never thought about in the American legal tradition. Does the prohibition against incest rest on a duty of respect? Is there a duty on the part of sexual minorities to keep their lifestyle to themselves out of "respect" for the sensibilities of others? My intuitions on these latter two questions are negative, but this unreflective response is but the beginning of the discussion. If American legal thought begins to move in this direction, a new chapter of legal theory will begin to unfold.

The basic question is whether it would be sensible to formulate the problem of flag burning not as a matter of the government's interest in passing a regulation curtailing speech, not as a collective right in public decency, but as an individual duty of self-restraint. I answer yes, even though the other approaches considered in this chapter could lead to many of the same legal results. The way we speak, the way we formulate issues, lend a spin to our analysis. The preoccupation with individual rights leads invariably to decisions protecting rights against the shared interest in solidarity. Speaking the language of duties could generate a different spin, one that would elicit what we have in common as opposed to the rights that separate us.

CHAPTER 8

Enlightened Loyalty

The case for loyalty requires modification. We could hardly insist on total commitment—regardless of the evil that might follow—to friends, family, community, country, or God. Loyalties, like religions, beget countless sins. Kinship ties prompt gifts and bequests that concentrate wealth in particular families. Nepotism favors friends over merit in filling important positions. The greatest sin of loyalty, of course, is war. Without both aggressive leaders and loyal soldiers, governments, in the wit of the 1960s, might "give a war and no one would come."

The problem is working out the limits of loyalty. What are the criteria, intuitions, and values that come into play to tell us when we have gone too far, in Søren Kierkegaard's words, toward "suspending the ethical?" There is no answer that immediately presents itself, but rather a host of solutions that have been used in different contexts at different times to accommodate loyalty in an overarching structure of virtuous and morally proper behavior. We canvass these proposed solutions in search of a mode of thinking about loyalty that best accounts for the sentiments we live by.

Loyalty to Loyalty

In his book on loyalty, Josiah Royce searches for the limits of loyalty in a manner that calls to mind John Rawls's strategy for accommodating conflicting assertions of liberty. As Rawls claims in his first principle of justice, each person is entitled to the maximum amount of liberty compatible with a like liberty in others. Claims of liberty must give way, in principle, when they diminish the liberty of others. Royce's strategy, in effect, is to claim that each person should exercise the maximum amount of loyalty compatible with respect for the loyalties of others. He captures this principle in the imperative: Be loyal to loyalty. Let Royce speak for himself:

> We set before you, then, no unpractical rule when we repeat our moral formula in this form: Find your own cause, your interesting, fascinating, personally engrossing cause; serve it with all your might and soul and strength; but so choose your cause, and so serve it, that thereby you show forth your loyalty to loyalty, so that because of your choice and service of your cause, there is a maximum of increase of loyalty amongst your fellow-men.[1]

Royce's account of loyalty suffers from the assumption that loyalty to causes is freely and autonomously chosen. He has no sense of the historical self that inclines individuals toward loyal commitments to their friends, families, countries, and religious communities. This flaw in his account of loyalty infects his theory of loyalty's limits. For there is nothing in the imperative to respect the loyalty of others that could accommodate the conflicting passions in our time of Jews and Palestinians, of Serbians and Croatians, and, even at the simplest personal level, the moral conflict of a child who discovers that her parent is in fact a criminal.

Recall the problem posed in the film *Music Box*: Ann Talbott, a criminal lawyer, decides to defend her immigrant Hungarian father, accused of war crimes and threatened with deportation. After winning his case in the good faith belief that he is innocent, she discovers that in fact he was guilty of heinous acts toward Hungarian Jews. What should she do? As her client's daughter, she bears one kind of loyalty; as his lawyer and confidante, she has a duty not to harm his case. She discloses the damaging evidence to the State Department, which discredits her father and terminates, one would assume, their familial bond. Her motives to act contrary to her duties of loyalty are complicated by an apparent concern about whether her son's upbringing will be affected by continued contact with a man whose past is replete with evil; in a suggestive scene before she reaches her decision she observes her father playing with the grandson he adores. Arguably, she acts of out of maternal loyalty and solicitude as well as a commitment to do the right thing.

In moral quandaries like these we encounter the limits of loyalty. The difficult questions emerge from conflicts of loyalties and from the confrontation of loyalty with moral axioms and intuitions. Royce's theory of "loyalty to loyalty" sidesteps these conflicts. He harbors an insouciant faith that one can simply choose the cause of one's "willing and thoroughgoing devotion." Missing in Royce is the sense of tragedy that inheres in conflicts of loyalty, tragedies born of fissures in the historical self.

Robert E. Lee was in fact loyal to the Union, and he was opposed to slavery, but he chose out of loyalty to his "kith and kin" to fight for the Confederacy. There is no way that a choice of this sort can be seen as anything but tragic, as the torturing of one dimension in the historical self for the sake of another.[2] Yet Royce seems to think that for Lee as well as for others caught in a conflict of loyalties, either choice is sound so long as it is "faithfully lived out in full devotion."[3] His advice to Ann Talbott, who must choose between loyalty to her client, fealty to her father, love of her son, and commitment to the truth, would be simply put:

> With all your heart, in the name of universal loyalty, choose and then be faithful to the choice. So shall it be morally well with you.[4]

This sounds strikingly modern. It reminds one of the pop psychology fostered in self-actualization therapy. Yet the naive faith in voluntary self-definition misses the dimension of historical integrity, of recognizing who one is and of adhering to the lines of possible action already embedded in the historical self. It also deprives the choosing agent of the humanizing sense of agony that flows from knowing that one has suppressed loyalties inherent in one's historical self. Robert E. Lee would hardly warrant our respect if he did not endure irremediable regrets and even guilt about having turned his back on the Union and on his principled opposition to slavery. Whatever decision the lawyer Talbott made, there would remain compelling arguments on the other side. This tragic view of our conflicting loyalties dignifies the human actor by recognizing his or her capacity to recognize the partial truths in conflicting demands. It is a better account of who we are than Royce's formula for channeling conflicted personalities into the "willing and thoroughgoing devotion" to one dimension of their historical selves.

Higher and Lower Loyalties

Many metaphors capture both our experience and our attempts to resolve conflicting loyalties. One could think of loyalty first to individuals (friends, lovers, family members), second to country, and third to God as planes in a hierarchy of ascending loyalties. In most cases loyalties on the higher plane trump those on the lower. The higher, more abstract values of God and country seem to have a greater moral claim on us than our more immediate attachments to family and friends.

But this structure of values often gets turned around, as illustrated by Robert E. Lee standing by his kith and kin and by the famous remark attributed to Camus: "I believe in justice, but I will defend my mother before justice."[5] Sartre put it slightly differently: If he had to choose between patriotic commitment to the French Resistance and caring for his aged mother, he would choose his mother.[6] The binding of Isaac is so compelling a moral tale because we all assume that Abraham should have been moved by loyalty to Isaac, the bearer of his genes. Though the higher, more abstract planes—justice, the Resistance, God—often compel our loyalty, we are blessed with the capacity to reject the sirens of abstraction and to commit ourselves to the bonds of our immediate and concrete lives.

Another possible technique for resolving conflict is to invoke the idea of the myth of a "true" abstract of the person or group that gains our loyalty. Standing by one's group when it appears to engage in heinous, unjust behavior is readily justified as loyalty to the group as it really is, its true face hidden behind a repellent surface. In his attempt to assassinate Hitler, Colonel von Stauffenberg arguably acted in the name of the true Germany. A mother's continuing to nurture a son turned violent criminal expresses a commitment to the good man behind the corrupt surface.

Maintaining faith in the goodness of the seemingly unjust turns out, sometimes, to be justified—at least in the legends of our culture. In the end, God does not carry through on his demand that Abraham sacrifice his son. In *East of Eden*, a touching adaptation of the story told at the outset of *Genesis*, John Steinbeck casts the God who turned away from Cain and favored Abel[7] as a cold, distant, and morally rigid father and Cain as a loyal son Cal who despite the most brutal and arbitrary rejection would not go "out from the presence of [his father] and dwell in the land Nod, on the east of Eden."[8] Eventually, on his death bed, the father's heart turns, and he seems to recognize the love that Cal has always tendered him. Does it ever turn out this way in real life? It is hard to know. It is to have great faith in the cycle of higher and lower loyalties holding each other in proper harmony.

Intersecting Circles

We typically find ourselves in a set of intersecting circles of loyal commitment. In the United States and indeed in virtually every modern culture, we are members of multiple groups that demand our loyalties. A typical American is a member not only of a family but of an ethnic group, a profession or trade, a particular firm, a church or religious community, the alumni circles of high school and university, and perhaps an amateur athletic team or the fan club of a local hockey or basketball team. Add to this list the special loyalties of veterans and the politically active, and you generate a picture of the typical American caught in the intersection of at least a half dozen circles of loyal attachment.

The term "multiculturalism" comes readily to the lips of Americans in the 1990s. What this term supposedly means is that one of these circles of identity—the one called ethnicity or race—dominates all the others. This may be true today for Arabs and Jews in Israel, for Walloons and Flemings in Belgium, and for Armenians and Azerbaijanis in the former Soviet Union, but in these cases the circles of religion, language, and historical consciousness tend to converge. Their internal cultural adhesion is solidly grounded, regardless of labeling by outsiders.

Despite the vast immigration of Hispanics and Asians in recent years, the coming out of gays and lesbians, the new assertiveness of feminist, Jewish and black leaders, one is hard pressed to impose on the cultural patterns of the United States the kind of enclaving that has existed for centuries in other countries. The pop culture of TV sitcoms, McDonald's, Peanuts, and Superman, the Dodgers, hating Saddam Hussein, feeling compassion for Magic Johnson, pondering the credibility of Anita Hill and Clarence Thomas—these are constitutive cultural experiences affecting virtually all Americans. Those who claim cultural rifts in the United States comparable to the endless tribal clashes of Eastern Europe, Asia, and Africa miss the beat of American life.

This is not to say that we should not, within the bounds of our unity, encourage diversity in our institutions and respect for all cultures in teaching history in our schools. The burden of my argument in Chapter 5 is precisely that the legal systems should appreciate and defer to the horizontal loyalty within the diverse groups that constitute American society. It does not follow from the principle of cultural autonomy, however, that we, the American people, are no more than distinct nations living side by side. We do not live, as some extreme multiculturalists claim, in a condition of Diaspora from some mythical home country. The excitement of America is that we are a diverse people bound together, on a deeper level, in a common culture.

These issues of multiculturalism and conflicting loyalty came to the fore recently in the controversy engendered by Harvard Law Professor Randall Kennedy in his carefully crafted article "Racial Critiques of Legal Academia."[9] I propose that we take a close look at Kennedy's argument as a case study in the problem of seeking to remain an individual as the society pushes one more and more toward group identification.[10] The target of Kennedy's critique is a series of law journal articles arguing that race and ethnicity by themselves lend a distinct and valuable perspective to the work of scholars coming from certain disadvantaged groups (among others, blacks, Hispanics, Native Americans). In other words, the source lends additional force to the message. The work does not stand on its own; the reader must know the author in order to evaluate the analysis and the argument.

Kennedy concedes that "in some situations race can serve as a useful proxy for a whole collection of experiences, aspirations and sensitivities."[11] This may be true, but it has nothing to do with evaluating written work. As Kennedy concludes:

[F]or purposes of evaluating a novel, play, law review article, or the entire written product of an individual, there is no reason to rely on such a proxy because there exists at hand the most probative evidence imaginable—the work itself.[12]

Kennedy has a vision of scholarship and creative writing that goes beyond bearing witness. It may be true that Elie Wiesel brings a distinctive voice to his descriptions of the horrors of Auschwitz. Yet as Stephen Crane and Leo Tolstoy wrote classic novels about wars they never experienced and William Styron adopted a persona beyond his skin color in *The Confessions of Nat Turner*, there is no reason why a black American cannot produce a memorable novel about the Holocaust. The world of the imagination is not cabined by a writer's limited experiences.

Kennedy's target is not the undeniable possibility that life experience enriches an author's voice but whether a set of experiences, particularly those defined by race and ethnicity, confine an author to a limited perspective. The dogma that everyone speaks from within a particular perspective, the view called "perspectivalism," has gained a disquieting degree of currency in American academic life.[13] Kennedy implicitly attacks perspectivalism; in the view that black scholars invariably speak as blacks, he sees a denial that individuals speak in their personal and distinctive voice.

The voice of a writer worth remembering is defined not by a set of experiences that he or she shares with an entire ethnic group but by the ability to transcend these experiences and write in a vein that speaks across history and across cultural lines. Ralph Ellison articulated the argument well when he objected to a critic who assumed that other black writers had a constitutive influence on his work.[14] Irving Howe had claimed that Richard Wright served as Ellison's role model. Ellison responded that his creative spirit was nourished by reading "Marx, Freud, T. S. Eliot, Pound, Gertrude Stein, and Hemingway. . . . It requires real poverty of the imagination to think that this can come to a Negro only through the example of *other Negroes*.[15] This argument had an obvious impact on Kennedy, not because Ellison was of the same "ethnicity" but because it is the voice of a writer who insists upon being read as an individual, as a spirit who moved beyond his origins and found a voice at once unique, personal, and universal.

The creativity individual voice does indeed become universal. It overcomes the bounds of genesis and reaches out to the humanity shared by all. The mode of reaching others may be the common ground of reason, but one need not be a Kantian to appreciate the universal appeal both of compelling argument and of great literature.

The foundation of the appeal could be the common emotions of human experience or, in the Kantian idiom, it could be the divine spark of reason shared by all human beings.

If all this is true, one cannot but be puzzled by a concession made at the end of an Op-Ed piece in *Newsday*, in which George Will, summarizing and endorsing Kennedy's article, notes:

> It is discouraging that, in the current militarized climate of academic discourse, it is journalistically necessary to note here that Kennedy . . . is black.[16]

Given the thesis of Kennedy's article, his own race or ethnicity should be irrelevant to the merit of his argument. Why, then, does Will think it important to mention that Kennedy is black? The reasons are important, for the same reasons that make Kennedy's race relevant in public disclosure also raise serious issues of his loyalty to other aspiring members of his community—be it the community of all blacks or the community of other aspiring academics of color.

Kennedy's critique undermines the claim that race is a distinctive qualification for employment under the traditional view that faculties should appoint the "best people" they can find. Kennedy's foes think that being a member of an oppressed minority per se makes a candidate more qualified for a teaching appointment, because by definition she brings a black, an Hispanic, an Asian, or some other "underrepresented" perspective to her teaching.[17] Having this perspective is a qualification akin to having an additional degree or some other form of relevant experience, such as clerking on the Supreme Court.[18] If race—or even the experience of oppression—is not a qualification, then obviously candidates who might benefit from this factor will receive fewer jobs. Whether Kennedy is right or wrong in his critique of the minority perspective as an academic qualification, his advocating this position arguably hurt his "people." This is precisely the point that both makes his blackness rhetorically relevant and allegedly disloyal to his "community."

Kennedy's race has a twofold rhetorical impact. First, it exempts him from the charge that his motives in challenging the perspectivalist thesis may be suspect. He is not likely to be deploying this argument because he is opposed, for covert racist reasons, to increasing the number of black law professors. And further, because his position seemingly hurts his own, his position is more credible. People do not ordinarily make arguments that run directly contrary to their personal and group interests.

Because of the way his arguments cut, Kennedy is subject to charges of disloyalty. Robert Williams, a Native American law professor in Arizona, reportedly said, "My first reaction was disbelief. . . . How different the life of a minority professor at Harvard is from life in Arizona."[19] The implication is that Kennedy has risen in the white man's system and then turned his back on his own. At the Columbia Law School, black students typically denounce Kennedy's article as a sign either of his shame about being black or as a disloyal gesture of support for the opponents of affirmative action.

Is there any substance to these charges of disloyalty? If Kennedy felt no commitment to the black community in the United States, his situation would arguably be comparable to that of William Joyce, who grew up in England but felt no loyalty to the culture that educated and nurtured him.[20] The question then would be whether one can fairly expect a (Jewish-, Hispanic-, Asian-, gay) American to feel a sense of commitment to the interests of his or her particular subculture in the United States. As nineteenth-century nation states demanded this loyalty from their constituent subgroups, the tendency toward dissolution of these larger entities today tends to impose duties of loyalty within self-defined subcultures. Membership a subgroup called African-Americans or gays may be as arbitrary as where William Joyce learned to speak English and went to grade school. Yet one's arbitrary membership in a group has never stood in the way of others in the group tendering loyalty and demanding it in return.

There is no doubt about Kennedy's commitment to promoting black interests and black culture as he understands those interests. He is the founder and editor of a significant new journal, *Reconstruction*, devoted to the high-level discussion of questions bearing on the lives of African-Americans. In his public statements, he displays a strong sense of commitment to causes that he regards as beneficial to blacks. How, then, should we think about the conflicts that Kennedy—or someone like him—would face in deciding whether to publish his "Racial Critiques of Legal Academia." In conclusion, he brings the issue into the open:

The militarization of discourse also increases pressure on intellectuals to "choose sides" and to display *loyalty* to the side chosen. . . . [D]isagreement becomes attack and dissent becomes *betrayal*. . . . The sense of isolation that many minority academics feel creates a particularly powerful demand for *loyal* conformity.[21]

In resisting this claim of loyalty, Kennedy has at his disposal three modes of proceeding. First, he could deny that it is in the true interests of minorities to remain silent on these issues. He senses a condescending attitude on the part of those who refuse to "take on" the minority scholars who argue race as a distinctive academic qualification. Respect is expressed, he correctly senses, in disagreement and debate. Those who are silent "are not moved to publicize disagreement because they lack the sense that those with whom they disagree are their intellectual equals."[22] True loyalty to his people (however defined) requires that he engage them in vigorous academic debate.[23]

The assertion of this version of loyalty suggests a second ground for resisting claims of academic loyalty. Kennedy identifies with an all-encompassing academic and intellectual community as well as with other minorities, particularly black lawyers and law professors. The ethic of the broader community is, as Ralph Ellison maintained, to learn from everyone and to disagree when respect requires disagreement and debate. Put in this way, the conflict is among intersecting circles of communitarian identification. In this light, the analogy between Kennedy's conflict and Joyce's alienation dissolves. Kennedy chooses an encompassing identification; Joyce chose loyalty to a bellicose enemy.

The argument for silence would be that one simply cannot trust the academic community to interpret one's views accurately and fairly, and thus in making an argument undercutting an advantage for minorities in the job market, one risks having one's views distorted and applied to contrary political purposes. The argument on the other side is that loyalty to the larger academic community entails faith in the fairness of interpretive reactions. To be part of the intellectual world, one must both trust the responses of colleagues and take the risk of good faith misreadings. Kennedy's experience suggests grounds for this faith. I know of no evidence that his white colleagues have exploited his articles for the sake of a political agenda that he would not share.

A third ground for resisting an alleged duty of silence would be that it would be immoral to become convinced of a position, as Kennedy has, and then suppress one's vision of the truth as an act of loyalty. Arguably, everyone—whether in the academic community or not—bears a moral duty to speak the truth. This way of seeking the limits of loyalty invites more general consideration, for it is indeed the question that has nagged us since we quoted MacIntyre at the outset of this essay that patriotism poses "a constant moral danger."[24]

Eventually we shall have to assess precisely which demands of morality stand in the way of our acting wholeheartedly on our loyalties. Even posing the question is problematic, for the ethic of loyalty is itself a species of morality. What, then, could it mean for a moral teaching to raise a "constant moral danger?" The term "moral" as MacIntyre and other professional philosophers use it invokes the tradition of impartial and universal moral principles that include, among other things, prescriptions requiring us to tell the truth, to treat others as equals, not to favor our interests over those of others, and not to act unjustly or exploitively toward others.

One species of morality to which loyalties clearly pose a constant danger is the duty to do justice, for, by common agreement, doing justice requires impartiality. Judges in athletic competitions would clearly act improperly if they brought their personal loyalties to bear in judging, say, a gymnast's or boxer's performance. Those who enter into competitive matches assume that the standard for winning and losing will be their performance and just their performance; their identity is irrelevant.

Much the same can be said of other instances of judging merit—examinations in a university, awarding the Nobel Prize, and most importantly, the judging of lawsuits. It is no accident that in the traditional representation of Justice with her scales, she is blindfolded. Justice on the merits of a competition or of a dispute should be indifferent to the identity, needs, biographies, and relationship of the parties to the judge. The principle comes forth clearly in *Leviticus* 19:15: "You shall do no unrighteousness in judgment: thou shalt not respect the person of the poor, nor honor the person of the mighty." Neither the poor nor the mighty deserve special treatment in judging—and this is true whether the stakes are first place in an athletic competition or winning a lawsuit.

The problem for the theory of loyalty is whether loyalties always conflict with the duty to do justice. Is there a proper domain of justice and a proper domain of loyalty? Once we resolve that conundrum, we shall return to the more general question whether and under what conditions loyalties are overridden by the duties of impartial morality.

When Justice Prevails

In a range of social institutions, we unquestionably expect certain decision-makers to put aside their loyalties and act on the basis of universal and impartial principles. John Rawls devoted his monumental book *A Theory of Justice* to elaborating and defending his two principles of justice as the "first virtue of social institutions."[25] If we assume for the present purposes that we can assent to these two principles,[26] the problem remains whether all institutions, all relationships, fall within the domain of justice. Some people have argued that justice is a jealous virtue. It claims the family as well as the institutions of the state.[27] On this view, justice controls intimate relationships as well as the duties of legislators and judges.

The countervailing reaction to Rawls found its stimulus in Michael Sandel's argument that insisting on justice in intimate relationships corrupts the sentiments that sustain friendship, love, and family bonds.[28] Sandel's claim is that the qualities of loving relationships—benevolence, shared ends, reduced "opacity of the participants"—should displace justice as the first virtue of communitarian social life.[29] In this regard, Sandel follows David Hume, who argued that "if every man had a tender regard for another . . . the jealousy of interests which justice supposes could no longer have a place."[30] The thrust of these arguments is to treat both law and justice as contingent necessities. Ideally, the models of love and family would provide all the guidance we need for regulating social relations.

The more sensible way to take this critique is to read it as an appeal for a limited understanding of "social institutions." Rawls's theory applies in a range of institutions where we confront each other as opaque citizens, as strangers, not as friends and lovers who exact reciprocal duties of loyalty. In the realm of loyalty, playing the lawyer and insisting on justice may well undermine the bonds of loyal sentiment. Equally true, letting loyalties intrude into the proper realm of justice brings about its own form of distortion.

We are left with the question, then, When should justice and when should loyalty prevail? The question is hardly new. Aristotle recognized both that justice was a moral virtue and that friendship "implies a virtue and is besides most necessary with a view to living."[31] In the shopworn terms of social theory, justice prevails under the conditions of *Gesellschaft* and loyalty, under the conditions of *Gemeinschaft*. These terms—society and community—hardly advance the discussion, for we are left with the conundrum of allocating relationships to one realm or to the other.

Clarifying the realms of loyalty and of justice requires that we appreciate the value both of personal bonding and of impartial detachment in the complex relationships that constitute modern society. The utopian ideal of personal bonding constantly beckons to those of us who suffer from the rootlessness and anomie of a society in which families disintegrate, friendships are hard to maintain, and working relationships are "cashed out" in the capitalist marketplace. Yet the failure to maintain detachment, particularly in the workplace, contributes to the contemporary outcry of injustice and harassment resulting from the aggressive search for sexual intimacy.

At the level of philosophical theory, it may be difficult to make the case for the ethic of loyalty. But at the level of practice, it is far more difficult, in many of our institutions, to defend the virtue of impartial detachment. In making hiring and promotion decisions, in deciding whose career to further and whose to hamper, we are governed all too often by sentiments of loyalty. Our commitments to excellence and to the just distribution of opportunities are compromised if we express our yearnings for community and solidarity at the wrong times and places.

Of all the arenas of conflict between justice and loyalty that come to mind, the most difficult is democratic voting for public office. There is no doubt that ethnic groups tend to vote for the candidates with whom they readily identify. The argument has been voiced as well that women should vote for candidates of their gender, regardless of their politics, simply in order to further the representation of women in positions of political power.[32] It might be naive to expect voters to put these sentiments of loyalty aside and vote for the candidate they perceive, all things considered, to be the best qualified for the job. Yet we cannot ignore the problem of principle in whether this should be our aspiration in voting.

Working out these respective domains of loyalty and of justice should be one of the central concerns of political theory. Yet we are still caught in a vacillation between extreme positions—between those who argue that justice should dominate all our relationships and those who argue with Hume that "tender regard" could take the place of justice.[33] Would that we had the wisdom to find the proper contours of these contradictory virtues.

When Impartial Morality Prevails

Let us assume that we are indisputably in the domain where duties of loyalty govern our relationships—to friends, lovers, family, community, or country. Let us assume further that the demands placed on our loyalty make us think we might be acting immorally. Examples are not hard to come by. Your closest friend confesses to you that she has committed a murder. She expects you to facilitate her escape. Do you call the police? Or to recall the dramatic conflict of *Music Box*, your father was a war criminal but since then has led an exemplary life. Do you turn your back on him? Or you are committed to a national or political cause, but you know that many leaders of the movement exploit the cause for private, dishonest ends. Do you speak out against their venality? Do you hurt a cause you believe in because others are corrupt? These are cases in which duties of loyalty reach their limits. Loyalty's bond loses its inner beat. The flattening pitch of moral impartiality overwhelms what we once thought were clear and compelling tones. One would like to think that there would be a formulaic response to these conflicts, a guide that would tell us something more specific than that we must do the right thing. The most we can do, however, is reflect on the difficulties of reaching decisions in these quandaries where loyalty and impartial morality collide.

Moral theory, as we understand it, is ill suited to resolving the pangs of conscience triggered by allegedly excessive loyalty. The impartial moral theories of the Enlightenment speak to the universal human condition. They are designed to transcend our emotional links to individuals and countries and to generate objective, universally shared reasons for our actions. It is not objective for me to say that I am engaged in particular action because the welfare of *my* friend or *my* company or *my* community is at stake. This is a subjective consideration, limited to me and to my sentiments, and therefore it does not speak to someone with a different set of attachments.

A good reason for helping someone would point to features of that person that would be visible to all—her intelligence, her character, her potential for a productive career. But it would hardly count as an objective reason to say, "She is my sister. I want to help her because she belongs to *my* family." Partiality and loyalty seem to run counter to the very notion of moral and just behavior.

Because the ethic of loyalty is so clearly at odds with universalist moral theory, it becomes difficult to think of the latter as a corrective to the excesses of the former. It is almost as though one wished to apply the Copernican vision of the universe as a corrective for the weaknesses of the Ptolemaic system. On some intellectual and ideological conflicts, one simply must choose the more compelling position. Yet in an anti-ideological age, we think that mixed systems are not only possible but desirable. As economists seek an accommodation of state planning and the free market, philosophers should be able to marry universal to relational ethics.

Let us suppose, then, that melding the two systems, the universal and the relational, the impartial and the partial, is conceptually possible. The problem remains whether the great eighteenth-century moral theories, deriving respectively from the work of Kant and Bentham, can teach us something about the proper limits of loyalty. To think about this possibility, we have to distinguish between the pure and applied forms of these universalist moral systems.

In their pure forms, I submit, neither Kant's deontological ethics nor Bentham's utilitarianism generates guides to human action. Both schools are inspired by a vision of ethics—deriving perhaps from the Sermon on the Mount—that makes moral conduct virtually unattainable. Though they take different paths, they both undermine the potential and the appeal of the moral life by making it available only to the saintly who are capable of imitating God's ways.

Kant's Utopianism

Though a Lutheran Pietist by background, Immanuel Kant sought to deliver a basis for moral judgments that would appeal to enlightened secularists. He exacted of his reader only a belief in reason, a rational capacity to know the truth, independent of the passions and the inclinations of the body. Reason is expressed in what Kant calls a good will. And it is only the good will, he insists at the outset of his *Groundwork to the Metaphysics of Morals* (1785), that can generate a moral act. Using an argument familiar to the critique of loyalty, every human impulse carries with it the potential for abuse. However noble the inclination, it poses a constant risk of excess. Only the good will, driven by pure reason, is pure and moral.

But what is reason? Kant's definition is essentially negative. We know what reason is not, but not precisely what it is. It is not submission to bodily impulse. It is not the response of our organisms to external stimuli. Yet Kant believes firmly that there is some way of acting that transcends the impulses of the world around us and within us. Acting out of duty, Kant submits, is the only way of abstracting ourselves from the worldly influences that affect our sentiments. This higher, pure way of acting requires an attentive ear to the voice of reason.

The connection between "reason" and "acting out of duty" leads Kant eventually to the notion of a moral law that commands the assent of reason.[34] The moral law is the categorical imperative, which prohibits us from acting on a maxim that we cannot universalize and imagine performed by everyone, everywhere. From this first formulation of the categorical imperative, Kant derives the familiar principle that we should never treat anyone merely as a means, but always as an end in himself. These propositions are guides to moral conduct. But the only truly moral act consists not just in following the moral law but in acting for the sake of duty, having one's actions express the purity of reason alone.

The theory lends itself to easy criticism for the formality of its conception of moral action or for the ambiguity of the injunction to respect others as ends in themselves. But these common attacks miss the point. According to Kant's theory, moral action is logically possible, but *not* readily accessible to humans who suffer from constant tension with their sensual impulses. In the final pages of

Groundwork, Kant concedes that there is no way of proving that any particular human action is indeed moral, that is, action born of duty rather than sensual impulse. Moral action stands as an ideal that we should seek to attain, but our failure to attain it is hardly a great failing. It is in our nature as human beings that we unsuccessfully seek the moral.

In the end Kant's moral teaching demands purity from all of us. We are not free to affirm our particularity, to visit our friends because we love them, but rather to be moral we must find the cause of our conduct in a realm of spirit abstracted from our worldly selves. Morality turns out to be a struggle of each person with himself to overcome the influences of personal attachment and sensual desire. This kind of morality rests on a yearning to think of human beings as agents wholly in control of themselves, who can act independently of their environment.

Kant's system breaks down when he turns from the theoretical grounding of morality to the resolution of practical conflict. He concluded in *Groundwork* that promising without an intention to perform the promise under a condition of distress would violate the categorical imperative. He extrapolates that all forms of deception are impermissible. Lying can never be a moral act. In the most extreme application of this view, he offers the following example. Suppose a murderer pursues your friend and your friend takes refuge in your house. Let us say the scene is Budapest in July 1944. The Gestapo agent knocks on the door and demands to know whether you are harboring Jews. According to the categorical imperative, you may not lie. For even if your telling the truth results in the death of your friend, the killing is not your act. The minions of the Gestapo are responsible for their heinous misdeeds; by telling the truth, you at least retain your integrity.

There could be no clearer collision with the ethic of loyalty. Who would want to live in a world in which it was wrong to lie to the Gestapo? That would be a world in which friendship was impossible, for surely the minimal condition of friendship is that one would do just about anything, which certainly includes lying to a murderer, in order to save the life of one's friend. There is something so obviously awry in Kant's thinking about lying that we hear the clock strike thirteen. It is hard to believe that the previous twelve bells intone a way of life that we should all follow.

Even if the innocent hiding in your home were not your friend, it should be permissible to lie in order to save her life. The doctrine of self-defense should come into play as a justification for using means, ordinarily illicit, in order to ward off the aggressor's design. If violent means are acceptable to fend off an unjust attack, then surely it could not be wrong to use words—even consciously false words—to achieve the same end. Yet the doctrine of self-defense has no place in Kant's moral system. He treats self-defense as a principle of the legal, not the moral order. Self-defense speaks to the way people must resolve real conflicts in the real world.

Kantian morality has a different agenda. Let law and justice govern the way people actually live. Morality addresses the spiritual aspiration to transcend the limitations of the passions, to live as do God and the angels, free of the heteronomous distortions of the real world. This way of thinking abandons morality and justice for the sake of *imitatio dei*. Only by subjecting oneself to the most arduous demands on our spiritual development can one hope to imitate God's love, achieve the unique causality of reason, and purify one's soul from the temptations of justice. Whether the path is one of love or of reason, only the saint can hope to negotiate it.

The confusion of the moral and the spiritual may be uplifting, but it marks an unhappy turn in the history of Western moral thought. It takes a conception of proper conduct that should be accessible to every normal person and perverts it into an occasion for incessant self-criticism.

Utilitarian Purity

If Kant is the chief perpetrator of the ideal of purity in moral thought, then one would expect his utilitarian opponents to be exempt from this uplifting vice. But if we look at utilitarianism closely, we find that it too shares in limiting moral conduct to the most virtuous among us.

If Kant turns away from human needs, Bentham enthrones them as his starting point. His psychology holds that all human beings seek pleasure and avoid pain. From this factual claim, he concludes in an extraordinary leap that the best social policy is the one that will bring about what people seem to want—the greatest pleasure and least pain. It is as though the entire society acted as single pleasure-seeking organism. The aim of social policy should be to maximize the utility of society, as measured by its pleasure and pain (its happiness), thus the label utilitarian for those who follow Bentham.

Let us leave aside well-known problems of measurement and assume that we can sum up the utility of diverse persons and compute what would be good for the society as a whole. The demand on each individual in the society is that he think of himself as having pleasures and pains that are important not because he or she feels them but because they are felt by someone, anyone. The only thing that matters is that these pleasures and pains occur.

Utilitarianism has many virtues. It teaches us that human suffering is relevant to moral action. It can easily account for lying when necessary to protect life or even to protect important relationships. The difficulty with utilitarianism is that the Benthamite calculus of pleasure and pain also generates some unpalatable results. It suggests that killing one innocent person would probably be all right to save two; if there is a net increase of pleasure over pain, more life is surely better than less. The same calculus implies that stealing from the rich would be all right to benefit the poor, for the pleasure to those starving would presumably be greater than the pain to the rich of losing redundant property. It even suggests that slavery in limited amounts would be desirable, for the pain to a few slaves might (all we need is the word "might") be less than the gain to their masters.

Some utilitarians struggle against these implications by limiting their claims of justification to the moral rules that we take for granted, such as those found in the Ten Commandments. In the long run, these rules serve social utility, and we can easily see why. Avoiding various forms of aggression (homicide, rape, theft, and so on) certainly contributes to a more stable, secure way of life. But as many critics have argued, there is no reliable utilitarian argument to explain why individuals in times of stress should not violate the rules. The principle of utility might explain why parents should be loyal to their children; but it cannot explain why, if given the choice between saving my own child and the significantly more gifted child of my neighbor, I should save my own. Utilitarianism generates prohibitions that are contingent on the computations of the moment.

For our purposes, however, the relevant point is that utilitarianism, like Kantianism, stands for an ethic of purity. In making moral decisions, individuals must think of the good for the collective organism called society. They may not think of themselves first. They may not rest their decisions on whether they bleed but rather on bleeding as abstracted from any particular artery in the society. The blood of all is of equal weight.

Utilitarianism proves, therefore, to be the teaching of altruism. The true follower of Bentham must think to himself or herself: The other is as important as myself, and many other persons overwhelm my insignificant existence with their collective capacity to feel plea-sure and pain. As Kantian thought submerges the individual in a transcendental world of reason, Benthamite theory loses the moral agent in a sea of social pains and pleasures. As no real human being can free himself of the demands of inner sensual impulses, no one with a healthy ego can give himself over to the altruistic demands of utilitarianism. One theory as much as the other exacts a purity that is not of this world. Moral conduct becomes as much a part of our daily lives as the perfect vacuum becomes the medium for experi-mental physics.

The purity exacted by both Kant and Bentham consists in imitat-ing qualities of the divine. For Kant, the imperative quality of God is reason exercised without distraction by bodily impulses. For Ben-tham, the quality of benevolence takes precedence, but it turns out that the theory demands the divine attribute of omniscience as well. The perfect utilitarian foresees the consequences of every act and calculates the costs and benefits of every alternative. However differ-ent their paths may be, Kant and Bentham share the Enlightenment impulse of grounding a moral theory in attributes of the human con-dition. In both cases, however, it turns out that the desired qualities are unattainable versions of God's perfection.

Impartial Morality: The Derived Maxims

Because they express a melding of morality and spiritual aspiration, the pure theories of Enlightenment morality have too little to offer in our quest for guidelines that would minimize the "permanent moral danger" of loyal commitments. Yet these impartial moral theories of the eighteenth century have had an impact on our moral thinking, not because they are used in their pure form but because they generate maxims or rules of thumb for resolving practical problems. Kantian thinking is associated with the following rules of thumb:

1. Never treat anyone merely as a means, but always as an end in himself or herself.
2. Respect the human dignity of others.
3. In order to assess whether conduct is right, think about the implications of everyone's doing it.

Utilitarian benevolence issues in the familiar techniques of cost/benefit analysis and assessing whether individual acts are good or bad for the society as a whole. These derivative forms of eighteenth-century moral theories unquestionably guide our thinking about social issues in the late twentieth century. And they might, in very rough terms, provide some understanding of the conditions under which we think excessive loyalty poses a moral danger. This danger is probably triggered by the sense that one's loyal acts toward a person, family, or nation threaten the dignity of outsiders or, alternatively, risk very high costs proportional to the benefits of remaining loyal. These approximate guidelines to the limits of loyalty may be all we can reasonably expect from the tradition of impartial moral theory.

There is a great danger, however, of confusing the limits with the foundations of loyal sentiment. At the breaking point, standing by a friend, lover, or community simply "shocks the conscience."[35] Virtue turns to vice; loving support becomes complicity in a crime. And it might even be possible to capture the shocking of our conscience as an injustice or immorality, per one of the maxims adopted from the tradition of moral philosophy. We might say something like: "I can no longer remain true to someone or some group that acts with so much contempt for humanity"; or "The costs of my loyalty have simply become too great." The former is a version of Kantian rhetoric, the latter, of utilitarian idiom. Either might be suitable as an epitaph to a loyal relationship. Yet epitaphs do not tell us why we act in the first place. The reasons for our exit do not inform us about the motives for maintaining a loyal voice for so long. The arguments of the breaking point do not tell us why the commitment was in place, and why we stayed loyal to the point at which it was no longer tolerable.

The ethics of loyalty doom us to a mixed system of independent but compelling systems of thought. Impartial morality and loyalty remain independently binding; neither reduces to the other. Loyalty cannot be seen as a version of impartial morality any more than impartial morality can be understood as deriving from loyalty. Contrasted at the level of pure theory, the differences between the ethic of loyalty and impartial morality are manifold. The former is grounded in our relationships with others; the latter is universal in its appeal. The ethic of loyalty brings to bear an historical self; impartial morality derives from the universality of reason or of human psychology. The former is pitched to humans as they are; the latter, to the spiritual aspirations of humans as they might be. Systems that are so radically different cannot be brought together within any single common denominator.

Is This the Final Word?

Who are the critics of loyalty? To whom must I make my case? The argument takes place on different planes, against different adversaries. At the level of moral theory, the opponent of loyalty is the entire tradition of impartial ethical theory, the pretentious claim that only the impartial can be moral. At the level of the real, the adversary changes. With those who live their lives in a constant struggle to do the right thing, the problem is not whether it is right to stand by others, whether it is good to be partial toward those who share our biographies. Outside the courts, sports, and other competitive arenas, partiality is assumed. The problem is not whether we should do more for those who are close to us. The problem is that we are likely to do too much. We are fearful not of excessive distance but of complicity in evil.

The ethics of loyalty is caught, therefore, between two extremes. It attends to the voices of Camus and Sartre, who favor their concrete loyalties over the demands of abstract justice. Yet the more we see the dangers of suspended critical judgment, the more we are driven back into the refuge of Kant and Bentham and their moral theory. The dialectic is unresolved. Absolute loyalty deprives us of our critical judgment; impartial ethics, of our human sensibilities.

The path of ethical thought in the future must recognize that neither the Kantians nor the utilitarians have much to teach us about how to lead our lives. Their ideal of moral purity is unattainable in social life as we know it. Even the watered-down versions of their views lead us astray. It is sometimes right to lie—as when necessary to save a life. It is even right to use others as means rather than ends—when the use is reciprocal, as in joint ventures. Nor does the Benthamite calculus of social costs and benefits account for human insights. There are some wrongs—such as slavery, exploitation, and degradation of others—that are perceived and understood only when human beings bring to bear a sense of their universal humanity. There is more in the world of moral conduct than can be captured either in Kant's abstractions of pure reason or in Bentham's disengaged calculus of pain and pleasure.

The great danger in my appeal for loyalty is that I am likely to win too much support from those who concur in my endorsing the role of the historical as well as the universal self as sources of obligation. This line of thought dovetails well with the emergent emphasis on multiculturalism, racial and ethnic particularism, and the often exaggerated claims that different genders and races necessarily think differently about the same problems. One peculiarity of the present political situation, at least in the United States, is that the political left can no longer see beyond the historical and communal self. The tragedy of the left in post-Communist politics is that they have abandoned the universalistic demand that a common humanity unite all cultures and races, men and women.[36] The dream of universal fraternity has been replaced by a turning inward in an effort to build solidarity with those who speak the same language or share the same history of oppression.

In the turn toward particularism, there is a great danger that the notion of truth itself will become pitched to particular communities. One can already see the outlines of this impending breakdown in discourse. The argument typically involves a confusion of sociological or psychological observations, on the one hand, and epistemology, on the other. From useful observations about boys and girls thinking differently,[37] it could be claimed that men and women have different criteria of truth. From the observation that different cultures support different and inconsistent religious beliefs, one might conclude that they are all true, each religion according to its own cultural premises. Truth, then, is reduced to belief. When beliefs become incontestable, we lose the capacity to say that some are better than others. Dissent loses its bite. Emperors without clothes—and propositions based on propaganda—have the same force as the supported scientific argument.

There are simple responses to those who would abandon the standard of universal truth and insist that each community has its own standards that are beyond questioning. The problem whether truth is universal or community based cannot be resolved by asking which community you are in. Those who say that truth depends on the convergence of belief mean to say something that is true for all communities, at all times, whether there is a consensus supporting their position or not.

Yet this argument is not likely to persuade those who are unwilling to think about the methodology of their claims. When rational discourse breaks down, the primary mode of argument is guilt by association. Those who believe in the universal criteria of truth are taken to be the naive inheritors of the religious tradition or of some other mode of thought that speaks in the idiom of humanity, but in fact seeks to oppress the latest group on the agenda of liberation. We have yet to appreciate the intellectual tradition of neutral and universal discourse that has enabled us, in our time, to think of liberating groups to whom we owe no loyalty other than that dictated by the bond of common humanity.

For an argument to be worth making, it must be cast in a language that appeals to those who have no loyalties to the proponent. When Carol Gilligan wrote about the way eleven-year-old girls think, she did so in a rigorous style designed to convince neutral observers. Although many feminists rely upon her work to argue that women think differently from men, nothing could be further from her approach than the claim: If you are a woman, you should be loyal and believe me. When loyalties begin to encompass the criteria of validation, we will have lost the necessary condition for making valuable arguments that can appeal to those who disagree with us.

Is it time, then, for an appeal against loyalty? Perhaps, for some. But for the many, the need is to recognize the legitimacy of loyal bonds in the ethical life. Loyalty, as I argued at the outset, inhibits exit, preserves institutions, and generates the need for politics. Loyalties represent a relational interest that should be protected from the state's interventionist hand. Loyalties stand opposed to the tradition of impartial morality that exacts a life of spiritual perfection. Loyalties recognize who we are in our friendships, loves, family bonds, national ties, and religious devotion.

The challenge for our time is uniting the particularist leaning of loyalties with the demands, in some contexts, of impartial justice and the commitment, in all contexts, to rational discourse. As much as I make this plea for loyalty, I make a stronger plea for the qualities of mutual respect and reasoned discourse that make this or any argument worthwhile. There is no point to an argument that would be accepted or rejected on the basis of personal loyalties. The text stands as an argument that, if worth making, has no ties to my time, my place, or my community. It is an appeal to discourse across time, across space, and across culture. We learn we have roots by transcending them.

Notes

Chapter 1

1. A. Hirschman, *Exit, Voice and Loyalty: Response to Decline in Firms, Organizations and States* (1970).

2. Id. at 30.

3. It appears that Hirschman ignores this important dimension of voice. He discusses, for example, Ralph Nader's role as a consumer advocate without noting Nader's reliance on lawsuits as a vehicle of protest. Id. at 42–43.

4. Id. at 98.

5. Id. at 96.

6. A. MacIntyre, *Is Patriotism a Virtue?* 15 (published as a pamphlet by the University of Kansas 1984).

7. This famous phrase comes from Stephen Decatur's 1816 toast: "Our country! In her intercourse with foreign nations may she always be in the right; but our country, right or wrong."

8. The great thinkers about morality have tended to avoid the subject of loyalty. The serious philosophical writings on loyalty include J. Royce, *The Philosophy of Loyalty* (1908, reprinted 1920); P. Pettit, "The Paradox of Loyalty," 25(2) *American Philosophical Quarterly* 163 (1988); J. Ladd, "Loyalty," 5 *Encyclopedia of Philosophy* 97–98 (1967); R. P. Wolff, "Loyalty," *The Poverty of Liberalism*, Chap. 2 (1968); A. Oldenquist, "Loyalties," 79 *Journal of Philosophy* 173 (1982); M. Baron, *The Moral Status of Loyalty* (1984); A. MacIntyre, *Is Patriotism a Virtue?* (University of Kansas 1984). Responses to MacIntyre include S. Nathanson, "In Defense of Moderate Patriotism," 99 *Ethics* 535 (1989); P. Gomberg, "Patriotism Is Like Racism," 101 *Ethics* 144 (1990). Also on patriotism, see M. Janowitz, *The Reconstruction of Patriotism* (1983); J. Schar, "The Case for Patriotism," 17 *American Review* 59 (1973). See also the collection of short comments about the meaning of patriotism today in the *Nation*, July 4, 1991.

9. Aristotle, *Nicomachean Ethics* 1155a.

10. Id.

11. Id. at 1156a–56b.

12. Id. at 1156a–58a.

13. Id. at 1156b.

14. Id. at 1155a (citing ancient proverb).

15. Id. at 1156b.

16. See Ladd, supra note 8, at 97. Ladd is one of the few people writing on loyalty who at least mentions Aristotle and perceives the analogy between loyalty and friendship.

17. They also commit idolatry, but in view of my using the term "idolatry" in the text to refer to absolute commitments to the concrete objects of loyalty, I will reserve the religious references to Chapter 4, where the ideas of loyalty to God and idolatry can be properly addressed.

18. Compare the special sense that "loyalty" acquired during the McCarthy period. See the discussion at pages 21–22 below.

19. Last words before being hanged by the British as an American spy, September 22, 1776.

20. Dante, *The Divine Comedy*, Canto 11, lines 50–60 (R. Bottrall trans. 1966).

21. W. Blackstone, 4 *Commentaries on the Laws of England* 75 (1765–1769).

22. These less than scientific conclusions about animals derive from assorted conversations I have had with people who work with animals, including a useful talk with Dr. Michael McGuire at UCLA's Neuropsychiatric Institute.

23. See MacIntyre, supra note 6.

24. Gomberg, supra note 8.

25. This is the way John Rawls presents utilitarian theory in J. Rawls, *A Theory of Justice* 22–27 (1971).

26. See Oldenquist, supra note 8, at 186.

27. See W. Godwin, 1 *Enquiry Concerning Political Justice* 126–27 (3d 1798).

28. See B. Ackerman, *Social Justice in the Liberal State* 54–59 (1980) (on the distribution of manna).

29. See R. Dworkin, "Liberalism," in M. Sandel, *Liberalism and Its Critics* 60 (1984).

30. Rawls, supra note 25, at 60–62.

31. This appears to be the highest state of moral development, according to Lawrence Kohlberg. See L. Kohlberg, 1 *The Philosophy of Moral Development* 383–84 (1988).

32. This theme is taken up in greater detail in Chapter 3 at 52–57.

33. See M. Buber, *I and Thou* (trans. W. Kaufmann 1970).

34. See generally C. Gilligan, *In a Different Voice: Psychological Theory and Women's Development* (1982).

35. Many of these committed American Jews lost their citizenship, for at

the time fighting on behalf of a foreign military was taken to be equivalent to voluntary renunciation of American citizenship. The assumption was that everyone had to be loyal to one and only one people. The topic of divided loyalties is taken up below in Chapter 8 at 155–62.

36. See Royce, supra note 8, at 102–6.

37. Rawls, supra note 25, at 60.

38. For a discussion of the problem of extending Rawls's analysis beyond particular societies, see T. Pogge, *Realizing Rawls* 240–80 (1989).

39. M. Walzer, *Spheres of Justice: A Defense of Pluralism and Equality* 39, 44 (1983).

40. See Oldenquist, supra note 8, at 177.

41. I. Kant, "On the Common Saying: 'This may be True in Theory, but it does not Apply in Practice," reprinted in H. Reiss (ed.), *Kant's Political Writings* 61, 74 (1970).

42. Id.

43. Id.

44. See the analysis of loyalty oaths below in Chapter 4 at 65–68.

45. C. Fried, "The Lawyer as Friend: The Moral Foundations of the Lawyer-Client Relation," 85 *Yale Law Journal* 1060, 1061 (1976).

46. A critique of Fried's article, supra note 45, is tangential to my case for loyalty. His argument that lawyers should think of themselves as friends of their clients is so clearly wrong, however, that I must take issue.

Fried's premise is that lawyers enter into "personal" relationships with their clients. Id. at 1071. From this dubious premise (who, after all, wants a *personal* relationship with the person we hire to get the job done?) Fried leaps to friendship. Implicitly involving Aristotle, he infers: "that like a friend he [the lawyer] acts in your interest, not his own; or rather he adopts your interests as his own. I would call that the classic definition of friendship." If a friendship arises between lawyer and client, it is surely a matter of convenience, the type that Aristotle regarded as the lowest kind.

Fried has two tactical reasons for relying on the model of friendship to explain the lawyer-client relationship. First, he wants to justify the special devotion that lawyers feel toward their existing clients at the expense of others in need of legal services. And second, he wants to deny that lawyers have a duty to serve the public good in making decisions about which clients they will serve. The notion that the lawyer has an obligation to work for the common good, for the welfare of all, strikes Fried as a "monstrous conception." Id. at 1078. It runs counter, Fried reasons, "to the picture of purely discretionary choice implicit in the notion of friendship."

Let us admit that the term "loyalty" prompts us to think of friendship and thus to conclude that lawyers should treat their clients the way we treat our friends. And then recall that at the outset of friendship everyone has a choice whether to pursue the relationship or not. It follows, supposedly, that lawyers can have it both ways. They can lavish the kind of attention on clients that we reserve for purely personal relationships, and further, they can choose their clients at will, regardless of the public interest. The fallacy of this association lies in forgetting that the duties of friendship do not arise just from the choice to let history deepen a desired relationship.

Fried forgets the elements of time and interwoven identity that bind friends together and thus make friendship plausible. His illusion that one chooses friends in the way one chooses a lawyer, or a lawyer in the way one develops a friendship, sidesteps reality for the sake of the argument. What Fried really wants is a free market in legal services. The model of voluntary contract accounts for everything he needs to say. First, if the terms of the contract are that the lawyer must act loyally toward his client, then by virtue of the voluntary agreement he comes under a duty of loyalty. Further, a free market permits those offering goods and services to choose their customers at will. But if lawyers are merely selling their services, they have no more claim to be a calling or profession than do butchers, bakers, and candlestick makers.

47. C. Fried, *Order and Law, Arguing the Reagan Revolution—A First Hand Account* (1991).

48. Id. at 189.

Chapter 2

1. Exodus 1:11–12 (King James translation).
2. M. Nussbaum, *The Fragility of Goodness* 63–79 (1986).
3. Id. at 57.
4. This point is well made by Nussbaum; id. at 65.
5. Genesis 29.
6. Pethihta to *Eikha Rabba* 24.
7. The rabbis used this tale of self-denial to raise questions, which will concern us in Chapter 4, about God's tendency toward jealousy. The *Midrash* continues:

> And if I, who am only flesh and blood, dust and ashes, was not jealous of my co-wife [anticipating her later marriage to Jacob] and did not permit her to be shamed and humiliated, then You, O living King, why are You jealous of idols that have no reality, and why have You exiled my children and allowed them to be killed by the sword and permitted their enemies to do as they wished with them?

Immediately God's pity was stirred, and he said, "For you, Rachel, I will return the Israelites to their place."

8. See supra note 6.

9. See Chapter 1, note 6.

10. These were published in *Time*, October 1, 1990, 42–49.

11. Id. at 46.

12. But it would not have been an act of loyalty to the Hungarian nation. See Chapter 1, at 17–18.

13. Genesis 22:1.

14. Genesis 3:8.

15. See God's making his covenant with Noah that "the waters shall no more become a flood to destroy all flesh"; Genesis 9:12.

16. See Abraham's challenge to God concerning the destruction of Sodom and Gomorrah: "Will not the Judge of the Universe act justly?" Genesis 18:26.

17. See M. Walzer, "A Note on Positive Freedom in Jewish Thought," I(1) *S'vara: A Journal of Philosophy, Law and Judaism* 7 (1990).

18. Exodus 3:6.

19. Exodus 20:2.

20. I return to these themes later in my analysis of idolatry as a breach of loyalty to God. See Chapter 4 at 71–75.

21. *L'Existentialisme est un humanisme* 39–42 (1970).

22. See also the decision by the midwives to resist Pharaoh's command and save Jewish babies; Exodus 1:17.

23. Aeschylus, *Agamemnon*.

24. See supra note 2.

Chapter 3

1. See M. Sharp, *Was Justice Done?* 100–5, 175–89 (1956). Khrushchev concedes that they were guilty in his secret tapes; *Time*, October 1, 1990, 47 ("I was part of Stalin's circle when he mentioned the Rosenbergs with warmth.").

2. Whether this duty is in fact limited to citizens is taken up below at pages 52–57.

3. See L. Gordon Crovitz, "Even Pollard Deserves Better Than Government Sandbagging," *The Wall Street Journal*, September 4, 1991, A13: "Mr. Weinberger's claim that Jonathan Pollard committed treason by spying for Israel was bad law or curious diplomacy."

4. Exodus 21:22. For interpretations of this passage, see the symposium in 2 *S'vara: A Journal of Philosophy, Law and Judaism* 48–71.

5. As quoted in Rosenberg v. United States, 346 U.S. 273, 311 (1953).

6. The statute also treats as conclusive on disloyalty specific acts that are

damaging to the realm, such as counterfeiting money. See 25 Edw. III, § 3, cl. 1.

7. T. Hobbes, *Dialogue between a Philosopher and a Student of Common Laws of England* 97 (London 1681) (the position of the philosopher, commonly taken to be a stand-in for Hobbes himself).

8. Crohagan Case, 79 Eng. Rep. 891 (K.B. 1634).

9. 3 *Coke's Institutes* 14.

10. Coke had conceded, however, that written words, presumably because of the greater danger they represented, could satisfy the overt act requirement. 3 Coke 14.

11. Kelyng 15 (1708 ed.).

12. Kelyng's own editor rejected his views. See id. at 15 note 1 (1789 ed.).

13. Laws of the State of New York, 4th Sess. ch. 68 (Poughkeepsie 1782).

14. Law, October 1776, ch. V, 9 Hening, Statutes at Large 170 (1823).

15. Hobbes, supra note 7, at 97.

16. See D'Aquino v. United States, 192 F.2d 338 (9th Cir. 1951).

17. There is a technical problem about whether Jane Fonda could have been prosecuted for treason. We never declared war against North Vietnam, and therefore it was not technically our enemy.

18. Exodus 20:17.

19. M. Maimonides, *Mishneh Torah: Laws of Robbery and Property*, Chap. 1, 9.

20. See the discussion in Chapter 4 at 69–75..

21. O. W. Holmes, Jr., *The Common Law* 3 (1881).

22. United States Constitution art. III, § 3, cl. 1: "Treason against the United States shall consist only in levying War against them, or, in adhering to their Enemies, giving them Aid and Comfort. No Person shall be convicted of Treason unless on the Testimony of two Witnesses to the same overt Act, or on the Confession in open Court."

23. Rosenberg v. United States, 346 U.S. 273 (1953).

24. United States v. Cramer, 325 U.S. 1 (1945).

25. See ex parte Quirin, 317 U.S. 1 (1942).

26. 325 U.S. at 55–56.

27. Justice Jackson concedes this point. 325 U.S. at 38–39.

28. Id. at 38.

29. United States v. Cramer, 325 U.S. 1 (1945).

30. Id. at 50.

31. Id. at 34–35.

32. For another instance in which Justices Black and Douglas disagreed with Justice Jackson about the demands of loyalty, see the discussion of Barnette v. West Virginia Board of Eduction, 319 U.S. 624 (1943), infra Chapter 6, at 116–20.

33. United States v. Haupt, 330 U.S. 631 (1947).

34. The question of Herbert's citizenship became an issue when he was tried before a military tribunal for committing an offense against the laws of war. See ex parte Quirin, 317 U.S. 1, 20 (1942). Crossing enemy lines in civilian dress for the purpose of committing hostile acts is a violation of the laws of war. The Court held that Herbert was guilty whether he was still an American citizen or not. Id. at 37.

35. United States v. Haupt, 136 F.2d 661 (1943) (of the six defendants, the three men were sentenced to death; the three women, to 15 years imprisonment).

36. Justice Frank Murphy was the lone dissenter. 330 U.S. at 646. He developed an ingenious argument, which I have found appealing at times, that the overt act of treason should be one that clearly manifests the required inner adherence to the enemy. Only acts that are fully incriminating, such as giving the enemy a map of military installations, should be enough for treason.

37. 330 U.S. at 641. This is the way the Supreme Court reports the instructions. The correct instruction would have been that unless they found beyond a reasonable doubt that Haupt's intention was to aid the German Reich, they should have voted for acquittal.

38. Herbert Haupt tried to invoke this principle of universality to save himself from the death sentence imposed by a military tribunal for his violation of the law of war; see supra note 34. The Supreme Court held that the Sixth Amendment right to a jury trial did not apply to offenses within the jurisdiction of military tribunals. Ex parte Quirin, 317 U.S. 1, 43–44 (1942).

39. See supra note 34.

40. Note the problem in *Quirin* was that Haupt claimed he was an American citizen.

41. This distinction is drawn nicely in Oldenquist, "Loyalties."

42. Plato, Canto 50b–c (H. Tredennick trans. 1961).

43. Id. at 50d.

44. See supra note 12.

45. It remains to be seen whether after the failure of the Yanaev coup in August 1991 the thirteen arrested conspirators will actually be convicted of treason. As of this writing, a trial appeared to be scheduled for October 1992; leading lawyers in Moscow predicted that conspirators could not be convicted of treason.

Chapter 4

1. Bostonians root for a football team called the New England Patriots; no American would ever identify with a term called the "Loyalists."

2. This topic is taken up in Chapter 7.

3. In 1977, as the Governor of Massachusetts, Dukakis asked the judges of the state Supreme Court for their opinion about the legality of the Pledge. Five of the seven judges advised him not to favor legislation that would impose sanctions against teachers who refused to conduct the Pledge in their classrooms. See Opinion of the Justices to the Governor, 372 Mass. 874, 262 N.E.2d 251 (1977). For more on this dispute see Chapter 6.

4. It is worth noting, however, that German constitutional language repeatedly invokes the term *Verfassungstreue*, which has a stronger connotation than loyalty to the constitution. It means something closer to "being faithful to constitutional values." Also, the phrase "treason to the constitution" was used early in American constitutional history to refer to judges avoiding their responsibility under the Constitution. See Cohens v. Virginia, 6 Wheat. 264, 404 (1821). ("We have no more right to decline the exercise of jurisdiction which is given, than to usurp that which is not given. The one or the other would be treason to the constitution. Questions may occur which we would gladly avoid; but we cannot avoid them.")

5. 384 U.S. 426 (1966). A more lawyerly statement of the case holding would be that the Court extended the Fifth Amendment privilege against self-incrimination (as applied to the states under the "due process" clause of the Fourteenth Amendment) to custodial interrogation in the absence of counsel.

6. Rogers v. Richmond, 365 U.S. 534 (1961).

7. Id. at 541.

8. Id.

9. Decision of the Federal Constitutional Court, February 25, 1975, 39 BVerfG 1.

10. For an insightful discussion of oaths and one slightly more sympathetic than that expressed here, see S. Levinson, *Constitutional Faith* (1988).

11. United States Constitution Art. II, § 1, cl. 8. The prescribed oath for the President reads: "I do solemnly swear (or affirm) that I will faithfully execute the Office of President of the United States, and will to the best of my Ability, preserve, protect and defend the Constitution of the United States."

12. Id. Art. VI, § 3, prescribing that all senators, representatives, and executive and judicial officers, state and federal, shall "be bound by oath or affirmation to support this constitution."

13. Note the controversy in Cummings v. Missouri, 71 U.S. (4 Wall) 277 (1866) about whether the Reconstructionist government in Missouri could demand, as a condition of employment, an oath from teachers that they had not been in sympathy with "armed hostility to the United States." A sharply divided court invalidated the oath as a bill of attainder, an imper-

missible legislative judgment inflicting punishment without a trial. Id. at 319.

14. See, e.g., Law Students Research Council v. Wadmond, 401 U.S. 154 (1971); Baird v. State Bar of Arizona, 401 U.S. 1 (1971); Connell v. Higginbotham, 403 U.S. 207, 209 (1971); Keyishian v. Board of Regents, 385 U.S. 589 (1967); Baggett v. Bullitt, 377 U.S. 360 (1964); Cramp v. Board of Public Instruction, 368 U.S. 278 (1961).

15. Cole v. Richardson, 405 U.S. 676 (1972).

16. Exodus 20:1. See Maimonides, I *The Commandments* 1 (C. Chavel trans. 1967). Significantly, God announces his existence, but does not command that one believe in him. Belief is presumed in accepting that it is God who has announced his existence.

17. The passage reads literally: "There shall be to you no other gods ahead of me [in my face]."

18. Exodus 20: 5–7: "For I the Lord thy God am a jealous God, punishing the iniquity of the fathers upon the children unto the third and fourth generation of those that hate me; but showing mercy to thousands of generations of those that love me, and keep my commandments."

19. My own thinking about idolatry has benefited greatly from studying the manuscript by M. Halbertal and A. Margalit, *Idolatry* (1992). The claims made in the text, however, differ from theirs, and the errors are mine.

20. Religious Jews do not pronounce the "four-letter name" (yud-heh-vav-heh) by which God is identified in the Bible.

21. Maimonides, *The Book of Knowledge*, Mishnah Torah Book I, 66a–66b (M. Hyamson trans. 1981)

22. Exodus 20:2.

23. The biblical text supporting the talmudic reflection is limited: "And they stopped at the foot of the mountain." Exodus 19:17. It seems obvious that the Jewish tradition preferred to see the covenant as imposed rather than as freely chosen. This conforms to the Jewish maxim "you should do and then you shall understand [and be in a position to choose]." For a meditation on what it means that the Good chose the Jews before the Jews chose the Good, see E. Levinas, *Nine Talmudic Readings* 30ff. (A. Aronowicz trans. 1990).

24. See *Encyclopedia of the Jewish Religion* 133 (Z. Werblowsky and G. Wigoder eds. 1965) ("no confirmation of the events from any other source").

25. Jeremiah 3:20.

26. As David Daube points out, the use of gender terms in theology often casts God as lover and husband and even as mother (see Luke 13:34), but never as wife. First Annual Gerald Goldfarb Memorial Lecture, University of Judaism, Los Angeles, California, January 20, 1991.

27. Matthew 5:28.

28. Babylonian Talmud, *Avodah Zara* 54b–55a.

29. Id.

30. Note that in this parable, Israel plays the part of the husband, not the wife. Cf. the thesis by David Daube discussed in supra note 26.

31. Ezekiel 16:62.

32. Hosea 11:9.

33. See *Midrash Sifrei on Deuteronomy* 306, as discussed in Margalit and Halbertal, supra note 19, at 38 (ms).

34. Babylonian Talmud, *Sanhedrin* 72a.

Chapter 5

1. L. Brandeis and S. Warren, "The Right to Privacy," 4 *Harvard Law Review* 193 (1890).

2. See Griswold v. Connecticut, 381 U.S. 479 (1965) (relying on the "penumbra" to the First, Third, Fourth and Fifth Amendments).

3. This is based on the facts in Blau v. United States, 340 U.S. 332 (1951).

4. J. Wigmore, 8 *Evidence* § 2332 (McNaughton rev. 1961).

5. See Trammel v. United States, 445 U.S. 40 (1980).

6. J. Bentham, 5 *Rationale of Judicial Evidence* 340 (1827).

7. Id. at 338.

8. See supra note 5.

9. The Court does not undermine the traditional common law rule so far as it permits a defendant to block testimony about matters communicated in confidence. 445 U.S. at 45 n.5. This is the form of privilege that clients and patients enjoy in their confidential relationships with those under a duty of professional loyalty.

10. See Idaho Code sec. 9–203(7) (Sup. 1986); Minn. Stat. Ann. sec. 595.02(1) (West 1986). These provisions apply only on behalf of parents.

11. See *In re* Ryan, 123 Misc.2d 854, 474 N.Y.S.2d 931 (Fam. Ct. 1984); Michelet P. v. Gold, 70 A.D.2d 68, 419 N.Y.S.2d 704 (1979).

12. *In re Grand Jury Proceedings (Agosto)*, 553 F.Supp. 1298 (D.Nev. 1983).

13. See Comment, "Parent-Child Loyalty and Testimonial Privilege," 100 *Harvard Law Review* 910 (1987); A. Stanton, "Child-Parent Privilege for Confidential Communications: An Examination and Proposal," 16 *Family Law Quarterly* 1 (1982); D. Coburn, "Child-Parent Communications: Spare the Privilege and Spoil the Child," 74 *Dickinson Law Review* 599 (1970).

14. See the discussion of this case in Chapter 3 at pages 48–51.

15. Wilson v. Rastall, 100 Eng.Rep. 1287 (K.B. 1792).

16. S. Levinson, "Testimonial Privileges and the Preference of Friendship," 1984 *Duke Law Journal* 631.

17. My description of the case draws on the opinion of the New Jersey Supreme Court in the Matter of Baby M, 109 N.J. 396, 537 A2d 1227 (1988) and the book written by Mary Beth Whitehead in collaboration with a journalist: M. Whitehead and L. Schwartz-Nobel, *A Mother's Story* (1989).

18. For the intellectual foundations of this view, see the discussions of impartial morality in Chapters 1 and 8.

19. See J. Mill, *On Liberty* (1859).

20. As reported in Whitehead and Schwartz-Nobel, *A Mother's Story* 17.

21. The court reviewed the New Jersey statutes punishing giving or paying money in connection with an adoption, N.J.S.A. 9:3–54a. 109 N.J. at 423–27.

22. Whitehead and. Schwartz-Nobel, *A Mother's Story* 26.

23. I have left out some details of the story that were highlighted in the popular press. It seems to be irrelevant that Elizabeth Stern had sensible medical grounds for refusing to bear her own child. Nor does it seem important that William Stern is the son of Holocaust survivors and therefore particularly concerned about continuing his blood line. With regard to the later point, it is worth noting that Mary Beth Whitehead was the one who favored giving the child a name with strong Jewish resonance.

24. According to the opinion of the Court, she threatened suicide and said that she would return the child in a week. 109 N.J. at 415.

25. According to the account in Whitehead and Schwartz-Nobel, *A Mother's Story*, the Florida court order was fraudulent. I am not in a position to verify this claim.

26. 109 N.J. 396 (1908).

27. 109 N.J. at 437.

28. See J. Goldstein, A. Freud, and A. Solnit, *Beyond the Best Interests of the Child* 16–17 (1973).

29. 109 N.J. at 450.

30. For a more elaborate defense of this conclusion, see the Amicus Curiae Brief submitted in the Baby M case by the Gruter Institute for Law and Behavioral Research; reprinted in M. Gruter and P. Bohanon, *Reader on Laws, Ethics and Biology* 217 (1991).

31. Some of these arguments emerge in B. Ackerman, *Social Justice and the Liberal State* (1980).

32. For an exposition of these three grounds of entitlement—acquisition, rectification, and voluntary transfer—see R. Nozick, *Anarchy, State and Utopia* 150–53 (1977).

33. See *New York Times*, January 6, 1992, B4 (specifically, the surrogate court judge ruled that contrary to the usual practice, the estate should not have to pay the taxes on the bequests to the lawyer and the nurse, but these two should have to pay their own taxes).

34. See the argument supra at page 82.

35. German Civil Code §§ 2303–2338A (*Pflichtteil*); Argentina Codigo Civil §§ 3577–3605.

36. As of this writing, the Supreme Court is scheduled to decide whether to uphold a lower court ruling that the Santeria religion may engage in animal sacrifice in violation of a local health ordinance. See Church of Lukumi Babalu Aye, Inc. v. Hialeah, 723 F.Supp. 1467 (S.D. Fla. 1989), aff'd 936 F.2d 586 (11th Cir. 1991), cert. granted 112 S.Ct. 1472 (1992).

37. Leary v. United States, 383 F.2d 851 (1967).

38. Reynolds v. United States, 98 U.S. 145, 164 (1879).

39. Minersville School District, Board of Education v. Gobitis, 310 U.S. 586 (1940), discussed in greater detail in Chapter 6 at 111–12.

40. There are at least three different ways of numbering the Commandments. I follow the Jewish system here. For more on worshiping graven images and the connection between the Third Commandment and idolatry, see Chapter 4 at 69–75.

41. The renewal of the *Gobitis* holding occurred in Employment Division, Department of Human Resources of Oregon v. Smith, 494 U.S. 872 (1990).

42. See West Virginia Board of Education vs. Barnette, 319 U.S. 624 (1943).

43. Id.

44. Sheldon v. Fannin, 221 F.Supp. 766 (Ariz. 1963).

45. See Wooley v. Maynard, 430 U.S. 705 (1977) (not required to use New Hampshire license plate that read "Live Free or Die"). See also Thomas v. Review Board of Indiana Employment Security Div., 450 U.S. 707 (1981) (Jehovah's Witness could receive unemployment compensation even though he quit his job because he did not want to participate in the armaments industry).

46. The primary winners under this line of cases have been Seventh Day Adventists. See Sherbert v. Verner, 374 U.S. 398 (1963); Hobbie v. Unemployment Appeals Commission of Florida, 480 U.S. 136 (1987).

47. See Frazee v. Illinois Department of Employment Security, 489 U.S. 829 (1989).

48. Wisconsin v. Yoder, 406 U.S. 205 (1972).

49. Romans 12:2.

50. Justice William O. Douglas concurred in a separate opinion stress-

ing the right of the children to decide for themselves whether they would attend public high school. 406 U.S. at 241.

51. 50 U.S.C. app. 456(j) (1988).

52. See Thomas v. Review Board of Indiana Employment Security Div., supra note 45.

53. All of the following decisions strike me as deplorable: Goldman v. Weinberger, 475 U.S. 503 (1986) (Jew in military service subject to discipline for violating dress code by refusing to remove *yarmulke* when indoors); Braunfield v. Brown, 366 U.S. 599 (1961) (Jew who closed shop on Saturday violated state "blue law" if he opened shop on Sunday); Estate of Shabazz, 482 U.S. 342 (1987) (Moslem inmates in state prison were denied permission, on grounds of prison security, to attend Friday afternoon services).

54. The most shocking case is Lyng v. Northwest Indian Cemetery Protective Assn., 485 U.S. 439 (1988), which held that even though the government's building roads over Indian burial grounds would have "devastating effects on traditional Indian religious practices," there was no need to defer to Native American religious claims. Equally disturbing is the case that terminated the entire jurisprudence of religious exemptions: Department of Human Resources of Oregon v. Smith, 494 U.S. 872 (1990) (Native American claim to use peyote in religious worship rejected). See also Bowen v. Roy, 476 U.S. 693 (1986). (This case strikes me as an easy one for rejecting the exemption, and the majority agreed, albeit in highly convoluted opinions, that a Native American could not assert a religious exemption from the general requirement that recipients of welfare have a Social Security number.)

55. Hernandez v. Commissioner of Internal Revenue, 490 U.S. 680 (1989) (payments made to church not deductible as contributions to a charitable organization).

56. See Leary v. United States, 383 F.2d 851 (1967).

57. 406 U.S. at 216.

58. Matthew 22:21.

59. One of the articles in the literature that shares this view of the religious life is Perry Dane's student comment, "Religious Exemptions under the Free Exercise Clause: A Model of Competing Authorities," 90 *Yale Law Journal* 350 (1980).

60. Bowen v. Roy, 476 U.S. 693 (1986).

61. Justice Byron White would have granted Roy's petition; 476 U.S. at 733. Justices Sandra Day O'Connor, William Brennan, and Thurgood Marshall dissented from various segments of the majority's reasoning, but not from the conclusion rejecting the claim for exemption.

62. 476 U.S. at 700. The point of the metaphor is to illustrate the

majority's thesis that however sincere and committed the religious belief, the free exercise clause "does not afford an individual a right to dictate the conduct of the Government's internal procedures." Id.

63. Thomas v. Review Board of Indiana Employment Security Div., 450 U.S. 707, 716 (1981).

64. 476 U.S. at 700.

65. Id.

66. Lyng v. Northwest Indian Cemetery Protective Association, 485 U.S. 439 (1988).

67. Id. at 459.

68. Id. at 442.

69. As described in an independent study. Id.

70. Id. at 449.

71. It is not that the dissenting opinion by Justices Brennan, Marshall, and Harry Blackmun did a much better job distinguishing the two cases. The dissent accepted the majority's distinction between the internal and external affairs of government and tried to argue against its application in this case. See id. at 470–71:

> Federal land-use decisions, by contrast, are likely to have substantial external effects that government decisions concerning office furniture and information storage obviously will not, and they are correspondingly subject to public scrutiny and public challenge in a host of ways that office equipment purchases are not.

72. See Matthew 13:57.

73. Genesis 22:1.

74. See United States v. Lee, 455 U.S. 252 (1982), which tested the belief of an Amish carpenter that because his religion required him to care for his own, he should not have to pay Social Security taxes on behalf of his employees. His scriptural support, I Timothy 5:8 requires him to provide "for those of his own house," but the Bible says nothing about refusing to pay taxes. Mr. Lee obviously had forgotten that the context in which Jesus instructed his followers to "render unto Caesar what is Caesar's" was a response to a question from the Pharisees about paying taxes. Matthew 22:15–22.

75. See Ohio Civil Rights Commission v. Dayton Christian Schools, 477 U.S. 619 (1986).

76. But see F. Gedicks, "Toward a Constitutional Jurisprudence of Religious Group Rights," 1989 *Wisconsin Law Review* 99, who is sympathetic to the Supreme Court's not intervening in the Dayton Christian Schools dispute.

77. See Bob Jones University v. United States, 461 U.S. 574 (1983).

Chapter 6

1. Apparently, New York was the first state to require the recitation of the Pledge in school, enacting the ritual in 1898, one day after the outbreak of the Spanish-American War. See Maryland v. Lundquist, 262 Md. 534; 278 A.2d 263 (1971).

2. See M. Quaife, M. Weig, and R. Appleman, *The History of the United States Flag* 154–55 (1961) (reporting that 12 million pupils took the Pledge in 1892).

3. As reported at id.

4. Public Law 396, 83rd Cong. 2d Sess.

5. For a description and critique of "value-free" education, see A. Gutmann, *Democratic Education* 30–41 (1987).

6. As reported by many firsthand participants, pupils in the Israeli schools (at least those for Jews) engage in widespread cheating. In grouping together against the authority of the teacher, the pupils learn a valuable lesson in loyalty that serves an important covert function in an embattled society.

7. Recall the comment by Alasdair MacIntyre, discussed in Chapter 1 at note 3.

8. The letter is dated October 27, 1989, and the issue, November 2–8, 1989. The five authors are Elizabeth Badinter, Régis Debray, Alain Finkelkraut, Elisbeth de Fontenay, and Catherine Kintzler.

9. The French *Conseil d'État* (Council of State) functions as the supreme court in France on the legality of administrative decisions. See L. Neville Brown and J. Garner, *French Administrative Law* 27 (3rd ed. 1983).

10. See *Libération*, November 7, 1989, p. 32.

11. Id. at 33.

12. Id.

13. Wallace v. Jaffree, 472 U.S. 38 (1985) (legislative history revealed covert religious purpose to minute of silence); McCollum v. Board of Education, 333 U.S. 203 (1948) (released time for voluntary religious education on school property held in violation of Establishment clause).

14. See Lewis v. Allen, 5 Misc.2d 68, 159 N.Y.S.2d 807 (1957), aff'd. 207 N.Y.S.2d 862 (App. Div. 1960), 200 N.E.2d 766 (N.Y. 1964), cert. den. 379 U.S. 923 (1964). (New York court gives short shrift to the argument that use of "under God" is unconstitutional.)

15. The use of the phrase on coins dates back to 1865. See A. Nussbaum, *A History of the Dollar* 116 (1967). This practice did not become obligatory until 1955 by Act of Congress.

16. See Edwards v. Aguillard, 482 U.S. 578 (1987) (state law requiring that creationism be taught if evolution is taught declared invalid for want of a secular purpose).

17. As reported in the *International Herald Tribune*, November 11, 1989, 2.

18. See G. Fletcher, *A Crime of Self Defense: Bernhard Goetz and the Law on Trial* 89 (1988).

19. The date of decision is November 27, 1989.

20. Minersville School District v. Gobitis, 310 U.S. 586 (1940).

21. Exodus 20:4,5. For an analysis of this Commandment, as it relates to idolatry, see the discussion in Chapter 4 at 69–75.

22. The renewal of *Gobitis* occurred in Employment Division, Department of Human Resources of Oregon v. Smith, 494 U.S. 872 (1990).

23. See Reynolds v. United States, 98 U.S. 145 (1879) (upholding a federal criminal prohibition against polygamy in the territory of Utah).

24. 494 U.S. at 879, relying on the passage in *Gobitis*, 310 U.S. 586, 594–95.

25. West Virginia State Board of Education v. Barnette, 319 U.S. 624 (1943).

26. 310 U.S. at 601, 606.

27. These thoughts provide a wedge for reasoning that *Barnette* did not overrule *Gobitis*, but merely shifted the debate from freedom of religion to free speech. If a problem such as liturgical peyote smoking is formulated as a problem of the free exercise of religion rather than as free speech, then arguably *Gobitis* is still controlling.

28. Chief Justice Charles E. Hughes and Justice James C. McReynolds had voted in the *Gobitis* majority. The former retired in 1941 and was replaced as Chief Justice by Harlan Fisk Stone, whose position as Associate Justice was filled by Robert H. Jackson. McReynolds retired in 1941 and was replaced by James F. Byrnes, who resigned in 1942, thus leading to the appointment of Wiley B. Rutledge. Justices Jackson and Rutledge voted in the new *Barnette* majority, along with Chief Justice Stone, who had dissented in *Gobitis*, and Justices Black, Douglas and Murphy.

29. See supra note 26.

30. 319 U.S. at 643. There follows in the quote a reference to Jones v. Opelika, 316 U.S. 584, 623 (1942), which is the only authority Black and Douglas cite in their *Barnette* opinion. And indeed they are not citing to the case as authority but to their own dissenting opinion in which all three judges, Black, Douglas and Murphy, signaled their shift of sentiment about *Gobitis*.

31. Some of the notable cases were Schechter Poultry Corp. v. United States, 295 U.S. 495 (1935) (regulation of a local poultry invalidated as beyond congressional power); United States v. Butler, 297 U.S. 1 (1936) (government subsidies to farmers in return for limiting production exceeded Congress's spending power); Carter v. Carter Coal Company, 298

U.S. 238 1936 (wage and hour regulations for coal miners not within commerce power).

32. 319 U.S. at 645.

33. Id.

34. Id. at 643.

35. Douglas v. Jeannette, 319 U.S. 157 (1943).

36. On the organization of the Jehovah's Witnesses, see D. Manwaring, *Render unto Caesar: The Flag Salute Controversy* 17–34 (1962).

37. See the remark made in Jones v. Opelika, supra note 3.

38. Douglas v. Jeannette, 319 U.S. 157 (1943).

39. Justices Douglas, Black, and Murphy and the newcomer Rutledge joined Chief Justice Stone who dissented in *Gobitis*.

40. See the companion case, Murdock v. Pennsylvania, 319 U.S. 105, 110 (1943).

41. Id.

42. Note, however, that only Stone agreed fully with Black. The other three, Murphy, Douglas, and Rutledge, joined in a separate concurring opinion locating their objection to the Struthers ordinance in the more specific ground of religious liberty. Martin v. Struthers, 319 U.S. 141, 149 (1943).

43. 319 U.S. at 146.

44. See Jackson's special opinion in the *Douglas, Murdock,* and *Martin* cases, 319 U.S. at 166.

45. The Court had already held, unanimously, in Chaplinksy v. New Hampshire, 315 U.S. 568 (1942), that a Jehovah's Witness could not, with impunity, call a public officer a "God damned racketeer" and a "damned Fascist" and thus intimated the "fighting words" limitation on freedom of speech.

46. See supra note 44.

47. 319 U.S. at 635.

48. This subtle point explains why Justice Scalia could plausibly revive *Gobitis* in his opinion in *Smith*, the peyote case. *Barnette* arguably did not overrule *Gobitis*; it merely shifted the grounds for resolving the problem of the Witnesses from religion to speech, thus leaving *Gobitis* intact in other free exercise cases.

49. In a later case, it becomes clear that Witness children are prepared to stand, respectfully, during the Pledge. See Sheldon v. Fannin, 221 F. Supp. 766 (Ariz. 1963).

50. 319 U.S. at 634. Cf. the concurring opinion by Justice Murphy: "The right of freedom of thought and of religion . . . includes both the right to speak freely and the right to refrain from speaking at all." 319 U.S. at 645.

51. Wooley v. Maynard, 430 U.S. 705 (1977).

52. 319 U.S. at 643.

53. Justice Murphy indicates that he "agree[s] with the opinion of the Court and join[s] in it." 319 U.S. at 644.

54. Prince v. Massachusetts, 321 U.S. 159 (1944)

55. 319 U.S. at 643.

56. A majority of the Court (Black, Douglas, Stone, Rutledge, and Reed) voted to uphold the statute on the ground simply that the state had the authority to pass legislation protecting the welfare of children. Prince v. Massachusetts, 321 U.S. 159 (1944). The argument under the First Amendment simply collapses under the weight of this legitimate state interest. In a separate opinion, joined by Frankfurter and Roberts, Jackson reiterates his views on the limitations of religious liberty: "I think the limits begin to operate whenever activities begin to affect or collide with liberties of others or of the public." 321 U.S. at 176.

57. 321 U.S. at 165. Cf. the dissenting opinion by Justice Murphy, 321 U.S. 171, 174: "If the right of a child to practice its religion in that manner is to be forbidden by constitutional means, there must be convincing proof. . . . [here Murphy cites *Barnette*]." For good reason, Justice Jackson's concurring opinion omits all reference to the authority of *Barnette*. Jackson's theory of free speech for all children supported the Witnesses' position.

58. In McCollum v. Board of Education, 333 U.S. 203, 232 (1948) (concurring opinion), he writes: "When a person is required to submit to some religious rite or instruction or is deprived or threatened with deprivation of his freedom for resisting such unconstitutional requirement . . . we may then set him free or enjoin his prosecution." The case holds that "released time" instruction on school property violates the prohibition against the establishment of religion.

59. 319 U.S. at 641.

60. 319 U.S. at 642.

61. See text supra note 5.

62. As is well known, the record of tolerance bears some flaws. See Korematsu v. the United States, 323 U.S. 214 (1944).

63. House Joint Resolution 359, approved December 22, 1942, 56 Stat. 1074 § 172.

64. 319 U.S. at 640.

65. The passionate commitment in *Barnette* to tolerance and diversity can be read as another example of decision-making as an affirmation of identity. For an analysis of the way these affirmations influence decision making, see the discussion in Chapter 4 at notes 5–9.

66. See supra note 7.

67. Tinker v. Des Moines School District, 393 U.S. 503 (1968).

68. Note that the Georgia Supreme Court recently upheld a ban on

adults wearing white hoods, the uniform of the Klan, in public. See State v. Miller, 260 Ga. 669 (1990).

69. 393 U.S. at 509.

70. See 393 U.S. at 507 (citing *Barnette*).

71. 393 U.S. at 506.

72. Hazelwood School District v. Kuhlmeier, 484 U.S. 260 (1988).

73. Id. at 266–67.

74. Note the first assumption in the analysis of *Barnette*, supra at page 117.

75. See the discussion of this point supra at note 51.

76. 393 U.S. at 520.

77. Russo v. Central School District, 469 F.2d 623 (2nd Cir. 1972).

78. Id. at 631.

79. It is difficult to predict which, of all the decisions discussed in this chapter, would carry the most weight with the Court's conservative majority. *Gobitis* may have been revived as a redundant makeweight. In view of the *Smith* decision on peyote smoking as the free exercise of religion, *Barnette* would probably not be reread as a case limited to the rights of Jehovah's Witnesses. Yet in view of *Tinker's* being undercut by later decisions on the free speech rights of children, *Barnette* could hardly be treated as affirming children's rights of conscience and free expression.

Chapter 7

1. 5 Record 656, quoted in Texas v. Johnson, 491 U.S. 397, 406 (1989).

2. Street v. New York, 394 U.S. 576 (1969) (reversing conviction for speaking contemptuously about the flag at the same time that defendant burned the flag); Spence v. Washington, 418 U.S. 405 (1974) (reversing conviction for "improper use" of the flag by affixing peace symbol and displaying it upside down); Smith v. Goguen, 415 U.S. 566 (1973) (as applied to defendant who affixed flag to seat of his trousers, the crime of treating flag "contemptuously" declared unconstitutionally vague).

3. All three dissented, along with Justice White, in Street v. New York, 394 U.S. 576 (1969). Note these particular comments: Warren, J.: "I believe that the States and the Federal Government do have the power to protect the flag from acts of desecration and disgrace." Id. at 605. Black, J.: "It passes my belief that anything in the Federal Constitution bars a State from making the deliberate burning of the American flag an offense." Id. at 610.

4. A *New York Times*-CBS poll indicated that in the summer of 1989, 83 percent of the public had no compunctions about punishing flag burners. *The Christian Science Monitor*, June 21, 1990, 13.

5. Public Law 101–131, 1989 H.R. 2978, amending 18 U.S.C. § 700.

6. United States v. Eichman, 110 S. Ct. 2404 (1991).

7. 110 S. Ct. at 2412..

8. See Chapter 1 at note 3.

9. *New York Times*, March 23, L25. Judge Dier of the state Supreme Court ordered that the lawyer Kurt Mausert be barred from participating in the state's indigent defense program.

10. *Chicago Tribune*, March 10, 1991.

11. The topic came up in my jurisprudence class at the Columbia Law School in March 1991. The virtually unanimous opinion of about thirty students, some of whom opposed the Gulf War, is as stated in the text.

12. But a Cincinnati judge did order that a museum curator named Dennis Barrie stand trial for having exhibited Mapplethorpe's work. See *Newsweek*, July 2, 1990, 46.

13. The German Constitution (*Grundgesetz*) distinguishes sensibly between freedom of speech, art. 5(1), and artistic freedom, art. 5(3). Without this distinction, we automatically classify all artistic efforts as "speech" under the First Amendment.

14. Bowers v. Hardwick, 478 U.S. 186 (1985).

15. Id. at 196.

16. Leviticus 20:13.

17. Note the remarkable statement in 36 U.S.C.S. § 177(j), prescribing the mode of expressing respect for the flag: "The flag represents a living country and is itself considered a living thing."

18. See, e.g., 1905 Uniform Flag Statute, § 2. See also the Nebraska statute quoted in full at infra note 21.

19. See 36 U.S.C.S. § 177(j): "No part of the flag should ever be used as a costume or athletic uniform."

20. Halter v. Nebraska, 205 U.S. 34 (1907).

21. The full text of the Nebraska statute, approved July 3, 1903, entitled "An act to prevent and punish the desecration of the flag of the United States," reads as follows:

§ 2375g. Any person who in any manner, for exhibition or display shall place, or cause to be placed, any word, figure, mark, picture, design, drawing, or any advertisement of any nature, upon any flag, standard, color, or ensign, of the United States of America, or shall expose or cause to be exposed to public view any such flag, standard, color, or ensign, upon which shall be printed, painted, or otherwise placed, or to which shall be attached, appended, affixed, or annexed, any word, figure, mark, picture, design or drawing or any advertisement of any nature, or who shall expose to public view, manufacture, sell, expose for sale, give away, or have in possession for sale, or to give away, or for use for any purpose, any article or substance, being an article of merchandise, or a receptacle of merchandise, upon which shall have been printed, painted, attached or otherwise placed a representation of any such flag, standard, color or ensign, to advertise, call attention to, decorate, mark, or distinguish, the article, or substance on which so placed, or who shall publicly mutilate, deface, defile, or defy, trample upon or cast contempt, either by words, or act, upon any such flag, standard, color or ensign, shall be deemed guilty of a misdemeanor, and shall be punished by a fine not exceeding one hundred dollars, or by imprisonment for not more than thirty days, or both in the discretion of the court.

§ 2375h. The words flag, color, ensign, as used in this act shall include any flag, standard, ensign, or any picture or representation, or either thereof, made of any substance, or represented on any substance, and of any size, evidently purporting to be, either of said flag, standard, color or ensign, of the United States of America, or a picture, or a representation, of either thereof, upon which shall be shown the colors, the stars, and the stripes, in any number of either thereof, or by which the person seeing the same, without deliberation may believe the same to represent the flag, color, or ensign, of the United States of America.

§ 2375i. This act shall not apply to any act permitted by the statutes of the United States of America, or by the United States Army and Navy regulations, nor shall it be construed to apply to newspaper, periodical, book, pamphlet, circular, certificate, diploma, warrant, or commission of appointment to office, ornamental picture, article of jewelry, or stationery for use in correspondence, on any of which shall be printed, painted or placed, said flag, disconnected from any advertisement." 1 Cobbey's Ann. Stat. Neb. 1903, c. 139

22. Ruhstat v. People, 185 Ill. 133, 57 N.E. 41 (1900).

23. McPike v. Van De Carr, 178 N.Y. 425, 70 N.E. 965 (1904).

24. 205 U.S. at 40–41.

25. The change came in Near v. Minnesota, 283 U.S. 697 (1931).

26. The language of the Uniform act, § 3, is identical to the quoted language from the Nebraska statute.

27. A search of the case law has failed to yield a decision after 1920 that treats advertising as desecration.

28. Model Penal Code § 250.9.

29. Id.

30. Texas Penal Code Ann. § 42.09(3)(b).

31. For a long list, see Leviticus 20. If it is true, as Chief Justice Burger opined in Bowers v. Hardwick, 487 U.S. 186, 196 (1985), that "Condemnation of those [homosexual] practices is firmly rooted in Judeo-Christian moral and ethical standards," one wonders why we don't also punish "a man who takes a wife and her mother." See Leviticus 20:15. Obviously, male homosexuality triggers strong psychological reactions that are not to be explained simply as the teachings of the Bible.

32. Texas v. Johnson, 491 U.S. 397, 414 (1989). The same line is endorsed in United States v. Eichman, 110 S. Ct. at 2410.

33. Cohen v. California, 403 U.S. 15 (1977).

34. Hustler Magazine, Inc. v. Falwell, 485 U.S. 46 (1988).

35. Flag Protection Act 1989, 18 U.S.C. § 700(b)

36. 110 S. Ct. at 2408.

37. 18 U.S.C. § 700(a)(2).

38. See generally L. Tribe, *American Constitutional Law*, Chap. 12 (1988) (listing following exceptions: advocacy of lawless action, fighting words and vulgarities, defamation, obscenity). See Brandenburg v. Ohio, 395 U.S. 444 (1969) (censorable speech must be "directed to inciting or producing imminent lawless action and [be] likely to incite or produce such action"); Chaplinksy v. New Hampshire, 315 U.S. 568 (1942) ("fighting words" censorable if "likely to provoke the average person to retaliate and thereby cause a breach of the peace").

39. Accordingly, I will not consider the argument, aired and rejected in the Supreme Court in the *Johnson* case, that flag burning can provoke a breach of the peace and therefore protecting public safety justifies the suppression of speech, even tantamount to censorship. This exception should be kept as narrowly confined as possible.

40. 391 U.S. 367 (1968).

41. Portions of the Reports of the Committees on Armed Services of the Senate and House Explaining the 1965 Amendment, as published as an Appendix to United States v. O'Brien, 391 U.S. 367, 387, 388 (1968).

42. Justice Marshall did not participate, and Justice Douglas dissented on technical grounds.

43. Id. at 382.

44. The Court sidesteps the question whether Congress was in fact so motivated. Id. at 383–85.

45. Id. at 377.

46. Id. at 382.

47. For a thorough analysis of the way these categories operate, see J. Ely, "Flag Desecration: A Case Study in the Roles of Categorization and Balancing in the First Amendment Analysis," 88 *Harvard Law Review* 1482 (1975).

48. Clark v. Community for Creative Non-Violence, 468 U.S. 288 (1984).

49. See 36 U.S.C.S. §§ 170ff.

50. 491 U.S. at 418, citing Spence v. Washington, 418 U.S. at 412.

51. Admittedly, the word "motive" is not quite right. If it were, the Court would have struck down the statute in *O'Brien*, where Congress's motive was rather clearly to suppress speech. The relevant notion is not the actual legislative motive but whether in some abstract sense the statute is directed *at* speech or *at* the action aspect of speech-in-action.

52. 319 U.S. at 642; see the discussion of this quotation in Chapter 6 at note 59.

53. 491 U.S. at 417.

54. 319 U.S. at 642.

55. See the discussion of Wooley v. Maynard in Chapter 6 at 118.

56. See the discussion of oaths in Chapter 4 at 65–68.

57. Compare the analysis of idolatry in Chapter 4 at 69–75.

58. Justices David Souter and Clarence Thomas have replaced two influential votes in the majority, Justices William Brennan and Thurgood Marshall. There is no way (at least for me) to predict how these strongly conservative but faceless personalities are likely to go on this issue. They are likely to follow the pro-flag line of Chief Justice William Rehnquist, but they could conceivably fall under the sway of Justice Antonin Scalia, who voted with the majority in *Johnson* and *Eichman*.

59. Thornhill v. Alabama, 310 U.S. 88 (1940).

60. See Stromberg v. California, 283 U.S. 359 (1931).

61. See Brown v. Louisiana, 383 U.S. 131, 142 (1966).

62. See the discussion of the *Tinker* case in Chapter 6 at page 142. Compare the wrongheaded reasoning in *O'Brien*, discussed supra at notes 40–47.

63. M. Nimmer, *Nimmer on Freedom of Speech* §3.06, at 3–45.

64. Texas v. Johnson, 491 U.S. 397 (1989).

65. 110 S. Ct. at 2410.

66. This doctrine could be pushed too far. In Cohen v. California, discussed at supra note 33, one might say that Cohen could have gotten his point across without using offensive language, that is, "Fuck the draft." I would limit the doctrine of "effective alternative means" to symbolic language. In the tradition of Justice Black's jurisprudence, I treat the actual use of language as an arena of nearly absolute protection.

67. See the Brief by Charles Fried and Kathleen Sullivan for the ACLU as amicus curiae, United States v. Eichman, 3. ("*Amici* do not contest the validity of a statute making criminal the destruction of the flag when it is government property or the property of another.")

68. See the leading case on this point, Vincent v. Lake Erie Trans. Co., 109 Minn. 456, 124 N.W. 221 (1910).

69. Some speech acts, such as criminal threats, criminal conspiracy, solicitation, and incitement, are prohibited on the ground that they contribute causally to the criminal acts of others. For a thorough review of these issues, see generally K. Greenawalt, *Speech, Crime and the Uses of Language* (1989).

70. Apparently, she was saying: "Read my body: no more taxes." See 10 *Encyclopedia Britannica* 515c (1969 ed.).

71. See supra at note 112.

72. See Model Penal Code sec. 251.4 (classified under Article 251: Public Indecency).

73. See the *Mephisto* case, discussed in G. Fletcher, "Human Dignity as a Constitutional Value," 22 *University of Western Ontario Law Review* 171 (1984). Other duties mentioned or implied in the *Grundgesetz* are the duty to respect and be faithful to the constitution (*Treue zur Verfassung*), art. 5(3); the duty of parents to care for children, art. 6(2); the duty of the state to support mothers and their children (*Jede Mutter had Anspruch auf den Schutz und die Fürsorge der Gemeinschaft*); the duty of men to serve in the military or its civil equivalent, art. 12a; the duty of property owners to use their assets for the common good, art. 14(2).

74. Strafgesetzbuch 90a.

75. Strafgesetzbuch 90a(2). The same duty of respect extends to the organs of government, but only if the speech act can be qualified as the first step in an effort to overthrow the constitutional order. Strafgesetzbuch 90b.

76. Robert Cover insightfully stresses this feature of Jewish law, contrasting it with American legal thought. See Cover, "Obligation: A Jewish Jurisprudence of the Social Order", 5 *Journal of Law and Religion* 65 (1987).

Chapter 8

1. Royce, supra Chap 1, note 5, at 138.

2. See D. Freeman, 1 *R. E. Lee* 372 (1934) (discussing Lee's rejection of slavery).

3. See Royce, supra Chap. 1, note 8, at 194.

4. Id.

5. As quoted in H. Lottman, *Albert Camus: A Biography* 618 (1979).

6. See J. P. Sartre, *L'existentialisme est un humanisme*, 39–42 (1970).

7. Genesis 4:3: "And it came to pass that Cain brought of the fruit of the ground an offering unto the Lord. And Abel, he also brought of the firstlings of his flocks and of the fat thereof; and the Lord had respect unto Abel and to his offering; but unto Cain and his offering he had not respect."

8. Genesis 4:15–16.

9. 102 *Harvard Law Review* 1745 (1989).

10. For reflections in a similar vein, see S. Carter, *Reflections of an Affirmative Action Baby* (1991).

11. *Harvard Law Review* at 1797 (quoting from C. Edley, "The Boycott at Harvard: Should Teaching Be Colorblind? *Washington Post*, August 18, 1982, A23, col. 3).

12. Id. at 1797–98.

13. See K. Crenshaw, "Foreword: Toward a Race-Conscious Pedagogy in Legal Eduction," 11 *National Black Law Journal* 1 (1989), who simply assumes that "perspectivalism" is the correct view of legal discourse.

14. See R. Ellison, *Shadow and Act* 146 (1972), discussed in Kennedy, supra note 9, at 1804–5.

15. Id. at 116–17 (emphasis in original).

16. *Newsday*, May 17, 1990, 80.

17. See Kennedy, supra note 9, at 1802–3.

18. Will reports Derrick Bell as having said, "Race can create as legitimate a presumption as a judicial clerkship in filling a teaching position." Id.

19. C. Rothfeld, "Minority Critic Stirs Debate on Minority Writing," *The New York Times* January 5, 1990, 6B, col. 3. According to Kennedy, Williams also publicly denounced him as disloyal at a discussion held at an annual conference of law professors.

20. See the discussion of the treason prosecution against William Joyce in Chapter 3 at 54–55.

21. See Kennedy, supra note 9, at 1815 (emphasis added).

22. Id. at 1819.

23. Note the comment attributed to Kennedy in an interview: "I spent 70 pages in the *Harvard Law Review* taking seriously people who in my view had not been taken seriously enough. I can't think of more of a tribute to their scholarship." *The New York Times*, January 5, 1990, 6B.

24. See MacIntyre, supra Chapter 1, note 6.

25. See Rawls, *A Theory of Justice* 3–4.

26. Id. at 60. The two principles read:

First: Each person is to have an equal right to the most extensive basic liberty compatible with a similar liberty for others;
Second: Social and economic inequalities are to be arranged so that they are both (a) reasonably expected to be to everyone's advantage and (b) attached to positions and offices open to all.

27. See S. Okin, *Justice, Gender and the Family* (1989).

28. M. Sandel, *Liberalism and the Limits of Justice* 15 (1982).

29. Id. at 172–73.

30. D. Hume, *A Treatise of Human Nature* 494 (1739).

31. Aristotle, *Nicomachean Ethics* 1155a.

32. William Safire has argued, "All other things on issues being roughly equal, women should strongly support women as women until some parity (i.e., equal representation in political office) is reached. Then, secure in a system in balance, they can throw the rascals out regardless of sex." *Chicago Tribune*, December 23, 1990.

33. See supra note 30.

34. See generally G. Fletcher, "Law and Morality: A Kantian Perspective," 87 *Columbia Law Review* 533 (1987).

35. This phrase was coined in Rochin v. California, 342 U.S. 165, 172

(1952), to capture the point at which state police misbehavior would rise to the level of a federal constitutional violation.

36. The conflict has peaked in the debate about multiculturalism in the United States. See Report of the New York State Social Studies Review and Development Committee, *One Nation, Many People: A Declaration of Cultural Independence* (1991). For a thoughtful critique, see A. Schlesinger, *The Disuniting of America* (1991).

37. See Gilligan, supra Chap. 1, note 34.

Index